IN WHICH
THEY SERVED

IN WHICH THEY SERVED

The stories of five men and women
of the Great War
as told by their medals

RICHARD CULLEN

UNIFORM

Published by Uniform in 2020
an imprint of Unicorn Publishing Group

Unicorn Publishing Group
5 Newburgh Street, London W1F 7RG
www.unicornpublishing.org

A catalogue record for this book is available from the
British Library

ISBN 978-1-913491-03-1

Printed and bound by Imprint Press, India

Cover design and typesetting by Uniform

Contents

For Zoë and Alex

Foreword

The centenary of World War One has prompted many people to put on record the stories they have uncovered about relatives or friends whose wartime experience might well have been lost to time. Such first hand accounts are an invaluable way of making the war real to us now in a way that battle-led histories never can. As archivist of the Oxford College that educated one of the most famous chroniclers of World War One, Vera Brittain, I am very familiar with first hand accounts of the war, many of which have emerged over the last few years in the wake of the centenary. (Indeed, Richard and I first met in 2014, when I was preparing for a WW1 community archiving project, collecting such stories from the relatives of those who had lived through it). Brittain's harrowing account of the War that killed her brother, fiancé and their friends, is familiar to many people if not through reading *Testament of Youth*, then through seeing the 2014 feature film of the same name.

Richard's book, however, is not about harrowing accounts (shocking though many of his statistics are), lost generations, or lived experiences of the horrors of war. It is about the lives – the whole lives – some extraordinary, some more mundane, of five people, only part of whose lives were bound up in World War One. It is a chance to record and remember some of the men and women who felt moved to make a contribution to the war effort and whose courage and determination meant that they were decorated and honoured for those contributions. But they are also people who had lives before and after the war – real people who are bound together by the Great War but not necessarily defined by it. By showing us to them in this way, Richard has managed to make their war achievements and experiences all the more real to us now.

Dr Anne Manuel
Fellow and Archivist, Somerville College, Oxford

Preface

*"God will not look you over for medals
degrees or diplomas, but for scars"*

Elbert Hubbard (1859-1915)

As a boy I collected miniature medals.* Much later on, my father gave me a small but well-chosen collection of medals worn by British soldiers in India during the 19th century. All lay forgotten until I retired some ten years ago, when I began at last to appreciate and build on his gift. I realised that medals have their own story to tell, and I began to research the lives of those who had worn the miniature medals in my collection.

My growing interest in research coincided with the build-up to the centenary of the Great War of 1914-18, and I focused on the lives of a few who were involved in one way or another. They had all been decorated for their service in the war – either for bravery or for service as a civilian. *They* lived to see the end of the war.

But thousands from all sides fell in the war and the fields of northern France and Belgium are criss-crossed with their final resting places. While some have marked graves, the identities of many will never be known. Some are buried as 'Unknown' warriors, but scores are interred *en masse*.

The Commonwealth War Graves Commission maintains graves at 2,044 cemeteries in France and Belgium. Some contain

---

* Smaller (+/- 18mm) diameter versions worn on 'dress' occasions

Padre Francis Tuke, 1916
(© Elizabeth Best)

the bodies of just one soldier: others have thousands.

The CGWC estimates that more than one million military personnel serving with the British Empire died during the Great War, and that altogether the conflict accounted for nearly 13 million military dead and another 21 million or so wounded. Countless civilians suffered in the maelstrom that the war unleashed on them.

There are ten major CWGC memorials in Belgium and France that were built to commemorate those who fell and have no known grave. The Thiepval Memorial in France and the Menin Gate Memorial in Belgium are examples.

My Great Aunt's husband Francis Tuke is one of the 72,185 named at Thiepval.[†] A shell blast blew him to pieces as he carried water along one of the trenches at the Somme. Remembered by his family and the members of his parish near Hereford to this day, *he* has a story that lives on.

But so little is known of many of those who died. They were far away from their homes: their families and loved ones were barely aware of what they faced in wartime, and their talent was lost forever.

Just as so many of the fallen remain anonymous, so are those many men and women who survived the war and whose lives are untold. While much has been done to unlock their stories as the centenary

---

† The Rev. Francis Henry Tuke. Died 20 July 1916 aged 49, Army Chaplain's Department (with 53rd Brigade)

of the end of the war approached, many deeds remain untold and a myriad of mysteries remain. I want this book to make a small contribution to closing this gap.

I started with five individuals about whom I knew virtually nothing. Imagine that I took five sets of medals and followed *their* own paths, rather than focus on Victoria Cross exploits, famous names or mighty battles. For that is what I have done. They led me to rich and unexpected territory – both in peacetime and in war.

Four of the medal groups that underpin this story came with some information about their owners. It took me two years to unmask the owner of the fifth.

They were in no way connected. Their motives and life expectations were different.

But, unknown to each other, they shared one thing: they were all caught up in the grinding stalemate of the Great War, and they all survived. Equally unknowingly, they overlapped from time to time in the to-and-fro progress that marked the war on the Western Front – three converging on the Somme early in July 1916. There the commonalities end.

They led very different lives and are but examples of the relatively invisible men and women who were caught up in the war, many of whom are buried in France; professional soldiers, airmen, volunteers, nurses and philanthropists. It just happens that, unlike the many who were not, *they* were noticed and decorated. (Of over six million British and Commonwealth men and women 'under arms' just over 197,000 received awards for bravery and a further 141,000 were Mentioned in Despatches – public recognition in some form for around just 5.5% of them.)[‡]

It did not take me long to realise that I knew more about these five persons than anyone else, even their relatives. And so, I decided

---

‡ Analysis of data in *British Gallantry Awards* by P.E. Abbott & J.M.A. Tamplin, Guinness Seaby: London 1971

to write their stories. In a small way I like to think of them as people whose occupations represent the millions more who gave up their lives almost anonymously to the war; to promote peace and security in Europe.

You will read of a pilot, a professional nurse, an ambulance driver, a philanthropist and a gunner. They range from a distinguished traveller, painter and writer who mobilised volunteer help for French casualties to a career artilleryman who rose from Boy to Lieutenant Colonel. They include one of the few women to win the Military Medal. Between them, they served in at least ten countries outside the United Kingdom ranging from the Western Front to Russia, Turkey and the Far East.

All five medal groups contained honours from either the United Kingdom or foreign countries and, in three cases, both.

One began as a young reservist in South Africa in 1900 and two went on to serve in the Second World War.

In Chapter 2 we shall meet Richard Trevethan, who served as an infantry officer, then a pilot and, 25 years later, on Royal Navy small ships.

Lucie Toller (Chapter 3) was a distinguished army nurse who wrestled with the care of casualties of the Somme in 1916, and whom the peacetime Army later treated very badly.

Gerald Andrewes (Chapter 4) was an insurance broker who volunteered in August 1914, aged 41: he drove ammunition trucks for the British Army and then ambulances for the French.

Emily Kemp (Chapter 5) was an explorer who gave unstinted support to the French medical services as a volunteer. Later on, she provided Somerville College at Oxford with a chapel.

Finally, William 'Jack' Nunn won the Military Cross twice in 1917 as a gunner. He served as a professional soldier for another 30 years. His brother's letters from 1917 amaze.

While I describe their experiences in the Great War, and the military context and conditions within which they served in some detail, I aim also to tell of their lives up until August 1914 and try to explain the paths and forces that led to their involvement in the war.

When commenting on their progress and related challenges after the war, many questions linger: did Lucie Toller manage to recover from the ignominious and premature end to her distinguished career? Or, did Richard Trevethan ever recover from the 'high' of surviving the aerial battles of 1917?

What made these otherwise ordinary people 'tick' away from the ghastly but essential glue that kept them going through the war? Were they happy or frustrated; dull or witty; conventional or rebellious? Did they have lovers? What did they 'feel'? How did they relate to others? How did they manage in tough conditions? Was it pure optimism that led Gerald Andrewes to keep his business alive throughout the war while so far away? Would Emily Kemp have achieved so much had she married? Why does she not have a biography? These are questions that I have often asked myself.

I have included the transcripts of several letters and first-hand accounts from other writers that reveal much both about the individuals themselves and also the social, political and military landscapes in which they lived. Backed up by maps and photographs, I hope that the resulting emphasis on context will open up many of the events of the war to relative strangers to warfare and the period, and that you will see Great War events on land and in the air through a new lens.

It is one hundred years since these five men and women came home from France. Unknown to them, *their* stories are no longer forgotten and have come to life. Here they are, in this book. I hope that I have shed a light on their lives without forgetting the million others who lie buried in France and Belgium. So that we do *not* forget...

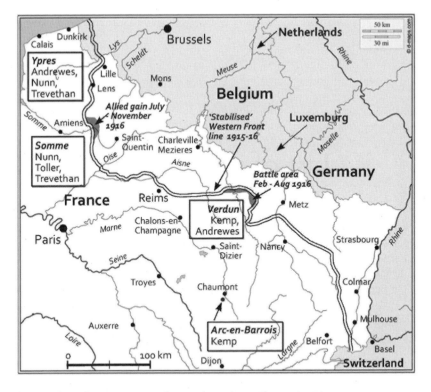

Base map: *https://d-maps.com/m/europa/france/nordest/nordest23.pdf* accessed 14 Feb 2019

Line of 'Stabilised' Western Front, 1915-16 traced from *180mm W-M 1.2.19 1173px-Western_front_1915-16* by US Department of History, US Military Academy West Point - The History Department of the US Military Academy West Point, Public Domain.jpg

The Western Front: The 'five' in France

List of illustrations

List of maps

List of abbreviations

2nd Lt	Second Lieutenant
2 RF	Second Battalion, Royal Fusiliers
6 SLR	Sixth Battalion, South Lancashire Regiment
8 SLR	Eighth Battalion, South Lancashire Regiment
AA	Anti-aircraft
ADMS	Assistant Director of Medical Services
AmTr	Ambulance Train
ASC	Army Service Corps (Royal Army Service Corps (RASC) from 1918)
AA	Anti-aircraft
BAC	British Ambulance Committee
Battn.	Battalion
BEF	British Expeditionary Force
BL	Breach loading [gun]
BRC	British Red Cross
BRCS	British Red Cross Society
BSM	Battery Sergeant Major
BMS	Baptist Missionary Society
BZM	Baptist Zenana Mission
CAMC	Canadian Army Medical Corps
CANS	Canadian Army Nursing Service
CCS	Casualty Clearing Station
CdeG	*Croix de Guerre*

C of E	Church of England
CIM	China Inland Mission
CLC	Chinese Labour Corps
CMS	China Missionary Society
CO	Commanding Officer
Coy	Company
CWGC	Commonwealth War Graves Commission
DAC	Divisional Ammunition Column
DAP	Divisional Ammunition Park
DGAMS	Director General Army Medical Services
DM	Diphenylaminechlorarsine
DoW	Died of wounds
EGK	Emily Georgiana Kemp
FANY	First Aid Nursing Yeomanry
FAU	Friends' Ambulance Unit
FRMetSoc	Fellow of the Royal Meteorological Society
FRGS	Fellow of the Royal Geographical Society
GH	General Hospital
GHQ	General Headquarters
GOC	General Officer Commanding
GSA	Gerald Stewart Andrewes
HAB	Heavy Artillery Brigade
HAG	Heavy Artillery Group
HB	Heavy Battery RGA
HE	High Explosive
HMHS	His Majesty's Hospital Ship
HMT	His Majesty's Transport Ship
HQ	Headquarters
IV DAC	Fourth Division Ammunition Column
IWM	Imperial War Museum

KIA	Killed in action
km	kilometre
KR	King's Regulations
LMG	Light machine gun
LMT	Lucie Mary Toller
Lt	Lieutenant
m	metre
mm	millimetre
MAC	Monro Motor Ambulance Corps
MC	Military Cross
MG	Machine gun
MIC	Medal Index Card
MID	Mentioned in Despatches
MM	Military Medal
MO	Medical Officer
NCO	Non-commissioned officer
NID	Northern Ireland District
NRRF	North Russia Relief Force
NTS	Night Training Squadron
NYDN	Not Yet Diagnosed Nervous
OC	Officer commanding
OCW	Officer Cadet Wing
OBE	Order of the British Empire/ Officer of the Order
OMFC	Overseas Military Forces of Canada
OR	Other Rank
pdr	pounder [e.g. as in 15-pounder gun]
PTSD	Post-traumatic stress disorder
QAIMNS	Queen Alexandra's Imperial Military Nursing Service
QAIMNS(R)	Queen Alexandra's Imperial Military Nursing Service Reserve

QARANC	Queen Alexandra's Royal Army Nursing Corps
QF	Quick firing
QMS	Quarter Master Sergeant
RA	Royal Artillery
RAF	Royal Air Force
RAMC	Royal Army Medical Corps
RE	Royal Engineers
RFA	Royal Field Artillery
RFC	Royal Flying Corps
RGA	Royal Garrison Artillery
RHA	Royal Horse Artillery
RMT	Richard Michael Trevethan
RNAS	Royal Naval Air Service
RRC	Royal Red Cross
SAA	Small Arms Ammunition
SB	Siege Battery RGA
Sqn	Squadron
SOS	Support or Suppression
SSA	*Section Sanitaire Anglaise*
SSY	*Section Sanitaire Yeomanry*
SVP	Small Vessels Pool
TF	Territorial Force
TNT	trinitrotoluene, an explosive chemical compound
TF	Territorial Force
VAD	Voluntary Aid Detachment
VC	Victoria Cross
VD	Venereal Disease
WJN	William John Nunn
WO	War Office
WRNS	Women's Royal Naval Service

Acknowledgements

I owe this book to many collaborators (most of whom I have never met), to the extraordinary resources present in our museums, archives, libraries and online, and friends who encouraged me, provided guidance and criticism, and commented on my drafts: notably Marion Williams, Robert Bullard and Moniek van de Ven.

Richard Trevethan's story is underpinned by the more personal and verifiable vignettes to his life held at the Imperial War Museum, where his Private Papers are catalogued as Documents 22390.

Mary Armour, a 'distant cousin' of Trevethan added obituary and other material, her own write-up of him, and much encouragement. She also pointed me to photographs of RMT in flying gear, and then to Dominic Gribbin. To Dominic I owe my thanks for permission to publish his grandfather's photograph of Trevethan in France and for confirmation that it was indeed him.

Others who gave willing help include John Sadden, archivist at Portsmouth Grammar School; Andrew Dennis of the RAF Museum, Hendon; Anne Barrett, archivist at Imperial College, London; Julie Carrington of the Royal Geographical Society; Stephen Nulty and other contributors to the Great War Forum who helped me with Trevethan's army service and to decipher sometimes illegible hand-written abbreviations in his RAF record; and Michael Carver and colleagues at the Falmouth Poly who revealed his post-war career.

Finally, Andrew Pool of the Royal Falmouth Yacht Club who knew RMT gave me priceless insight to his last years.

The late Sue Light deserves special mention. Through her website about British military nurses 'Scarletfinders' she has championed the role of British Military Nurses in the Great War. Apart from her patient and helpful replies to my own questions, by giving us all access to the official war diary of the Matron-in-Chief of the British Expeditionary Force she led me to valuable references to **Lucie Toller**, her progress and her achievements as seen by others.

I happily acknowledge the welcome, help and encouragement from Martin Wyer, **Gerald Andrewes**'s step-grandson and Martin's wife Margaret, including their recollections, and access to original documents and photographs.

Lesley Koulouris of the Berkhamsted School Archives very helpfully provided information about Gerald and his brother. Paul Handford, SSA1 enthusiast and researcher, was generous with his background information and personal photo collection.

Anonymous members of the Victorian Wars, Anglo-Boer War and Great War forums; all helped to add flesh to what began as a very skeletal story.

While there is much to learn of **Emily Kemp** from her own writings and from various commentators of the Baptist church and missionary world, there is general silence in published sources about her life in general, and her work in the Great War in particular. Fortunately, there are fertile sources elsewhere.

I am particularly grateful to the Principal and Fellows of Somerville College, Oxford for their permission to access the college archive and reproduce related material. Anne Manuel and Kate O'Donnell at the archive led me to the chronology of Emily Kemp's life (and directed me to where I should look) and gave me access to the correspondence related to the Somerville Chapel, the college's obituary and Margaret Roberts' charming letter of 10 January 1940.

Marjorie DesRosier PhD, international nurse historian – whom I found via the Great War Forum – was generous with her knowledge of the history of the hospital at Arc-en-Barrois and Kemp's involvement there. She steered me clear of numerous errors in my earlier attempt to chronicle the birth of the hospital at Arc-en-Barrois and its related political wrangles, and greatly added to its depth.

Tessa Morris-Suzuki, who traced most of Emily's footsteps in Manchuria and Korea, and Elaine Hunt, a keen Meiklejon family researcher unlocked the mystery of May MacDougall's identity for me.

Liz Bruchet through the Slade Archive and Robert Winckworth at UCL Records Office were instrumental in helping me to unpick details of Emily's life in London in the 1880s.

Sarah Mitchell and Amy Taylor at the Ashmolean Museum enabled me to handle Emily Kemp's paintings and lanternslides and reproduce some of them here.

Finally, Emily's great-great-nephew Jonathan Kemp, the 3rd Viscount Rochdale has been generous with his insights to the Kemp family and his photograph archive.

The late Paul Rocky, the grandson of Jack's sister Nell, inspired **Jack Nunn**'s story. He sent me Fred Nunn's letters and two exceptional photographs of Jack himself. Later, his sister Virginia further encouraged me to continue with Jacks' story and added to it. I am very grateful to both of them for their generosity in providing me with this material and for allowing me to quote from the letters and reproduce the images.

Through a combination of the Great War Forum and the Orders & Medals Research Society I have come to know Dick Flory, who researches Royal Artillery officers in the Great War. Dick has been generous with his time, digging up information about Jack Nunn and his units that I would never have found myself; he also carefully reviewed an early draft of Nunn's story. I much appreciate his friendship, interest and support.

I was fortunate to be able to access the archives at the Royal Artillery Museum at Woolwich before it closed in 2016. Mark Smith, the curator and his colleague Paul Evans were unstinting with their time and resources. I enjoyed Paul's explanations about trumpeters and his insight to the value of the education that they received as boy soldiers.

Finally, Phyllida Shaw very generously allowed me to reproduce some of the trench-life sketches by Morris Meredith Williams from her book *An Artist at War*.

Richard Trevethan

The airman: Richard Trevethan

Old Trevethan ... 26 months' active service, twice wounded and still happy

Richard Trevethan's group of miniature medals (Military Cross, 1914-15 Star, British War Medal 1914-20, Victory Medal with Mention in Despatches oak leaf, 1939-45 Star, France & Germany Star, Defence Medal, British War Medal 1939-45, Coronation Medal (GRI), General Service Medal 1918-62 with 'SOUTHERN DESERT IRAQ' clasp [wrongly positioned], Imperial Russia: Order of St Anne, 2nd Class with swords)

'Come on chaps! Let's have another go...' The pilot looked up at the ring of New Zealander soldiers who surrounded him. 'We can't just leave the old girl here. There's enough fuel in the reserve tank to get us home.' His observer – a wry Englishman, who had just shot their German assailant down in flames, hesitated: the bullets that had severed the main tank fuel lines

and brought them down had struck just a hair's breadth away
from him. Thoughts of 'Bloody April' 1917, and those friends
lost to superior German planes and pilots, were not far away. *
Was his novice pilot, with only two previous operational flights,
completely crazy?

They looked at the ungainly bi-plane lying in the hollow in
no-man's land where the pilot had managed to touch down. They
remembered the German shells that had greeted their earlier
attempt to start the engine and this interruption to what might
have been a quiet day.

The infantryman relented. 'Bugger it – is this the only way we
can be rid of you?' He and his men left the safety of their trench
and crept into no-man's land, back to the aircraft. They carried
wooden ammunition boxes, which they used to chock the plane's
wheels. Having persuaded them to hang on to the wings, the pilot
started the engine, revving it up to full throttle. The 'Fee' rocked.†
The pilot signalled the New Zealanders to pull away the chocks
and let go of its wings. The plane staggered into the air, narrowly
missing balloon cables; a miracle. Dodging small-arms fire from
the German lines, the pilot and his observer hedgehopped the
30km westwards to their base. Safely back on the ground they
learned that they had been reported dead. Their CO had already
started to write to their next of kin at home…

What makes someone thirst for speed and risk?

This longing punctuates the life story of a Cornishman born
on 24 January 1895 in Park City, near Salt Lake City USA. His
name was Richard Michael Trevelyan Trevethan. My interest
in him began in 2011, when I bought an unattributed group of
miniatures that included a Military Cross and the Russian Order
of St Anne. I describe my efforts to attribute the miniatures later on

---

* 'Bloody April' – a period related to the dog fights associated particularly with the
Battle of Arras in which more than 240 British planes were lost to enemy aircraft
or ground fire, with more than 300 airmen killed, wounded or missing. (*FE 2b/d vs
Albatros Scouts* 44)

† 'Fee' – RFC nickname for the FE2d two-seater aircraft

RMT as portrayed on an identity card, Turkey 1921
(IWM: Documents 22390)

but – although missing hard evidence of some medals in the group – I strongly suspect that Trevethan is 'my' man.

The Trevethans were a long line of Cornishmen from the parish of Perranzabuloe in north Cornwall. They were miners. As Park City was built on the back of silver mining in the mid-1800s, perhaps it was mining that took Richard's father to America, and explains why Richard Trevethan was born there. But he was in

Cornwall for his christening at Truro on 1 May 1985, and he always considered himself an Englishman. By 1901 he, his parents and his elder sister Gertrude were resident at 29 Baldhu in the Civil Parish of Kea in south Cornwall. Baldhu is near Truro, and 20km from Falmouth, Trevethan's last home.

After a stint at Falmouth Grammar School, Trevethan completed his schooling at Portsmouth Grammar School. He played a very full and active role in school life and was a member of the Navy Form, the curriculum of which was intended to prepare pupils for officer training. Although small, he clearly excelled at sport, showing determination, enthusiasm, and perhaps a degree of recklessness.

Considering that he boxed as a bantamweight in 1921, he was probably small, skinny and very lithe. (A typical bantamweight boxer weighs 118lb (53.5kg) and is 5'5" (1.65m) high.)

As a member of the first soccer team he was described as 'a very determined tackler, but should learn to restrain his exuberance. An unfriendly critic might, perhaps, characterise his play as "wild"… at the back, Trevethan takes a lot of beating.'[1] He was a good cricketer and a formidable sprinter as well as winning most of the other athletic events. He also found time to play the piano.

Trevethan joined the Old Portmuthian Club after leaving school, and served on its committee. He played in the old boys' football club and did well as a sprinter in the 1913 and 1914 old boys' races.

While he had originally expected to join the Paymaster Branch of the Royal Navy, it was the army to which he turned when the Great War erupted. He was commissioned as a Second Lieutenant in the Sixth Service battalion of the Prince of Wales's Volunteers (South Lancashire Regiment) in September 1914 (6 South Lancs). His battalion had formed at Warrington in August 1914 as part of Field Marshall Kitchener's K1 Army Group. This was one of the first 'New Army' units.

A battalion can be described as the basic tactical infantry unit of the British Army in the Great War. At full strength it numbered some one thousand men, of whom 30 were officers.[2] It consisted of a battalion headquarters and four companies named, in 6 South Lancs' case, A, B, C and D. Each company was divided into four platoons, each commanded by a subaltern such as Trevethan. Platoons in turn were each divided into four sections. From February 1915, each company was allocated a machine gun section.

Trevethan's battalion moved to Tidworth in Hampshire, under command of 38th Brigade in 13th (Western) Division. In January 1915, it transferred briefly to billets in Winchester before moving on to Blackdown near Camberley, Surrey, where 38th Brigade trained extensively. On 14 March 1915 Trevethan landed in France while attached to another unit, but may only have been there for only a few days.[3]

Rather than being deployed to the Western Front, the battalion was one of those destined to fight at Gallipoli in Turkey.

Gallipoli 1915

Richard Trevethan's Medal Index Card shows his participation in the Gallipoli campaign, and that he set foot there. There is little first-hand evidence about his specific involvement, but his battalion's activity there is well recorded.

RMT's Medal Index Card (TNA WO 372/20/6715 ©TNA)

When war broke in August 1914, the Central Powers facing the Allied Powers consisted of Germany and the Austro-Hungarian Empire. That same month, the Ottoman Empire forged a secret alliance with Germany. (Germany needed the Ottomans on her side to secure easier access to her African colonies.) On 28 October 1914, the Ottoman Empire publicly joined the Central Powers and declared war on the Allies. Bulgaria followed in 1915. Britain and France declared war on Turkey on 5 November 1914.

The Gallipoli campaign was the land-based element of a plan to allow Allied ships to pass through the Dardanelles, capture Constantinople [now Istanbul] and ultimately knock Ottoman Turkey out of the war.[4] Allied success in the campaign could have weakened the Central Powers, allowing Britain and France to support Russia and to secure British strength in the Middle East.

As naval operations earlier in the year had failed, it was decided to deploy troops to neutralise Turkish guns that prevented any further progress at sea. On 25 April 1915, the Allies landed at six beaches on the Gallipoli Peninsula – Australians and New Zealanders at a small cove south of Ari Burnu later known as 'Anzac Cove', while the British and Indians landed at four beaches at Cape Helles at the southern tip. French troops made a diversionary landing at Kum Kale on the Asian shore, before re-embarking to hold the eastern area of the Helles sector. Although not strong enough to repel the landing forces, the Turkish defenders inflicted heavy injuries on the invaders. Critically, in what can only be described as a heroic and virtually suicidal defence, the Turkish 57th Infantry Regiment held the heights of Chunuk Bair, the second highest peak in the Sari Bair range of high hills that separated the eastern half of the Peninsula from Allied attackers hemmed in to the west.

Operational success depended on Turkish opposition crumbling quickly. This did not happen. Instead, the assault quickly developed into trench warfare. The Turks held the commanding heights inland. Allied casualties were very high. Trevethan's battalion was one of the units deployed to reinforce the Gallipoli operation and regain the Allied initiative.

On 13 June 1915, 6 South Lancs sailed from Avonmouth in HMT *Ausonia*, and reached Lemnos on 2 July, having stopped off at Alexandria and Malta.[5] Lemnos is a Greek island some 90km to the west of the Gallipoli Peninsula, and 6 South Lancs bivouacked on a hillside near the village of Mudros. On the evening of 6 July, the battalion shipped east, landing on W Beach on the tip of Cape Helles early the following morning – about two and a half months after the initial landings there.

Clement Attlee, then commanding 'B' Company of 6 South Lancs, and later to defeat Winston Churchill in the 1945 General Election, landed at Helles on 1st July – six days before the bulk of his battalion.[6] In view of their friendship, forged in 1915 as soldiers and continuing well into the 1950s (*q.v.*) it is tempting to think that Trevethan was one of his platoon commanders, and that he too landed on 1st July. As a leader he was inexperienced and untried in battle. He had much to learn.

Gallipoli was extremely inhospitable. Attlee recalled later that the heat, stench, insects, dysentery and monotonous field diet made his time at Helles quite horrible. Mosquitos, snakes, thirst, shelling and shrapnel added to the oppression.

The battalion spent July gaining experience of trench warfare, supporting but not participating directly in any major operations.[7]

After rest back at Mudros, the battalion returned to Gallipoli, landing at Anzac Cove on 4 August as part of a large force. This took place in parallel with a new landing at Suvla Bay north of Anzac, all of which was aimed at breaking the stalemate that had now gripped the campaign. One component of this was to re-energise the earlier attempt to seize the Chunuk Bair heights.

Two companies of Trevethan's battalion fought on the heights alongside Gurkha troops in a heroic action on 9 August. Acting on their own initiative (the main attacking force had lost its way) they advanced alone towards a saddle between Chunuk Bair and an objective called 'Hill Q.' They then stormed trenches that overlooked the Turkish side of the Sari Bair ridge, and occupied them.

Without support, and unable to withstand the overwhelming Turkish counter attacks that followed, they were forced back down to the earlier Gurkha positions, with heavy losses. A third South Lancs company moved up to support, and together they defended the position until Royal Warwickshire soldiers relieved two of the companies.

The failure to hold on to their position was tragic, as the Turks also contained the other two attacking columns attacking the Sari Bair ridge on 9 August.

The next day, 10 August, was a black day for 6 South Lancs. The Turks launched mass frontal attacks on the unreinforced Gurkha positions. Fire from the defenders devastated the Turks, who in turn responded with crippling enfilade machine gun fire. By midday the Gurkha, South Lancashire and Warwickshire men had been forced to retire to their original positions.[8]

The Turkish counter attack of 10 August across the whole front and related loss of earlier allied gains brought the assault on the Sari Bair ridge to an end. Losses on both sides had been severe. Water shortages were acute.

General Sir Ian Hamilton, British Commander in Chief at Gallipoli, declined to risk mobilising his reserve troops and extend the assault any further.

On 11 August, a decimated 6 South Lancs and the remnants of the Royal Warwickshire Regiment took over the line held by the 14th Sikhs. In the days that followed, water continued to be very scarce, with major outbreaks of fever. Around 500 of the 700 men deployed at the beginning of August had become casualties, including five officers missing and believed killed, and nine wounded.

Was Richard Trevethan one of the lucky few to emerge from the Battle of Sari Bair unscathed? His RAF records tell us that he was admitted to hospital in Alexandria on 10 July with typhoid.

Then, on 10 September, he was hospitalised in Malta for eight days suffering from neuritis, after which he returned to England, where he was admitted to the Hall-Walker Hospital for Officers at Sussex Lodge in Regents Park, suffering from tonsillitis. ‡

I think that Trevethan moved on to Gallipoli from Alexandria, and that he was there until the first week of September. Was he fit on 9/ 10 August, and engaged in the fury of Sari Bair? Was his 'neuritis' the result of severe combat stress? I do not know.

His battalion remained on Gallipoli until the very end, acting as rear-guard in the evacuation of Allied troops from Suvla Bay on 19 December 1915. Men of 6 South Lancs were the last to leave, and Clement Attlee was the last but one officer to do so. The evacuation was carried with such stealth and deception that the Turks were unaware that the allies had left. Ironically, this operation was hailed as the finest piece of military planning and execution of the whole campaign.

By this time some 480,000 Allied troops had served on Gallipoli, of whom some 252,000 became casualties, including 48,000 killed in action or died of wounds or sickness. Australia and New Zealand bore 73% of the casualties, of whom one third died. Total Turkish casualties in what was Turkey's greatest success of the war were around 250,000 with some 65,000 dead.[9]

Once out of hospital, Trevethan remained in England while 6 South Lancs completed its deployment on Gallipoli. The battalion moved on to Egypt and then Iraq, where *inter alia* it played an important role in the relief of Kut.

Battle of Albert

By April 1916, Richard Trevethan, still in England, had transferred to the Eighth Battalion, South Lancashire Regiment (8 South Lancs), acting as Brigade Signalling Officer to the 4th (Reserve) Brigade, based at Prees Heath in Shropshire on the staff of a young Officers' Company, training them in signalling.[10] He had by then been accepted for flying duties and awaited transfer to the Royal Flying Corps.

‡ Neuritis is a term used to describe an inflammation of a nerve that results in pain, sensory disturbance, or the ability of the nerve to 'react' properly. Among the many types of neuritis are optic, interstitial, and brachial. The condition can be exacerbated by battlefield-related trauma.

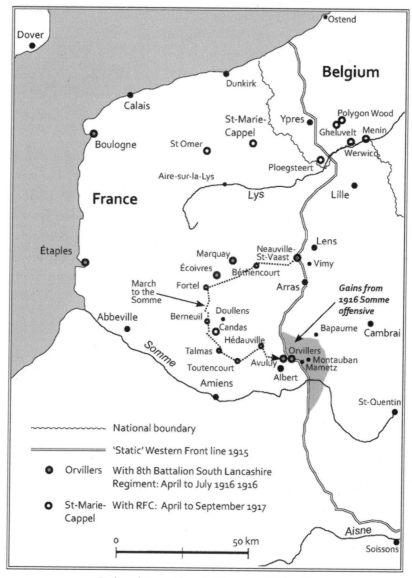

Richard Trevethan in France, 1916 – 17

In the meantime, he returned to France and the Western Front. The battalion, very much part of Kitchener's New Army, had been in France since September 1915, mainly around Ploegsteert ('Plug Street' to the Tommies) south of Ypres. It mouldered in the humdrum, uncomfortable but dangerous routine of trench warfare.[11]

Then, in the following spring, the battalion deployed north of Arras as part of measures to repel the German attack on Vimy Ridge.

After a spell at training grounds at Étaples, on 5 April 1916 Trevethan and 15 ORs joined 8 South Lancs at Marquay, a small village 30km WNW of Arras where the battalion rested in reserve. On 28 April it moved back to the front line and took over trenches at Neuville St Vasst, a small town just north of Arras.

After well over a year of trench warfare, both opposing sides had established a series of parallel trenches facing each other. The tract separating the opposing front line trenches was called 'No Man's Land,' the borders of which were protected by barbed wire fences. In some cases, No Man's Land was as narrow as 100m. Parallel first, second and perhaps third defence lines were linked by a series of communication trenches running roughly at right angles to them. Along these moved men, equipment, ammunition and food. Men slept in dugouts in the front system trenches.

Those in the trenches faced attack from snipers, shelling, mortars, machine gun fire, bombs and raiding parties and, from April 1915, poison gas. As the war progressed, both sides extended and improved their trench systems and related defences. There was a never-ending cycle of work to maintain the trenches and repair damage from shelling. Life in the trenches deteriorated grimly when rain turned the soil into mud and flooded the walkways.

The following extracts from the battalion war diary sum up Trevethan's first period at the front, when 'things soon became lively.'[12] You see a routine of about five days manning the front-line trenches (being shelled and bombed, retaliating, repairing damaged dugouts and trenches) interspersed with similar periods in the reserve lines along with working parties of one kind or another. Nerve-wracking. There was a steady trickle of casualties, even when in reserve.

On 2 June the battalion marched west out of the line to a billeting area in Béthencourt to join the 75th Brigade for training. Following the brigade's formal transfer to X Corps of the Fourth Army on 14 June, it began the two-week process of looping anticlockwise

'Edgeware Road', a communication trench in the Loos sector 1916,
(Morris Meredith Williams/ © Phyllida Shaw)

'Asleep on a fire step', Loos sector 1916
(Morris Meredith Williams/ © Phyllida Shaw)

round to the area to the south around Albert. They often marched by night as part of measures to conceal heavy troop movements from air observers. Rest days along the way were punctuated by spells of training. Altogether they marched some 75km, arriving at Hédauville, a commune seven kilometres northwest of Albert, on 1st July. This coincided with the disastrous first day of the Battle of the Somme, which had kicked off as the battalion reached the outskirts of Albert.

Extracts from 8th Battalion War Diary – April and May 1916

Dates	Place	Comment
28 April 1916	Neuville St Vasst Trenches 0.60-0.62 §	Took over line E. of Neuville St Vasst. V. active enemy trench mortar & bombs fire. Enemy blew up mine burying 3 of C. Coy and wounding 3 other ORs.
29 April	Neuville St Vasst Trenches 0.60-0.62	Owing to the near proximity of the enemy not possible to recover bodies of the 3 dead [from the explosion]
30 April	Neuville St Vasst Trenches 0.60-0.62	Enemy artillery v. active, shelling D Coy (in reserve), wounding 1 man. Remainder of day passed in exchange of bombs etc.
1 – 4 May	Neuville St Vasst Trenches 0.60-0.62	Damage to communication trenches from heavy shelling, trench mortars, aerial torpedoes & rifle grenades; 1 officer & 9 ORs wounded + 1 died of wounds (DoW)
5 – 10 May	Neuville St Vasst	Relieved by 2 S. Lancs and in Brigade reserve. 2 casualties. 30 NCOs and men received from Étaples.
11 – 16 May	Neuville St Vasst Trenches 0.60-0.62	Back at 0.60 – 0.62. Routine onslaught from heavy shelling, trench mortars, aerial torpedoes, shrapnel and rifle grenades which between them caused damage to trenches and casualties (three privates wounded of whom one died). British artillery also very active, causing considerable damage to enemy trenches. Those not involved in sentry duty largely employed on repairing trenches and digging communication trenches. Relieved by second battalion South Lancs on the night of 16th but then remained in Parallel VIII until 8pm and then proceeded trench digging afterwards; marching back to Écoivres in Divisional Reserve

§.   0.60 – 0.62; their section of the trench line; between markers 0.60 and 0.62 miles.

17 – 20 May	Écoivres	In reserve. Provided digging parties. Two privates wounded.
20 – 24 May	Trenches	Took over the trenches at about 2200. Enemy rather quiet for first two days. A little exchange of grenades. Companies working on wiring up the observation line and building up the resistance line. Considerable damage to trenches on 22nd and 23rd from heavy enemy shelling, trench mortars and rifle grenades. Strong retaliation with our trench mortar and rifle grenades supported by our artillery, which damaged their trenches. Our casualties seven wounded and one KIA. 24th relatively quiet with one NCO wounded. Relieved at 2200 and returned to Brigade Reserve in the cellars at Neuville St Vasst.
25 May – 1 June	Neuville St Vasst	In Brigade Reserve, supplying two companies working for the RE and the other two as carrying parties and doing general fatigues. Casualties: 1 KIA, 1 DoW, 2 wounded. 8 No. 2nd Lts joined Battn.

The Battle of the Somme was a joint Anglo-French initiative, intended to relieve the pressure from the Germans on the French at Verdun, and also break the stalemate at the western half of the front. It marked a baptism of fire for those thousands who had volunteered to fight in 1914 and 1915 and who formed the bulk of the BEF's Fourth Army under General Rawlinson. Charged with implementing the Somme offensive and had over half a million men and 1,500 guns at his disposal, he sent eleven divisions into action on 1st July along a 23km front running from Maricourt on the left bank of the River Somme in the south to Serre in the north. This, the Battle of Albert, parked the first phase of the Somme offensive.

Pressure from General Haig, his superior, constrained Rawlinson's instincts as an infantryman to advance step-by-step. (In this way, gains could be consolidated and supporting artillery support given time to move forward). As a result, objectives were overambitious and, even when achieved, were not generally sustainable. Rawlinson exacerbated the risk by counting six-inch calibre guns with those heavy guns *over* six inches (those with the capability to destroy enemy barbed wire and deep dugouts) when assessing the density of heavy guns available for pulverising the enemy trenches.[13] And so, the mighty barrages that preceded the battle did not have the devastating effect on the German defences that the infantrymen were led to expect: unsuspecting, untried soldiers walked into murderous machine gun and artillery fire from an angry enemy that had survived days of incessant shelling in the shelter of bunkers that had not been destroyed, and remained shielded by barbed wire defences that had not been cut. As Lieutenant Stefan Westmann, a German medical officer, wrote:

> Then the British army went over the top. The very moment we felt that artillery fire was directed against the reserve positions, our machine gunners crawled out of the bunkers, red eyed and dirty, covered in the blood of the fallen comrades, and opened up a terrific fire.[14]

In spite of displays of enormous courage, the Fourth Army suffered 57,470 casualties on the first day, of which 19,240 men were killed.[15] It is sobering to realise that many of these casualties were caught by shellfire while marching *towards* the front line, and never actually 'went over the top.' As they moved along overcrowded communication trenches towards their jump-off points, they were often exposed to heavy shrapnel and machine gun fire. Wounded men moving in the opposite direction added to the confusion.

While British and French forces achieved successes at the southern end of the assault on the first day of the battle, operations north of the line between Albert and Bapaume failed.[16]

These setbacks did not deter Rawlinson from continuing the attack. On 2 July 1916, the British 30th Division, holding the newly won Montauban Ridge repulsed two determined German counter-attacks. Both British and German commanders recognised it was here, in the cramped southern sector of the battlefield, that offered the most likely opportunities for further exploitation. Nevertheless, in the immediate aftermath of 1 July Rawlinson sanctioned repeated assaults against unbroken German defences over the battle-strewn uplands of the *entire* line of his original attack.

The period 2-13 July was characterised by a series of grindingly slow and costly British subsidiary attacks made to secure the flanks for a later major assault on the German second line positions. These were principally in the southern end of the line. In a succession of bloody encounters, the Fourth Army sought to secure Trônes Wood, Mametz Wood and Contalmaison; operations characterised by vicious hand to hand fighting, devastated villages and shell-thrashed woods riddled with concealed strongpoints. Heavy rain on 3 and 4 July produced the first quantities of the infamous Somme mud and pointed to the difficulties that terrain and weather would pose later in the campaign.

As the war diary shows, men of the 8 South Lancs moved from reserve in Aveluy Wood to the Unsa Tara Line – a defensive system astride the Albert-Bapaume road.[17] At 0400 on 8 July, the battalion went over the top in an attack close to Ovillers. Two days of solid fighting followed before relief by men of the Cheshire regiment.

Extracts from 8th Battalion War Diary – July 1916

Dates (1916)	Place	Comment
1 – 2 July	Hédauville	Waiting
2 July		Left Hédauville for Aveluy Wood thence at 2330 for the trenches South of Thiepval as support to the other battalions of the brigade in the attack on the German line carried out at 0615 on July 3.
3 -4 July	Trenches	The Batt^n. took over the line from Johnson's post to Hamilton Avenue and on the night of the 3/4 July the battalion took over the line held by the second battalion South Lancs Regiment, the Duke of Wellington's West Riding Regiment TF being on our left and the 8th Border Regiment on our right.
4 – 5 July		On the night of 4/5 July the Batt^n. was relieved by the 1/7 Worcestershire Regiment and went back to Aveluy Wood.
5 – 6 July	Aveluy Wood	Bivouacked In reserve.

Dates (1916)	Place	Comment
7 July	Unsa Tara line	Moved to Unsa Tara trenches by day via Crucifix Corner north of Albert, arriving about 1730. Batt[n]. stayed there until 2330 and then moved to take up position for an attack on German line just south of Ovillers to the ridge south of Nash Valley and north of La Boisselle
8 July	Attacked German trenches	Attacked around 0400 and took the front-line trench practically without opposition. Touch was obtained with the East Sussex on our left and the 11th Lancashire Fusiliers on our right. During the day we occupied the German second line trench as far as a point about 150 yards south of the southern edge of Ovillers and a part of the third line trench as far as Point 18
9 – 10 July	Trenches near Ovillers	During the day the work of consolidating the ground gained was continued and about 1730 a bombing attack on Point 24 was made supported by two platoons attacking from different directions but was unsuccessful. At 2000 in pursuance of direct orders from brigade an attempt was made to capture the remainder of German third line by a determined rush across the open. This attack did not reach its objective owing to heavy machine-gun fire from Ovillers, which completely enfiladed the ground to be crossed and the quagmire condition of the terrain due to recent heavy rainfall. On the night of 9/10 July the battalion bombers cooperated in an attack by one company of the 11th Cheshires on Point 24. This attack was not pushed owing to strong opposition being encountered.
10 – 12 July	Unsa Tara line	The Batt[n]. was then relieved by the 11th Cheshires and went back to the Unsa Tara line where they stayed until the night of 12/13 July

After a day of relatively easy advance, we can see that 9 July developed into a day full of seemingly suicidal attacks. C and D Companies, tasked with capturing the remainder of the German line in the evening assault, were ravaged by enfilade machine gun fire as soon as they left their trenches. There were heavy casualties, including three subalterns from C Company.[18] Richard Trevethan was one of the victims – shot in his thigh.[19]

After treatment at a casualty clearing station, Trevethan was moved to hospital at Boulogne on 10 July, and then shipped home to the 3rd Echelon hospital at Wandsworth. So ended his days as a front-line infantryman. Once recovered, he would be ready at last to become a pilot.

The battalion continued on through several of the stages in the Battle of the Somme that followed, adding honours for the battles of Bazentin, Pozières and Ancre Heights to its honour for the Battle for Albert. The slaughter in July was such that the battalion diarist no longer recorded each casualty by name, day by day; there were too many to list.

Just sixteen weeks...

Air warfare as we know it today was a completely new and unexplored concept in 1914. The British Committee of Imperial Defence had established an inter-service Royal Flying Corps (RFC) in 1912 from which, in mid-1914, the Royal Navy separated its flying arm to form the Royal Naval Air Service (RNAS). This left the RFC as the Army's aerial arm when war broke out in August 1914. It was essentially an Army unit, and structured as such.

Early in the war, aircraft and balloon use developed into essential reconnaissance and artillery spotting tools. But it was not long before opposing pilots began to shoot at each other, and antagonism set in. Pilots' fortunes were dependent on two key factors: their training and the quality of their aircraft. There were ebbs and flows in technical advantage; superior German machines in 1915 gave way to Allied advantage in 1916, only to be reversed when the Germans introduced the Albatros DII and DIII scouts near the end of that year ('Scout' being the Great War name for single-seater fighter). In time operational differences evolved; for tactical reasons, the RFC chose to operate aggressively on the German side of the line, allowing the Germans a more manageable, defensive role. By this time too, the RFC progressed from the earlier purer focus on reconnaissance to attack.

The casualty rate amongst RFC pilots was high, particularly in those periods when they lacked superiority in aircraft quality and numbers. Pilot training time shrank as the call for replacements grew, and the life expectancy of new pilots arriving in France could be measured in weeks rather than months. Pilot casualties jumped from 332 (20% of the service) in 1915 to 1,410 (34%) in 1916.[20]

Such loss rates were unsustainable, and in 1916 the RFC realised that pilots simply had to be better trained and prepared before becoming operational.

To improve the quality and quantity of new pilots, a dedicated Training Division equipped with many more training aircraft was established on 1 January 1917. In parallel an Officers' Cadet Wing (OCW), aimed at providing two months of classroom training in readiness for actual flying training, was set up. OCW training was then to be followed by a three-month course of elementary flying instruction, leading on to advanced flying school.

Flying instruction had changed too, catalysed by Major Robert Smith-Barry, who pioneered a new approach to pilot training in 1916. This was tested at the Gosport Flying School in January 1917 and then rolled out for general use. This process, involving aircraft with twin controls 'owned' by the trainee pilot, pushed trainees to experience the limits of their aircraft. They practised stunt flying in parallel with wide instruction in aerial combat. Then, once operational, their COs were to provide advanced training before committing them to action.

On 25 February 1917 the South Lancashire Regiment transferred Richard Trevethan to No. 1 School of Military Aeronautics at Wantage Hall, Reading. There he underwent four weeks of instruction in such subjects as aerial photography and spotting, gunnery and wireless communication.[21] He followed this with two weeks of flying training at No. 47 Reserve Squadron, based at Lincoln before moving on to No. 46 Reserve Squadron at Tadcaster, west of York in mid-April. On 14 May 1917, the Central Flying School at Upavon in Wiltshire certified that, having completed a 'course in the Military Wing,' he was 'qualified for service in the Royal Flying Corps.'[22] By the time he left Tadcaster, he had experienced barely more than seven weeks of flying instruction.

He was one of the lucky ones; accidents were common, and more than 2,000 pilots were killed in training accidents during the war.[23] He also timed it well, missing what became known as the 'Bloody April,' of 1917, when insufficiently trained pilots with even less than the-then requisite 15 hours of flying solo were hastened into action in the face of mounting pilot losses. For every 30 German aircraft destroyed between March and May 1917, the RFC lost 203.[24]

Trevethan duly reported at No. 2 Aircraft Depot, BEF at Candas – a dispersal point for aircraft flown to France, some 20km north of Amiens. Candas also acted as a pool for new pilots. There, Trevethan waited for posting to an operational squadron.

This came on 27 May 1917, when he joined No. 20 Squadron, stationed at Sainte-Marie-Cappel, some 20km east of St Omer, in northern Flanders. The squadron had deployed to France early in 1916, then equipped with FE2b two-seater aircraft. It was tasked to perform fighter-reconnaissance work. Ste Marie-Cappel was also home to 45 Squadron, equipped with two-seater Sopwith aircraft.

Squadron Leader Cecil Lewis MC, a distinguished fighter pilot, regarded the FE2b highly. In *Sagittarius Rising* he gives his view on the aircraft while training as a pilot early in 1916:[25]

> The FE2b was a pusher (that is, the engine pushed it from behind), a development of the Vickers Fighter, made by the Royal Aircraft factory. It had a 160 HP Beardmore engine... It was a fine machine, slow, but very sturdy, and carried a pilot, with an observer before him, in a boot which stuck out in front of the machine... Forward, therefore, it had a fine arc of fire and, attacked head on, was extremely formidable. Attacked from the rear, it was necessary for the pilot to stand up in his seat, hold the stick with his knees and use his own gun, which fired backwards over the top plane – not an easy job, but frequently resorted to in a dogfight.

RMT at Sainte-Marie-Cappel, France, 1917; on the reverse of the photograph are the words *'Old Trevethan. The senior pilot on my flight. 26 months active service, twice wounded and still happy.'*
(© Dominic Gribbin)

With good battle tactics, a flight of these machines was very deadly, even to an enemy with far greater speed and manoeuvrability. FEs were used for bombing raids and long reconnaissances, and time and time again they would fight their way home from 20 miles beyond the lines, continually circling to protect each other's tails, surrounded by enemy scouts. It's no joke to be shot up by a dozen machine guns for half an hour, engaged in a running fight in which the enemy can outpace you, outclimb you, and outturn you. It needs a lot of guts and a cool head... They [the pilots] soon had the respect of the Huns, who would never risk attacking unless they outnumbered them by two to one, and did wonderful work right through 1916 and on into the summer of 1917, when the FEs were scrapped as obsolete and the DH4s and Bristol Fighters took their place...¶

By the time that Trevethan reached his unit, the squadron had been re-equipped with an updated version, the FE2d, now powered by a 250hp Rolls-Royce engine. At first sight this relatively ponderous aircraft might appear to offer little opposition to the Albatros fighters that they faced. In *FE2b/d vs. Albatros scouts*, James Miller compares the two opponents:

Technical comparison between FE2d and Albatros DIII aircraft

Feature	FE2d	Albatros DIII
Wingspan (m)	14.6	9.0
Length (m)	9.7	7.3
Loaded weight (kg)	1,549	894
Armament	3 x 0.303in Lewis guns	2 x 7.92mm Maxim guns
Engine	250hp Rolls-Royce	158hp Mercedes
Maximum speed (km/h)	150 at sea level	174
Climb (seconds)	2,384 to 3,048m (FE2b with earlier 160hp engine)	660 to 3,000m

Apart from these stark differences – the FE2d being a heavier, bigger and slower opponent that took ages to gain height – there

¶ To watch an FE2B in flight, visit *www.youtube.com/watch?v=F4uzJuHG6jM* and *www.youtube.com/watch?v=JdyxPCCuQaQ*

were two defining and inter-related differences that tended to even out the odds.

The prominence of 'pusher' aircraft resulted largely because the RFC's aircraft earlier in the war were not armed with fixed machine guns that could fire forward through a nose-mounted propeller. This rendered the two-seater aircraft required to carry out aerial photography defenceless against oncoming hostile aircraft. In 1915, the Germans introduced the Fokker '*Eindecker*' monoplane, equipped with forward firing machine guns synchronised to fire safely. These aircraft had virtual control of the skies in 1915, punishing the RFC with heavy losses of machines and pilots.

As Cecil Lewis recalled, placing the engine behind the pilot freed up space to move the observer of a two-seater aircraft in front of the pilot. By equipping the observer with two Lewis guns – one facing forward and one, higher up, facing backwards over the wing – the FE2s were capable of both forward and rear defence.

In contrast, an Albatros pilot had to line his target up ahead to shoot him down and had no defence against an adversary behind him. Some FE2ds also deployed a fixed, forward-firing Lewis gun for the pilot. That said, RFC observers had no safety harness; standing up to fire a rear-facing Lewis gun at heights of 3,000m in an aircraft that was being thrown about the sky by a pilot doing his best to evade an attacker must have been perilous in the extreme. And in 1917 neither pilot nor observer had parachutes.

FE2d of 20 Squadron at Sainte-Marie-Cappel, France, 1917; showing the three Lewis guns and the precarious contortions required to enable the observer to fire backwards over the wings
(IWM Q 69651/ © IWM)

We can get a better view of No. 20 Squadron's operational role from the introduction to a note that Second Lieutenant T.A.M. Lewis wrote, following a remarkable escape while severely wounded during a famous dogfight on 27 July 1917. Describing the FE2d he wrote:

These machines were used chiefly for bombing, photography, and fighting, but their observers did such observation of the enemy as was possible on these trips.

A job which was really a combination of all these duties, was that known as the 'offensive patrol', and it entailed patrolling an area not less than 5 miles east of the 'lines', up and down, north and south between certain given points about 20 miles apart in Hunland.

Usually six or eight machines composed the formation detailed for the job, and their duty was to patrol at a given height (about 10,000 feet [3,050m]) for two hours, 'looking for trouble' in the shape of German aeroplanes, and to prevent them attacking our low-flying buses serving for the artillery. Though the Hun Albatros Scouts were much superior to the FE2ds in speed and manoeuvre, their respect for the fighting qualities of these British machines was such that they would rarely attack them unless in greater numbers (at least 2 to one) than the FEs, while the latter could not chase the Hun, being of inferior speed.

Trouble was always found, too, from 'Herr Archie [anti-aircraft fire]' who delighted to give his closest attention to the FEs on account of their large size and comparatively low pace, which makes them an attractive target, so that during the whole period patrol there was rarely a minute unpunctured by less than half a dozen 'Whooff, Whooff's' of black shell bursts around the formation, and often so close as to cause the pilots at once to change their course, height and speed, as 'Archie' is not to be trifled with. While no chances are given him, almost always on the return of the

FEs, effects of his shell fragments would be found in holed fabric, split struts or severed wires. [26]

Richard Trevethan flourished as a new pilot. After just one week, he flew on an offensive patrol that engaged eight Albatross scouts. Together with his observer, Sergeant John Cowell, they shot down the leading Albatross in flames. Cowell was to emerge as the highest FE2 'scorer,' with sixteen victories.[27] Had Trevethan been teamed up with this seasoned crewman to give him a 'soft' landing? He went on to forge a winning partnership with Lieutenant Campbell Hoy, who became the third highest FE2 'scorer,' with ten victories.[28] The top nine FE2 scorers all flew with 20 Squadron.

We appreciate more of Trevethan's character and skill from an uncredited note written in the early 1950s:

Pilot R.M. Trevethan served with No. 20 Squadron, amongst others, but it was this Squadron that gained the highest total of confirmed air victories in World War I for 2-seater aircraft.

Soon after joining No. 20 in 1917 he was on patrol with 5 other FE2ds and as was the custom he attained combat height on the reserve tank before switching over to the main tank which was operated by pressure [i.e. pumped] – the reserve tank being operated by gravity.

Shortly after, contact was made with the Germans over Ypres, and in the Dogfight that ensued, a bullet pierced the main petrol link releasing the pressure thus stopping the flow to the engine & forcing him to descend and break away from the formation.

This was observed by an Enemy fighter whose pilot was indiscreet enough to attack. ~~Captain C. A. Hoy~~ [Trevethan's correction?] was the gunman in the FE and soon the fighter was seen to be in flames by the remainder of the formation who mistook it for the FE2d and reported on return to St

Marie Cappel. However, Trevethan continued to descend and was forced to land between the lines, luckily in a hollow.

They abandoned the aircraft and rushed to the British lines, then occupied by New Zealand troops who welcomed them and gave them breakfast. Unsuccessful attempts were made to contact the Squadron by telephone and eventually, getting rather bored, they went back to examine the F.E.2D. The reserve tank still had petrol in it, so they started the engine

This attracted shellfire, and the engine was hurriedly stopped, and they returned to the trenches when again boredom caused them to arrange with the New Zealanders to chock up the wheels with ammunition boxes and hang on to the wings while the engine was again started. It was a lovely warm morning. As soon as the powerful RR engine was running full out the New Zealanders were signalled to pull away the chocks and release the aircraft which staggered into the air missing balloon cables etc. and the two returned to Ste Marie Cappel to find that they had been reported as having been shot down in flames

Incidentally Trevethan is one of the ~~only~~ [Trevethan's correction?] surviving members living in Cornwall of the list of air aces of World War I published in 1938. [29]

As Hoy was Trevethan's observer on all but three of the occasions when his victories were recorded, this event could have occurred on 2 or 9 June and 12 July. As the latter two records describe their victims as being 'destroyed in flames' near Ploegsteert, it is tempting to assume that this event took place on 9 June or 12 July – perhaps the former in view of the reporter's 'soon after joining No. 20 in 1917'? Ploegsteert is 15km south of Ypres, so that fits. (Gheluvelt, the scene of the 2 June action, is about 9km to the east of Ypres). Furthermore, Trevethan's victory on 12 July was timed at was timed at 5.25 p.m., which does not tally with the references to 'breakfast' and the 'warm morning.'

As the fighting moved on into July, Richard Trevethan and his observer, frequently Hoy, continued to dispose of enemy aircraft.

On 27th he racked up his eighth victory during a legendary dogfight where 'a formation of FE2ds of 20 Squadron acted as 'bait' for the whole of the Army Wing.' Their instructions were to fly over Menin, then about 30km over the lines and 45km west of St Marie-Cappel, and to stooge around until they attracted sufficient German aircraft to lure them 20km northwest to Polygon Wood. There a concentration of British and French fighters would await them in ambush. In the event, the squadron attracted about 20 Albatross scouts in the Polygon Wood area at a height of around 3,700m. Half deployed to the west to cut the FE2s' route home, and the others attacked from the rear. The odds were around three-to-one in the Germans' favour. As their objective was to lure the enemy in the direction of the Allied scouts, who in the event arrived 45 minutes late, the FE2s did not adopt the practice of flying in defensive circles as described earlier. Rather they remained in linear formation and engaged the enemy in a running battle until the scouts arrived.

That evening, No. 20 Squadron accounted for six enemy aircraft (including one to Trevethan) for no losses of its own. Between them, the RFC and RNAS accounted for 30 enemy aircraft throughout the day.[30]

As a rookie airman, Trevethan had done remarkably well. Not only was he still alive, but also by destroying five enemy aircraft he soon achieved 'Ace' status. This was not unnoticed, as his CO's recommendation led to the award of the Military Cross in August. General Plumer presented him with the MC ribbon on 17 August.

The 'official' citation for his MC was published in the London Gazette on 19 September 1917, the day after a wound took him out of active service for the rest of the war in France. It reads:

T./2nd Lt. Richard Michael Trevethan, Gen. List and R.F.C. MC 'For conspicuous gallantry and devotion to duty when on offensive patrols. He has continuously displayed the greatest dash and determination in attacking enemy formations, regardless of their superiority in numbers, and has shot down at least four, driving others down out of control.'

Trevethan gained quite a reputation within No. 20 Squadron. On a photo taken at Ste Marie-Cappel by Captain Harold Satchell, we see a laughing Richard Trevethan in his fur-lined flying boots; apparently care-free and relaxed.[31] On the back of the photo are the words 'Old Trevethan. The senior pilot on my flight. 26 months active service, twice wounded and still happy.'[32] It reminds us that they were barely more than boys, forging strong camaraderie in extremely difficult and dangerous times.

In August, No. 20 Squadron began to replace its FE2d equipment with Bristol F2b fighters – far superior two-seater aircraft that were to remain in RAF service until the early 1930s.

On 18 September 1917 Richard Trevethan's luck ran out; he was wounded while flying an F2b. Following admission to hospital at St Omer suffering from a lacerated scalp and severe concussion, he was moved to Étaples two days later before evacuation to hospital in London.[33] In spite of the improvements in pilot training and aircraft, the RFC was still a very dangerous arm in which to serve. RFC officer casualties in France reported during the two weeks when Trevethan was wounded were as follows:[34]

Casualty variations between RFC officer ranks – September 1917

Rank	Killed in action		Reported missing		Admitted hospital (wounded)		Totals	
Major	1		0		0		1	
Capt	2		3		7		12	
Lt	5		15		7	(including RMT)	27	
2nd Lt	31	(79%)	55	(75%)	24	(63%)	110	(72%)
Totals	39		73		38		152	

Source: Analysis of data in AIR 1/864/204/5/508

Those killed in action included two who died of wounds, one who 'died of injuries' and four killed accidentally. The first injury is dated 2 September and last 25 September.

Casualties for RFC NCOs and ORs on flying duty were light in comparison. Just seven NCOs became casualties in the same period compared with 152 officers. New, junior pilots bore the brunt – Second Lieutenants accounting for 72% of the total.

Trevethan himself had barely lasted sixteen weeks. But some sixteen weeks! Here is a summary of his victories as a pilot in that short time:

Victories credited to R.M. Trevethan

No.	Date	Time	Aircraft	Observer	Opponent	Location
1	2 Jun 1917	0945	FE2d (A6480)	Cowell	Albatros D.III (destroyed)	Gheluvelt
2	9 Jun 1917	0600	FE2d (A6341)	Dudbridge	Albatros D.III (destroyed in flames)	E of Ploegsteert
3	2 Jul 1917	1245	FE2d (A6523)	Hoy	Albatros D.III (out of control)	Comines-Houthem
4	7 Jul 1917	1900	FE2d (A6528)	Hoy	Albatros D.III (destroyed in flames)	Wervicq
5	12 Jul 1917	1725	FE2d (A6528)	Arkley	Albatros D.V (destroyed in flames))	E of Ploegsteert Wood
6	17 Jul 1917	1955	FE2d (A6512)	Hoy	Albatros D.V (destroyed)	Ploegsteert Wood
7	22 Jul 1917	1650	FE2d (A6528)	Hoy	Albatros D.V (destroyed in flames)	Menin – N of Wervicq
8	27 Jul 1917	1945	FE2d (A6528)	Hoy	Albatros D.V (out of control)	Lille-Menin
9	28 Jul 1917	0915	FE2d (A6528)	Hoy	Albatros D.V (out of control)	Kezelbars
10	8 Aug 1917	1030	FE2d (A6527)	Hoy	Albatros D.V (out of control)	E of Messines
11	8 Aug 1917	1040	FE2d (A6528)	Hoy	Albatros D.V (destroyed)	E of Messines
12	9 Aug 1917	0950	FE2d (A6527)	Hoy	Albatros D.V (out of control)	Becelaere-Roulers[35]

By October 1918, RFC casualties in its four war theatres (France, Italy, Middle East and East Africa) totalled 10,484. Of these 32% were killed or died of wounds, 41% were wounded, 17% were 'missing' and 10% became prisoners of war. If you include the 'missing' with the dead, all but half of the RFC casualties died.[36]

Trevethan did not return to the fighting in France. His fellow pilots missed him. In recognition of his service and friendship, they presented him with a handsome officer's sword inscribed 'Presented to Lt. R.M. Trevethan M.C. by the Officers and Men of 20th Squadron R.F.C.'

He was discharged from hospital early in December. Following sick leave, he resumed flying as an instructor at 187 Night Training School at Retford, near Sheffield.

No. 20 Squadron went on to become the highest scoring 2-seater squadron in the RFC. In March and April 1918 'during the retreat of the Army in the south and along the Somme, the squadron still stationed at Marie Cappel, took part in the bombing and shooting up of enemy troops and transport, flying down to Bray each morning at daylight and working from the aerodrome there, returning at dusk.'[37]

Early RAF days

In April 1918, RFC and RNAS merged to become the Royal Air Force. On 1st April 1918, Lieutenant 'A' Richard Trevethan became one of its first officers. On 1st October 1919, he was granted a permanent commission as Flying Officer.

Almost a year after his injury in France, Trevethan crashed again – this time flying a BE2e from the night training squadron at East Retford, in Nottinghamshire. He was hospitalised in Sheffield, suffering from contusions of the scalp and his left knee. A Court of Enquiry followed, which judged that while 'he turned too near the ground in very rough weather... and failed to flatten out sufficiently when landing', the ground surface where he landed (traversed by a newly filled-in drain trench) was very bad. There were no disciplinary repercussions.[38]

He returned to Retford early in December 1918, remaining there for another four months. And then, in July 1919 he returned to operations – this time in North Russia as part of a unit called 'Syren Force.'

North Russia

By 1917 Russia had been fighting the Central Powers on the Eastern Front for well over two years. Within Russia, the war and Tsar Nicholas II had become increasingly unpopular, paving the way for the February Revolution at St Petersburg. The Tsar abdicated on 15 March 1917, and a provisional government was formed. This government, led from July 1917 by Alexander Kerensky, determined to continue to fight the Germans on the Eastern Front. The unpopularity of the war continued to grow, and a German offensive in June led to mutinies and desertions. This contributed to the rise of the Bolsheviks and their overthrow of Kerensky's government during the October Revolution. Russia formally withdrew from the war through the Treaty of Brest-Litovsk, signed by the new socialist government and Germany in March 1918.

The Germans were now free to occupy former Imperial Russian territories in Belarus, the Southern Caucasus and Ukraine. Moreover, they could now release some 30 German divisions from the eastern front in time to strengthen the Spring Offensive in France that came perilously close to Paris: it was necessary to force these troops back to the eastern borders.[39]

Meanwhile, 'White Russian' opposition to the new Bolshevik government was growing, establishing a volunteer army in the process.

Thus, German expansion in eastern Europe and the need to keep Germany fighting on two fronts, west (in France and Belgium) and east (against Russia and her allies), led to Allied support for the White Russian cause in what became the Russian Civil War. There were also fears that Finnish troops allied to Germany would take the ice-free ports at Murmansk and Archangel and use them as U-boat bases to threaten the transatlantic convoys bringing vital American troops to France. Both ports had been used to supply Russia with military equipment throughout the war, as had Vladivostok in the extreme east of Russia. The two arctic ports held large stockpiles of weapons and munitions that the Bolshevik government was shifting to Moscow. Winston Churchill, among others, saw Bolshevism as a serious threat, to the extent that several countries including Britain, France, Japan and the USA resolved in 1918 to support the White Russians in what became known as the 'Allied Intervention' in the Russian civil war.

British involvement in Russia began in March 1918, when a party of Royal Marines landed at Murmansk. They were soon fighting Finnish troops in Karelia. Initially the Bolsheviks remained neutral, but in August 1918 British and French troops attacked and occupied Archangel, in open defiance. In time Serbian, Czech, Italian, Polish, Canadian and American troops would engage Bolshevik troops in North Russia and Siberia in support of the White Russian forces.

The troops in northern Russia fought through a bitter arctic winter, and Bolshevik counter-attacks in January 1919 recovered earlier allied gains around Archangel. Would they succeed in cutting off Murmansk from Archangel and then annihilate the Archangel force? Conditions were harsh and attempts to reinforce the British at Archangel from ice-free Murmansk were frustrated by the frozen White Sea and a shortage of icebreakers. In general, troops could only cross by sleigh.

The question of how and when to reinforce Archangel persisted throughout the summer of 1919. Consequently, the decision was taken to withdraw before enduring another winter, and a North Russian Relief Force (NRRF) was formed to smooth this process. The NRRF performed well, enabling the evacuation of British Forces from Archangel and then Murmansk by early October 1919. It inflicted serious damage on Bolshevik forces in the process.

Britain also deployed training contingents to Siberia, operated Russian gunboats on the Kama River in central Russia, and sent army and RAF units to train and equip White Russian forces in the Crimea and Southern Russia. The Royal Navy was also very active in the eastern Baltic Sea and also engaged on the Caspian Sea. America and Japan deployed large forces to Vladivostok in the Far

North Russia, 1919

East. The extremely complex politics and related manoeuvres, first to make peace with the Bolsheviks and then to enable sufficient support to the White Russians to overthrow them, were tortuous. Collectively these moves did little to impede the Bolsheviks' progress; over-optimistic expectations that these separate regional initiatives would somehow link up and gain some critical mass proved a pipe dream.

Major General Sir Charles Maynard was the commander of the allied forces at Murmansk, code named 'Syren Force.' It was incumbent on him to hold the railway line from Murmansk to the south to continue overland access to Archangel and maintain the security of the force there. In February 1919 he had been able to reinforce Archangel with two columns of men from the Yorkshire regiment. They undertook a 300km journey by horse-drawn sledge, following the southwest shoreline of the White Sea from Soroka on the Murmansk-Petrograd line to Obozerskaya on the Archangel-Vologda railway line.[40]

During the latter stages of the campaign, Maynard sought permission to gain a hold on Lake Onega, the large water body between the White Sea and Lake Ladoga to the south. The Murmansk railway ran along the western shore of Lake Onega to the Bolshevik port stronghold of Petrozavodsk, continuing to the former capital city at Petrograd, as St Petersburg was renamed at the outbreak of war in 1914.

To succeed, Maynard needed to establish and maintain a viable naval force on the lake. He achieved a tactical framework for this by assembling a force of British, French, Italian, Serbian and Russian troops along with American railway men. In an offensive from 1 to 21 May, they took Medvyeja Gora, a strategic town at the north end of Lake Onega.[41] The Americans played a key role by rebuilding bridges and relaying tracks in a very hostile environment that was exacerbated by marshes and rushing streams created by the thaw.

The flotilla that Maynard established on 4 June was far from convincing; it comprised six motor patrol boats and two steamers which 'slow as they were, and with engines on which continued reliance could not be placed, were better than nothing, and could usefully be used for patrol work.'[42] Fearful of opposition from Bolshevik vessels (which would soon be free from lake ice), he needed air support.

The RAF effort in Murmansk region had not impressed Maynard. It had begun with the supply of six RE8 two-seater biplanes in December 1918 but lacked both a suitable airfield and spare parts. It achieved little more than a few reconnaissance flights, and by late June only one RE8 was still flying.

In his frustration, Maynard requested the RAF to provide two flights of seaplanes: he wanted to fly them from the base that he intended to build on his new foothold on Lake Onega.[43] Their purpose was to protect the naval flotilla, through aerial reconnaissance and bombing, and to attack ground targets.

These aircraft were eventually shipped aboard the seaplane carrier HMS *Nairana* at Sheerness, from where she sailed on 22 May 1919.[44] (*Nairana*'s aircraft had frightened the Bolsheviks out of Archangel the previous August). She reached Murmansk on 29 May. After three days of unloading, the RAF team and its equipment entrained and moved almost 800km south to the railhead at Medvyeja Gora. There, they began on 4 June to unpack and assemble one flight of Fairey IIIC seaplanes and one of Short 184s. The first aircraft flew two days later. Two days after that, they were in action, supporting the naval flotilla in its first engagement in which it successfully took on four armed Bolshevik vessels that threatened Medvyeja Gora. These retreated amid total surprise at being attacked from the air.

The RAF set up their seaplane base at Medvyeja Gora on a narrow stretch of the Lake Onega shoreline. Nestling between thick forest and the water were an assortment of prefabricated hangars with curved corrugated iron roofing, Nissan huts, bell tents and crates of equipment. Simple wooden jetties reached out into the water, and shallow sloping ramps provided the means to winch the seaplanes up into the hangar areas for maintenance.

Russian Karelia in the summer is a pleasant place to be – the sun does not set for forty days, and temperatures of 20°C in in July and August are not unusual. But September temperatures generally fall by up to 10°C, after which snow and sub-zero temperatures dominate from October to April. Extreme temperatures of minus

RAF seaplane base at Medvyeja Gora, 1919
(J. Sewell/ *Murmansk Venture* 286)

30° C occur – hence the urgency to evacuate the Allied forces before the winter set in.

The Fairey IIIC biplane was the third variant of a two-seater reconnaissance aircraft originally designed to fly from aircraft carriers. Powered by a 280 kW (375 hp) Rolls-Royce engine, it had been modified as a bomber/reconnaissance floatplane and could carry a useful bomb load.[45] Armament consisted of a fixed forward-firing Vickers machine gun for the pilot and a single movable Lewis gun on a Scarff ring mount for the observer.[46] First flown in July 1918, the IIIC came into service too late for the Great War, but proved its worth in North Russia.

As for the Short 184 seaplane, one ex-Sopwith Camel pilot described it as like 'driving a bus after driving a motorbike,' commenting that it was difficult to take off, particularly getting the tail float to 'unstick.'[47] It climbed and turned very slowly. The Fairey IIIC in turn was also a particularly 'blind' machine, as the floats limited the pilot's vision; accurate aerial photography was difficult.[48]

All in all, the transition from conventional aeroplane to seaplane must have been challenging, although the IIICs were better powered than the Shorts. As an ex-FE2d pilot, Richard Trevethan had the advantage of experience with heavy two-seater biplanes.

And at least the propeller was at the front. Trevethan flew both types of seaplane during his operations from Medvyeja Gora.

The rail link from Murmansk to Petrograd was strategically very important at this late stage in the Murmansk operations. In his determination to prevent (or at least delay) Bolshevik attacks from the south, Maynard tasked the RAF with maximising disruption to the Bolshevik lines of communication. In particular, its aircraft were to 'pay special attention to the docks and railway centre at Petrozavodsk and enemy vessels on the lake.'

He also instructed them to 'make it their constant endeavour to break... one of the largest railway bridges between Petrograd and Murmansk [over the Suna River].'

Richard Trevethan joined RAF 'Syren' on 14 July and flew on many of these operations.[49] He was one of 20 officers in the Seaplane Unit, which was affectionately known as 'Duck Flight.'[50]

Trevethan's operational duties lasted from 31 July to 20 September, during which he flew 22 sorties. His observer on eight of these was Lt Harvey who, on 30 June, had the dubious distinction of crewing the only IIIC to be brought down by enemy gunfire.

Duck Flight's activities all contributed to Maynard's overall objective, including attempts on the Suna railway bridge that, as Trevethan's observer noted on 8 September, was a well-defended and small target. Eventually, an enterprising army unit managed to destroy it.[51]

As White Russian troops progressed on the Shunga Peninsula, it became imperative to disrupt Bolshevik ships on Lake Onega that frustrated Russian attempts to take the port of Tolvoya. This involved a joint operation on 3 August between Maynard's lake flotilla (newly reinforced with six sub chasers armed with 3-pounder guns and six motor boats carrying machine guns), and four of the RAF Fairey IIICs. Trevethan flew one of them. He and the other three pilots bombed the Bolshevik vessels, causing general panic among their crews in the process: one ship ran aground, while two others surrendered to the sub-chasers that harried their escape. White Russian and Allied troops then captured Tolvoya.[52]

We see from his observers' reports that Richard Trevethan flew on various support activities including reconnaissance, disruption at Petrozavodsk, attacks on shipping and also the controversial use of 'smoke bombs' (*q.v.*). The work was hazardous, and flights of two hours or more were not unusual. On the plus side, flying over islands and lakes and the many wooden churches and other buildings for which the area is still famous must have been a refreshing distraction from the hazards of anti-aircraft fire.

Extracts from Trevethan's Observers' Reports – August and September 1919

Date	Observer	Flight time	Objective	Summarised remarks; some (in quotes) verbatim
8 Aug 1919	Miln	114	Bomb Suna Railway Bridge	230lb bomb apparently damaged bridge supports; machine gunned siding and Kivatch Station; then Vremeny Post; AA [anti-aircraft] fire
8 Sep	Bloomer	120	General recce of Koikori-Ussuna – Suna – Siding 7	'Fairly accurate AA fire; 100 rounds MG on church. Trenches, houses & carts in Koikori; 100 rounds MG on trains of 16 covered trucks at Suna Bridge'; 'fairly accurate and heavy AA fire from eastern side of bridgehead. Two other guns located to south of bridge'; 2x112lb bombs on small steamer at Kondopoga. (RMT added by hand 'Steamer at Kondopoga large enough to carry 500 troops.')
14 Sep	Jones	95	To drop special smoke bomb over Mikheeva Selga	Dropped 30 special smoke bombs over village: several direct hits obtained, other bombs falling in and around village. Slight movement observed 100 yds south of village and MG fire directed on machine – we returned fire with 100 rounds. Movement observed 4 versts [about 4.5km] W of village – also enemy MG fire – this was also returned. Much smoke seen issuing from forest NW of village, Smoke bombing ceased at 061...

| 14 Sep | Jones | 170 | Recce of steamers at Klimenski & bomb if found | Sighted enemy vessels S of Konda heading for Petrozavodsk – 1x4-funnelled destroyer, 6 chasers, 2 barges. 'The destroyer appears to be a fast and good vessel and was firing from forward and aft. Much AA Fire was encountered from flotilla. On approach of seaplane the vessels zigzagged. One 230lb bomb and 2x20lb bombs dropped on destroyer. 230lb bomb was apparently seen by this vessel, which veered, thus avoiding it. Bomb fell about 30 ft from destroyer covering stern with splash. When last sighted flotilla was heading for Petrozavodsk at 1445 hours. 150 rounds MG directed at destroyer and other vessels' |

Source: Abstracts from AIR 1/1768/204/143/2

The last flight by a British pilot took place on 25 September. Air operations closed down, and the RAF handed over the planes and equipment to the Russians whom they had been training, and who duly took over the operational work. While some of the Russian pilots were excellent, there was insufficient time before the evacuation to complete the training of Russian mechanics. This was an inauspicious moment: 'it was a great pity that it should have been necessary to leave them at a juncture when a few weeks' more training would have made such a great difference to the efficiency of their air service.'[53] The official record summarised:

> Between 6 June and 17 September 1919, the Seaplane Unit of the Forward Wing RAF 'Syren' made 297 recce flights totalling 536.5 hrs of recce and 57 hrs of communications & 52 hrs of test flight (646hrs); dropping 989 bombs (27.75t) and 241 gas bombs, firing 45,928 rounds of MG ammo, photographing about 250 sq miles and dropping 25,000 propaganda leaflets.[54]

The wording is interesting. The euphemism 'smoke bombs' has been more properly translated as 'gas bombs.' These featured a new type of gas called diphenylaminechlorarsine and code-named 'DM,' an irritant agent designed to cause uncontrollable coughing.

These bombs were first used at Archangel on 27 August. Deployed more widely in September, they were not considered effective, blamed partly on the damp autumn weather (but probably too because the Bolshevik troops wore gas masks). As the CO at Kem recorded following the raid on the enemy headquarters at Suna Station on 14 September:

> The effect of these bombs [on 13 & 14 September] appears to have been only morale, as no enemy were captured in the condition that this particular form of gas is designed to produce; they had the effect however of driving the enemy out of his positions in the same way as on the Archangel Front. [55]

Once again Richard Trevethan's flying attracted high level attention. He was one of eight seaplane pilots and observers singled out for particular courage and performance, and he was gazetted as being Mentioned in Despatches for North Russia on 22 December 1919.[**] The Russians also recognised his services by awarding him the Order of St Anne, 2nd Class with swords. He appears in a list signed by Major General Skobeltsin, who had taken command of troops in the Murmansk district in June 1919. [56]

The RAF contingent boarded *Nairana* at Kandalksha on 30 September. She sailed for Rosyth via Murmansk after a few days and docked at Devonport three weeks later. Trevethan was home.

The British operations in the Archangel and Murmansk sectors between the spring of 1918 and October 1919 claimed the lives of

---

[**] Mention in Despatches (MID): a military recognition announced in the *London Gazette*. It originates from the despatches submitted by military commanders to the War Office to report on progress with operations, and the custom of listing individuals who deemed worthy of particular mention. Formerly there was no tangible award, but it was decided during the Great War that an oak leaf emblem could be worn on the Victory Medal to denote the mention. The practice continues today with all three Services; the emblem being worn on the riband of the war or campaign medal in question. (*https://www.longlongtrail.co.uk/research-mention-despatches/*, accessed 10.09.2018)

41 officers and 286 other ranks. A further 65 officers and 591 other ranks were wounded. The Army estimated the total cost of these operations at over eighteen million pounds.[57]

While relatively a side show compared with the near-disaster at Archangel, General Maynard's efforts had enabled forces at Murmansk to push south to Lake Onega – but no further: Petrozavodsk remained in Bolshevik hands.

What should have been the peace

Once back at home, Richard Trevethan fell into the routine of service life and the peripatetic existence that goes with it. He spent five months at the Grand Fleet School of Aerial Gunnery and Fighting at RAF Leuchars in Fife, Scotland, moving on in April 1920 to 210 Squadron at Gosport for duty with the Coastal Battery Corps.

While at Gosport, this dashing, decorated pilot met Muriel Doris Graham Moon, who was living at the Empress Club in Dover Street, London. Muriel was the granddaughter of the Rev. Sir Edward Graham Moon, 2nd Baronet. Her mother was the daughter of Sir Alexander Frederick Bradshaw, and her brother, Sir Arthur Moon, had inherited the 4th baronetcy in 1911.[58] This was a very well-connected family.

Richard and Muriel married at the St George Register Office in Hanover Square, London on 22 December 1920, in circumstances that must have raised an eyebrow or two at tea time; four months later, Muriel gave birth to a son, Gerald Michael, at Axbridge in Somerset.

The following October, Richard had another flying accident. This time, landing a DH9A at Delny in Scotland, he struck the top plane [wing] of another DH9A. He was uninjured. The Court of Enquiry that followed concluded that his record should not be adversely annotated.[59]

Shortly after this, Trevethan made the first of what were to be several appearances in court for speeding, when he was prosecuted for dangerous driving at Warsash; 'defendant came around a sharp and dangerous bend at between 20 and 25mph; defendant and his wife put the speed at about 11 mph; fined 30/- and another 10/- for not producing his licence at the time.'[60]

On 28 November he moved from Hampshire to 207 Squadron at RAF Bircham Newton, some 25km north west of King's Lynn, where he continued to fly DH9As. Promotion to Flight Lieutenant followed in January 1922.

Muriel became pregnant once again. Their second son, Richard Graham, was born at King's Lynn that summer.

In September 1922, the Turkish Army led by Kamal Ataturk, buoyed by their recent success at driving Greek troops from Izmir on the eastern coast of Turkey, threatened to attack British and French troops at Çanakkale who were guarding a demilitarised zone around the Dardanelles. This was part of a move to regain control of Istanbul and the whole of what is now European Turkey – then under allied occupation. In what became known as the 'Chanak Affair,' a knee-jerk reaction from the British almost resulted in a war with Turkey. This was fortunately diffused by British agreement to hand over East Thrace (that part of modern Turkey in south east Europe) to the Turks. This effectively forced the Greeks to give it up without a fight. Negotiations that concluded on 11 October resulted in an armistice that held back a British attack on Turkey with a few hours to spare.

These events deflected Richard Trevethan for what would have been an assignment at the RAF School of Photography, as the RAF sent No. 207 Squadron to Turkey as part of the rapid military response to the Chanak threat. [61] As commander of an advance party, Trevethan sailed for Turkey in the SS *Eboe* on 28 September. The squadron, under the command of Squadron Leader A W Tedder (later Marshall of the Royal Air Force, Lord Tedder) had a fairly dismal time. It operated from an airfield at Yeşilköy, a village on the Marmara Sea just to the west of Istanbul. The airfield was in abominable shape, suffering alternately from floods and frost. The facilities were poor, and the squadron's DH9A aircraft suffered in turn.

Fortunately, there were no further political disruptions, and after October 1922 the situation quietened down to permit Trevethan and his fellow airmen to return to England the following summer.

On 22 October 1923, he was posted to No. 39 (Bomber) Squadron, also flying the DH9A, based at RAF Spitalgate near Grantham in Lincolnshire. He remained there until reassigned to the RAF Depot at Uxbridge on 24 August 1925. Before then he was back in court again for speeding during one of his journeys south – this time at Horley in Surrey. He collected a fine of £3 for exceeding a new 20mph limit and antagonised the magistrates by giving the impression that that 'he is one of those persons who think the law should be altered.' [62]

Then came a change from flying duties; Trevethan undertook an RAF-arranged course in meteorology at Imperial College, London from October 1925 to September 1926.

The day after finishing his studies he sailed from Southampton to join the RAF Headquarters for Iraq in Baghdad as Senior Meteorological Officer. During his tour there he researched weather patterns in Iraq, particularly relating to winds.

His *Times* obituary reported that he carried out 'a vital role in the forging of links between Iraq and Britain' and that he had himself 'planned the system of weather reports and forecasts for Imperial Airways through to India.'[63]

Iraq had more than its fair share of disturbance during the revolt against the British colonial rule that followed the Great War. This continued for over a decade at various levels of intensity, including a countrywide Iraqi uprising in 1920. The RAF was prominent in the many attempts at pacification, often bombing settlements in the process.

From January to June 1928, Britain retaliated against Akhwan tribes in the southern desert of Iraq. This was primarily an RAF affair, involving Nos. 30, 55, 70 and 84 Squadrons and a small number of British officers and men with the Indian and Iraqi armies.[64] The RAF's task was to find and then bomb Akhwan raiders from the Najd desert in Saudi Arabia who aimed to destabilise tribesmen in the vicinity of the Iraqi border and Kuwait. The operation concluded in May 1928 when Ibn Saud, the first monarch and founder of the Kingdom of Saudi Arabia, undertook to restrain his tribes from raiding. A report on these events noted extremely difficult climatic conditions throughout the disturbances. These varied between snow early on in the campaign and extreme heat and severe dust storms later on. These made conditions for the personnel at the desert flying bases very stressful.[65]

Sound meteorological forecasting was critical for maintaining air operations in an area where dust storms, sudden strong winds and changes in wind direction presented a serious flying hazard; a tall order for Trevethan and his staff. For example, March 1928 in the Southern Desert began with abnormally low temperatures, with hard frosts, strong winds and snowstorms. Then, two days after south and southeast winds in the middle of the month fuelled sudden high temperatures, there was then an abrupt return of north winds and low temperatures.

In the middle of all this, Richard and Muriel Trevethan faced tragedy back in England. On 17 March 1928 fire broke out at a nursery school at the village of Salfords, not far from Horley in Surrey. The Trevethans had arranged for their two children to board there while they were in Iraq. Graham, the younger boy was one of eight children in the dormitory next to the bedroom of Miss Tucker, one of the two principals who ran the school. Fanned by strong wind, the fire took hold quickly. Frantic and brave attempts to rescue the sleeping children from the smoke-filled room followed. While three of the eight were saved, four boys and one girl died from suffocation.[66] Graham Trevethan was one of them; he was five. At the inquest that followed there was inconclusive discussion about an oil heater in Miss Tucker's bedroom and a related suspicion that a fault in an oil heater that caused the blaze.

Muriel Trevethan's stepfather represented the family at the funeral, when the five small children were buried in a single coffin.

The press reported the inquest that followed at some length. One extraordinary feature by today's standards was the widespread and uncritical support for the school principals and their courage in the rescue attempt. Trevethan himself had cabled the principal, writing 'Terrible news. Deep sympathy with you and Miss Young [the other principal].' There appears to have been a reluctance to attach any blame. Muriel's stepfather was quoted as being 'satisfied that the brother of Graham [Gerald] is being left in her [Miss Tucker's] charge' in spite of this dreadful event.

It is hard to imagine the effect that this calamity would have had on young Gerald and his parents. Apart from anything else, the marriage did not survive. When Muriel refused to accompany Richard when posted to India early in the following year, he sailed alone to Bombay on 26 January. Muriel went home to England and refused to join him when he returned in April. They never lived together again.

From early June he was stationed at RAF Bicester with No. 100 (Bomber) Squadron, following which he returned to RAF Leuchars in October to train on Blackburn aircraft. This led to a posting to the Fleet Air Arm, commanding No. 449 Flight on HMS *Courageous* and then No. 440 (Fleet Spotter Reconnaissance) Flight, flying Fairey IIIF biplanes. He served in various ships, including the carrier HMS *Hermes*, and at shore bases in the Far East.

While home in June 1931 he met his wife at Portsmouth, and 'she then finally told me that she was never going to return to me and asked me again to give her evidence so that she could divorce me.' He decided to comply, and on 11 July:

> I went up to London and met a woman whose name I cannot now remember and stayed the night and also the following night with her at the Hotel Belgravia... and committed

adultery with her. I have never seen this woman since, and I have never committed adultery with anyone else. I sent the Hotel Bill to my wife...[67]

Considering her later behaviour, this must have proved very galling; so much for doing the 'decent' thing.

Promoted to Squadron Leader on 1 December 1932, he continued his Far East service, shuttling between Hong Kong and Singapore, where he re-joined HMS *Hermes* on 19 November. He sailed home from Singapore on the *Kaisar-i-Hind* on 6 January 1933, reaching London early in February.

By this time his wife Muriel had left England. Since the beginning of October 1932, she had been living with a man called William McLellan on a farm at Thompson Falls, a scenic spot some 180km north of Nairobi in Kenya.

Back in England, Trevethan languished. He spent the first half of the year recovering from illness and was then put on half pay in July for a short while. In August he took command of No. 99 Squadron, during which he attended courses on twin-engined bombers and anti-gas measures. In May 1934 he then became supernumerary once more, ending back on the half-pay list early in July.

Meanwhile, he had to cope with a divorce, and finally filed a petition on 13 August 1934. In this he cited his wife's 'habitual' adultery with McLellan at the Thompson Falls farm, and on numerous occasions between December 1932 and April 1934 at the Norfolk Hotel at Nairobi. He also sought custody of their son Gerald. Muriel would not play. She denied adultery and stuck to her much earlier insistence that he admit adultery so that she could divorce him. This he duly did on 22 October 1934, along with a clear description of the events that had led him to his actions at the Hotel Belgravia in July 1931.

Richard Trevethan's days with the RAF were numbered. Reinstated on 27 August, he spent three months on general staff duties, followed by six months on flying duties at the Home Aircraft Depot at RAF Henlow in Bedfordshire, commanding the Flying and Parachute Test Squadron.

It appears that by mid-1935 he had had enough; he left the RAF on 1 June, aged 40. He had not, however, lost his interest in flying; The Royal Aero Club awarded him an Aviator's Certificate a few months later.

To shore up his prospects for civilian life, he successfully applied for membership of the Royal Geographical Society, which elected him as a Fellow in April 1936.[68] Interestingly, one of the grounds for his acceptance was that he had 'laid out and marked the chain of meteorological stations for the proposed demonstration flight of the [airship] R.101 [in 1929].' He was already a Fellow of the Royal Meteorological Society.

By this time, the nightmare of his divorce was just about over. After much torment he was granted a Decree *nisi* on 9 July 1935, and the divorce became Absolute on 20 January 1936. Muriel married McLellan soon afterwards. They too divorced in 1949.

Whether a symptom of depression or anger, or not, his changed lifestyle began to tell. Around the time that he petitioned for divorce, he was back in court for dangerous driving on the Kingston bypass. Fined £15, his driving licence was suspended for five years, but restored in 1936. Then, in August 1937 he was prosecuted for dangerous and drunken driving late at night in King's Road, Portsmouth. He pleaded guilty. A doctor testified that, following his examination, Trevethan was 'quite incapable of giving a rational account of where he had been.'[69] He was fined £10 and banned from driving for five years. Having pleaded that he had been unemployed since his disqualification and that he had been offered two positions that required him to able to drive, he managed to persuade the Portsmouth magistrates to restore his licence in October 1938.[70]

Trevethan's progress then becomes less clear. He based himself at the RAF Club at 128 Piccadilly and did find time to co-author a book called *Theory of Flight*, published around 1939.[71] (In his entry for the 1939 Register he described himself as an author.) His obituarist at the *West Briton & Cornwall Advertiser* recorded that:

> Wing Cmd. Trevethan left the RAF to become air adviser to the Chinese Government in 1937, and in the 1939-45 War served as mate and second officer in Royal Navy small ships. He was a keen sportsman and flying enthusiast, held the non-stop flying record from Scotland to the South Coast for several years, was a wrestling champion of the three services, and an RAF boxing champion.[72]

The link to China is puzzling. Beyond awareness that there was British involvement in the build up of the Chinese air force in the period up 1937 when the Sino-Japanese War broke out I can find nothing to substantiate this.[73]

The reference to 'Royal Navy small ships' however has more credibility. Trevethan was a keen sailor, and a skilled navigator. On 31 July 1944, eight weeks after the D-Day landings in Normandy, he received a telegram from 'Walker' at the Admiralty instructing him 'LEAVE CANCELLED RETURN TO DUTY DORLAND HOUSE IMMEDIATELY.'[74]

Clearly, he was attached to the RN in one form or another. I suspect that this was connected with the Small Vessels Pool (SVP), an organisation that had its roots in the evacuation from Dunkirk in 1940. Organised around over 1,560 volunteers, the SVP ferried small ships around the British coast for the navy. The volunteers – all attracted to the sea – came from all walks of life: 'the retired and the disabled, the elderly and the youthful; in brief, all done by men who wanted to have a hand in the war, but for whom no active employment existed, and whose use did not interfere with the man-power of the nation.'[75]

Between them they ferried around 1,000 vessels, yachts, tugs, launches, lifeboats and fleet tenders, regardless of weather or danger. Some were engaged in the Normandy landings. One, Major T.

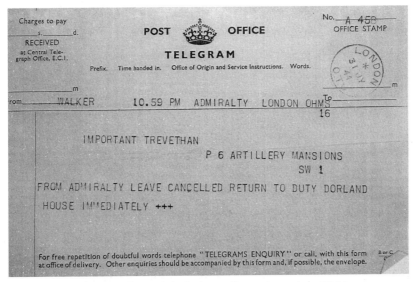

Telegram from Admiralty to Trevethan, July 1944
(IWM: Documents 22390)

J. May, had served in the Boer and Great wars, and was aged 76 when he served as an assistant beach master during the landings. He had joined the Home Guard at the outbreak of war, worked for the Ministry of Supply from 1942-43 and then been called up for service with the Royal Navy SVP in 1944-45. I think that Richard Trevethan, then a mere 49-year old, followed a similar route.

Return to Falmouth

During the war he met Mabel Alice Lina Grew, a civil servant and private secretary who helped him to rebuild his personal life.[76] The two married in Kensington, London at the end of 1943. At some point they settled at Falmouth, the town to which Richard's parents had returned from the USA at the turn of the century. His sister Gertrude, two years older than him, was married there in 1919. His mother had died there in 1939.

Falmouth is a pretty, small town and port that lies on the southern coast of Cornwall at the mouth of the River Fal and its exceptionally deep waters. Steep paths and lanes still lead straight up from the quayside road to the hill above the town. Perhaps large by Cornish standards, the population in 1951 was around 17,000. During the Second World War, maritime activity at Falmouth mushroomed. Thousands of Dunkirk survivors landed at Falmouth from small boats and rescue craft. The St Nazaire raiders sailed from there in 1942. There was a steady stream of crippled ships that came into port for repairs and refitting, which in turn prompted heavy enemy air raids. The Fal estuary was particularly important during the preparations for D-Day, providing extensive training grounds and embarkation facilities for the invading troops.[77] Falmouth also played an important role in the development and deployment of the Mulberry harbours that transformed the delivery of supplies to the Normandy beaches after the landings. As this high level of wartime activity and related bomb damage abated, an intensive programme of regeneration and rebuilding followed in the 1950s.

Trevethan had himself renewed his links with the town in March 1920. He became a freemason, joining the 'Lodge of Love and Honour.' The lodge continues to flourish, and functions from the Masonic Hall at Church Street, Falmouth.

In 1947, then living at Onslow Gardens in London, Richard needed a job. He applied successfully to become a member of the Royal Institution and looked for opportunities to apply his specialisation in meteorology.[78]

For many years there had been an observatory at Falmouth. Its history is interesting, having been instigated in 1867 when the Meteorological Committee of the Royal Society decided that a series of meteorological stations was needed around the British Isles to advance the study of the weather. Falmouth would be the site of one of the seven stations proposed: as the most southerly of the seven, it would have particular maritime importance regarding storms coming up the English Channel. The observatory had a ready champion in Falmouth in the shape of the Royal Cornwall Polytechnic Society (RCPS), founded in 1833 to 'promote the useful and fine arts, to encourage industry, and to elicit the ingenuity of a community distinguished for its mechanical skill.'[79]

Having operated first from a tower built on Bowling Green Hill in 1868 and leased from the builder, it began the rigorous programme of climate-related measurements required by the Meteorological Office in London. These extended to measurement of sea temperatures, reflecting the importance of weather information to Falmouth's fishing fleet.[80]

In 1882, the Meteorological Council decided to withdraw the grant that sustained the observatory. A year later it agreed under pressure to continue the grant for a further five years on condition that the RCPS build a suitable new observatory at its own expense. Consequently, it established a new building at 27 Western Terrace in 1886.[81] The old tower, at 1 Victoria Cottages, was returned to the builder. Many years later it became Richard Trevethan's home.

In 1948 the Falmouth Observatory Joint Committee of the RCPS appointed him to succeed a Mr Hooper, who had been superintendent of the observatory for twenty years.[82] The Committee also appointed Mabel Trevethan as his assistant. As the Observatory Joint Committee recorded, it had 'found a Cornishman educated at Falmouth... worthy of Mr Tregoning Hooper's long record of painstaking work.'

Not only had Trevethan found a job, it came with a home attached. The 1886 observatory was extensive, with ample grounds to house the full suite of climate measurement instruments. Apart from an office on the ground floor and an extensive loft area, the building included three-bedroomed accommodation for the superintendent and his family. To extend the observatory's reach, Trevethan initiated readings of ground temperature (of particular interest to agriculturalists) and evaporation (a notoriously difficult parameter both to measure and to apply, but important for managing crops.)

Each year the Superintendent prepared a 'Meteorological Note' for inclusion in the RCPS's annual report. This would summarise monthly statistics for all the measurements – barometric pressure, wind, temperature, rainfall and sunshine, and also related observations such as snow, hail, thunder, fog and ground frosts.

Richard Trevethan was interested in climatic anomalies and extremes and enjoyed reporting on them. In 1948 – 'The aurora borealis was seen with great brilliance in October.' In 1949 'lunar haloes on seven occasions in January.' In 1950 he noted, 'on Sept 26th the sun and the moon both had a remarkable blue appearance. This has been ascribed to the effect of the dust from forest fires in Canada having been carried in the atmosphere across the Atlantic. '

When asked about the reported sighting of a flying saucer, he must have enjoyed telling the honorary secretary to the RCPS Observatory Committee that it was probably a radio sonde balloon that had just been released from the Meteorological Station at Cambourne (it was later recovered in France).

According to the natural order of things, children bury their parents – not the other way around. Richard Trevethan however had lost his younger child at the age of five. As he was then 5,000km away, on duty in Iraq, he had not even been able to attend the funeral. Twenty years later, no sooner were his feet firmly settled underneath his desk at Falmouth, than fate intervened again.

On 19 January 1950 Gerald, his elder son, who had survived the fire that killed his brother, was found dead on the railway line between Littlemore and Cowley, outside Oxford. Gerald, a Cambridge graduate who had been a Captain in the Royal Electrical and Mechanical Engineers, had contracted tuberculosis while serving in Germany three years earlier. He had worried about his health and feared that he would infect others. This led to a nervous breakdown, following which he became a voluntary patient at Littlemore Hospital after a series of spells in various hospitals and sanatoria. While there, he had talked of joining his father at Falmouth to work out together how to further his career. The day before he died, he spoke optimistically about the future with Nora Kekewich, his great aunt. He had lived with her since he was ten.

The inquest that followed examined the possibility of suicide, but the court heard of nothing to suggest that he had contemplated taking his own life. He had been used to taking late night strolls and, as his great aunt had said, was almost blind in one eye. Asked whether his poor eyesight combined with the high winds blowing at the time might have preventing Gerald from realising that a train was approaching, the Medical Superintendent at the hospital stated that this was a possibility, but no more. He added that 'I feel convinced that this unfortunate boy did not commit suicide. I am firmly of the opinion that he had no intention of taking his life.' The jury agreed, returning a verdict of accidental death.[83]

Richard Trevethan had worried about Gerald for some time; tinged, probably, with guilt that his son had spent more of his life growing up with his great aunt rather than with his parents. He had shared his anguish with no less than Clement Attlee, his friend from Gallipoli days, who was then Prime Minister. In a letter from 10 Downing Street, addressing him once more as 'My dear Trev,' Attlee wrote of his sorrow on hearing of Graham's death.

Fortunately, he had Mabel to support him through this difficult time.

On top of all this, the financial viability of the observatory became increasingly precarious: the warning signs were clear in the 1948 Annual Report, and Richard probably took on the job realising that it might not last long. The RCPS took every opportunity to promote the value of the station and its observations, its educational value, and the extent of its contribution to the environment and economy – both locally and more widely in Cornwall. But this was not enough. By 1952 the building itself needed major and unaffordable refurbishment, and it was sold the next year. Trevethan's tenure lasted just four years. Measurement of the instruments in the observatory grounds continued until May 1953, after which they were all crated up and returned to the Meteorological Office in London.

Richard then went on to become Superintendent Registrar of Falmouth, a post he held for well over ten years – possibly up until his wife's death. As such he was responsible for both statutory and non-statutory registration services, performing marriage ceremonies, registering births, deaths and marriages, and issuing related certificates. His work also extended to licensing buildings for marriages and also for authorising buildings that had been built for worship to be used for other purposes.[84]

The old observatory tower where Trevethan then lived remains a landmark building in Falmouth. Set on a hill, the tower dominates the Falmouth skyline, and is famous for top floor windows that afford a spectacular 360° view to weather observers and the camera obscura that it houses.[††]

In retirement, Trevethan enjoyed showing the 'camera' to visitors. It consisted of a chamber at the top of the tower with a mirror that reflects light from objects outside downwards through a series of lenses on to a flat table. To select an image, Trevethan would have used two knobs to move the mirror; one to adjust the horizontal angle of view, and the other to set the declination. Refurbished with great care a few years ago, the tower is now a holiday home.

Old observatory tower at Falmouth in 2018

The downside of the tower was that, set on five levels with one room on each, there were many stairs. Andrew Pool, who met Trevethan professionally early on in his career as a chartered surveyor in the 1960s, recalls a small man who had been a keen sailor; by then, approaching his seventies, the stairs at the old tower had become a real difficulty. At some point Richard moved to Montague House at 31 Greenbank. This is a grand semi-detached building on the sea front that overlooks Falmouth

††   *Camera obscura* – dark/darkened room

Harbour and beyond to the Fal estuary. It also happens to be conveniently close to the Royal Cornwall Yacht Club, of which Trevethan was a keen member.

Mabel Trevethan died in 1966, aged 70. Richard never really recovered from the loss of his wife, and he spent the rest of his life as an unhappy man. To ease this, he returned to his old drinking habits that, from time to time, led the stewards at the yacht club to help him to stagger up the 160 or so steps back to his home.[85] He died of bronchopneumonia on 13 December 1971 and was buried at Falmouth.

When I look back over Richard Trevethan's life I can't help wondering how it played out the way it did. What, or perhaps 'whom' do we see – a young, brave adventurer who somehow lost his way? Without any first-hand knowledge it is perhaps unfair to conjecture, but did his early competitiveness give way to aggression with some arrogance thrown in? That elite of RFC pilots was trained to see themselves as knights of the sky. Would a decorated pilot in his early twenties propped up by family money and who had survived fear, danger and wounds have anything to lose by living for the moment – perhaps recklessly? He had survived while many of his companions, soldiers and flyers alike, had died. Did he end the war with some sense of invincibility that itself prompted bouts of wild abandon? Regardless of not being from the likes of Eton or Harrow, he clearly mingled with those in society. He married the sister of a baronet in a blaze of what would inevitably have been seen as indecent haste. Would life seem rather humdrum after all that? Did his divorce jolt him into severe depression?

As one of the RAF's first officers he survived the heavy cut in numbers that followed the end of the Great War. His career in the RAF had progressed well. And then, possibly triggered by the death of his first son, his life began to unravel. His marriage failed progressively over the next seven years, and his long absence in the Far East cannot have helped. His elder son spent much of his life living with his aunt rather than his parents.

And, for some reason, Richard became disenchanted with the RAF at a time when, with his impressive record, he might well have been slated for high office. Or perhaps the RAF became disenchanted with him — it put him on the half-pay list twice. Perhaps he was not a team player? His Second World War antics in small boats suggest that he certainly never lost his courage.

Falmouth and his second wife seem to have calmed him, or at least found him a new niche. He became a well-known, respected and active member of the community. Sadly, neither of his children survived him, and he had no nephews or nieces. What stories he would have been able to tell them! There can't be many to have served their country with such distinction in the air, on land, *and* at sea. Like all fearless cats, he had used up most if not all of his nine lives...

Attributing Richard Trevethan's miniatures

When I began my attempt to attribute these miniatures, I had hoped that the medal roll for the General Service Medal with clasp 'SOUTHERN DERSERT IRAQ' would help. This got me nowhere, as there does not appear to be a roll for RAF personnel, beyond an informal list said to include recipients with surnames up to 'M.' There is a roll for the small group of army participants, but that does not include anyone with the same combination of British Great War medals; hence my conviction that the miniature medals belonged to an RAF officer. The Service Personnel & Veteran's Agency of the Ministry of Defence was unable to expand the net.[86]

My luck changed when I managed to obtain a copy of Ray Brough's book *White Russian awards White to British & Commonwealth Servicemen during the Allied Intervention in Russia 1918-20*. This lists 56 officers with the RAF who were awarded the Order of St Anne for their services in both north and south Russia. Of these all but twelve (five 1st Class and seven 3rd Class) *either* received another Russian award *or* were not mentioned in despatches.[87]

Of the twelve, Michael Maton in *Honour the Officers* has listed five who received decorations throughout the Great War period.

Richard Trevethan is the *only* one of the five listed as a *single* Military Cross recipient. A second, Flying Officer L. C. Hooton, won a second award, and so does not count. The other three received combinations of the Distinguished Service Order, Distinguished Flying Cross and the Air Force Cross, so that rules them out too.

Trevethan's full-sized Military Cross, three Great War service medals and the Russian award were sold at auction on 18 June 1997. However the lot description does not state if they were mounted for wear, or loose. The group of miniatures that I bought also contains six other medals:

a. General Service Medal 1918-62 with 'SOUTHERN DESERT IRAQ' clasp (wrongly positioned second from the right in the mounted group)

b. 1939-45 Star

c. France and Germany Star

d. Defence Medal

e. British War Medal 1939-45

f. Coronation Medal (GRI)

Regarding Medal (a.), Trevethan was in Iraq from 1926 to 1929 and I have every reason to believe that he was directly involved in the 'SOUTHERN DESERT IRAQ' operations.

Regarding Medals (b.) to (e.), the Ministry of Defence has not been able to provide details of Trevethan's WWII campaign medals, as I am unable to obtain the Next of Kin consent required to arrange this.

However, assuming that my understanding that he was active in the SVP in 1944 at the time of D-Day is correct, I do have evidence that another SVP member (Major T.J. Grey CMG) received the same medals (b., c., d., e.) for his service related to the 1944 allied landings in Normandy.[88]

So far, I have been unable to locate Trevethan's name in the rolls for the 1937 Coronation Medal.

Looking at the whole picture and related probabilities, I remain convinced that Richard Trevethan is 'my man.'

Notes

1 Falmouth Grammar School archives (pers. comm. John Sadden 8 Jun 2015)

2 The Long, Long Trail, 'What was a battalion of infantry?', *http://www. longlongtrail.co.uk/army/definitions-of-units/what-was-a-battalion-of-infantry/*, accessed 24 Aug 2016

3 TNA WO 372/20/76715 Medal Card of Trevethan, Richard Michael; entries in the 'Theatre of War' box read 'France 14.3.15' and 'Gallipoli – 1915'

4 Imperial War Museum, 'What you need to know about the Gallipoli campaign', *http://www.iwm.org.uk/history/what-you-need-to-know-about-the-gallipoli-campaign*, accessed 8 Nov 2016

5 WO 95/4263-4359, War diary for 6 Battalion South Lancashire Regiment, Jul. 1915 – Dec. 1917 as transcribed by Stephen Nulty, March 2011

6 John Bew, *Citizen Clem* (2016) 81

7 Brian Mullaly, *The South Lancashire Regiment: The Prince of Wales's Volunteers* (1952) 189

8 WO 95/4263-4359, 6 Battalion South Lancashire Regiment

9 Firstworldwar.com, 'Battles – The Evacuation of Anzac Cove, Suvla Bay and Helles, 1915-16', *http://www.firstworldwar.com/battles/evacuation_dec15.htm*, accessed 5 Feb 2017

10 *The Portmuthian*, April 1916 42

11 Mullaly, *The South Lancashire Regiment*, 201

12 Henry Whalley-Kelly, *'Ich dien'; the Prince of Wales's Volunteers (South Lancashire) 1914-1934* (1935) 207

13 Experience in earlier battles had defined a notional density of heavy guns required to achieve effective damage to deep dugouts. Relaxing this 'rule of thumb' meant that 6-inch howitzers could be included in the density calculations along with the 7.2, 8.0, 9.2 and 12-inch guns deployed in the RGA siege batteries, thus falsely giving the appearance of sufficient numbers of effective guns (Hugh Sebag-Montefiore, *Somme – Into the Breach* (2016) 32-3

14 Max Arthur, *Forgotten voices of the Great War* (2002) 59

15 'First Day on the Somme', Wikipedia, *https://en.wikipedia.org/wiki/First_day_on_the_Somme*, accessed 4 Feb 2017

16 Hugh Sebag-Montefiore, *Somme – Into the breach* (2016) 7

17 Whalley-Kelly, *Prince of Wales's Volunteers*, (1935) 208

18 ibid. 209

19 RFC Casualty card for R.M. Trevethan

20 Robert Morley, *Earning their wings: British pilot training 1912-1918*, MA thesis, University of Saskatchewan (2006), Canada and AIR 1/39/15/7, 'RFC/RAF Casualties for Entire War,' and Peter Lewis, *Squadron Histories: RFC, RNAS and RAF since 1912* (London: Putnam, 1959) 197

21 Chris Ashworth, *Military airfields of the Central South and South-East*, (1985) 245

22 IWM, Documents 22390 Sqdn Ldr R M Trevethan; CFS Upavon Graduation Certificate, numbered 4448 and dated 14 May 1917

23 Chris Hobson, *Airmen Died in the Great War 1914–1918: The Roll of Honour of the British and Commonwealth Air Services of the First World War* (1995) ??

24 Morley, Earning their wings, 78

25 Cecil Lewis, *Sagittarius rising* (1936) 30-31

26 TNA, AIR 1/733/185/4, An account of an air-fight by a formation of FE2ds of No. 20 Squadron over Menin (Flanders) on Friday, July 27th, 1917, in which 2nd Lts G T W Burkett and T A M Lewis were wounded

27 Norman Franks, Russel Guest and Gregory Alegi. *Above the War Fronts: The British Two-Seater Bomber Pilot and Observer Aces, and the Belgian, Italian, Austro-Hungarian And Russian Fighter Aces 1914-1918* (1997) 10-11

28 ibid 26

29 IWM, Documents 22390, Sqdn Ldr R M Trevethan

30 TNA, AIR 1/733/185/4

31 Harold Satchell was a fellow 20 Squadron pilot (grandson of Dominic Gribbin)

32 pers. comm. Dominic Gribbin 12 Feb 2017

33 RFC Casualty card for R.M. Trevethan)

34 TNA, AIR 1/864/204/5/508, Return of casualties to all ranks of the RFC, British Army in France, for the fortnight ending 30 Sep 1917

35 Adapted from The Aerodrome, 'Richard Michael Trevethan', http://www.theaerodrome.com/aces/england/trevethan.php, accessed 2 Dec 2016

36 Analysis of data in AIR 1/39/15/7, Casualties RFC-RAF August 1915 – October 1918

37 TNA, AIR 1/167/15/156/1, History of 20 Squadron RFC

38 RAF Casualty card for R.M. Trevethan – accident on 8 Sep 1918

39 Damien Green, '*Imperial British Involvement in Russia 1918-1920*', http://www.russiansinthecef.ca/russiansinthecef/damien.shtml, accessed 3 Dec 2016

40 Damien Wright, *Churchill's Secret War with Lenin* (2017) 45

41 Christopher Dobson & John Miller, *The day we almost bombed Moscow* (1986) 222

42 Sir Charles Maynard, *The Murmansk Venture* (c1928) 233

43 Briton C. Busch (Ed.), *Canada and The Great War: Western Front Association Papers*, 'Ch. 12. Canadian Airmen and Allied Intervention in North Russia, 1918-19 by Owen Cooke.' (2003) 229

44 Naval History, 'The Voyages of HMS Nairana 1919', *http://www.naval-history.net/OWShips-WW1-04-HMS_Nairana.htm*, accessed 18 Jan 2017

45 'Fairey III', Wikipedia, *https://en.wikipedia.org/wiki/Fairey_III*, accessed 24 Nov 2014

46 Owen Thetford, *British Naval Aircraft since 1912* (1962) 107

47 Recollections from Ronald Sykes, IWM Interview No. 301, Reel 5, recorded 13 Mar 1973

48 TNA, AIR 1/472/15/312/167, N Russia – Syren – General returns Photography – Report on difficulties, 22 Jun 1919

49 Transcribed details from the Record of Service for Squadron Leader Richard Michael Trevethan MC, RAF'

50 Busch, *Canada and The Great War*, 229

51 Busch, *Canada and The Great War*, 230

52 ibid 225

53 Report for September 21010 from the OC, North Russian Expeditionary Force

54 TNA, AIR 1/472/15/312/167, N Russia – Syren – General returns

55 ibid, Monthly air operations report for Sep 1919, 5

56 DNW Lot description, 18 Jun 1997

57 Dobson & Miller, *The day we almost bombed Moscow*, 231

58 The Peerage, 'Sir Arthur Wilfred Graham Moon, 4th Bt.', *http://www.thepeerage.com/p51643.htm#i516425*, accessed 27 Jan 2017

59 RAF Casualty card for R.M. Trevethan – accident on 8 Oct 1921

60 *Portsmouth Evening News* 25 Oct 1921

61 Flight Global Archive (7 Sep 1922), 'Royal Air Force Intelligence', *https://www.flightglobal.com/pdfarchive/view/1922/1922%20-%200521.html*, accessed 27 Jan 2017

62 *Surrey Mirror and County Post* 19 Jun 1925

63 *Times* 7 Jan 1972

64 John Hayward, Diana Birch & Richard Bishop, *British battles and medals (7th Ed.)* (2006) 519

65 TNA, AIR 10/1839, Air Ministry, 1928 Report on the Operations carried out in the Southern Desert in Connection with the Iraq-Najd borders, November 1927-May 1928 20

66 *Surrey Mirror* 23 Mar 1928

67 TNA, J 77/3349/2270, Divorce Court File: 2270. Appellant: Richard Michael Trevelyan Trevethan. Respondent: Muriel Doris Graham Trevethan. Co-respondent: William Francis Bryan McLellan. Type: Husband's petition for divorce [HD].

68 RGS/FC – Trevethan, Richard, (pers. comm. Julie Carrington, RGS-IBG 13 Feb 2017)

69 *Portsmouth Evening News* 27 Aug 1937

70 *Portsmouth Evening News* 15 Jul 1938

71 With Henerson R.B. & Houndsfield F.H.C., *Theory of flight*, Danite Press Ltd, circa 1939

72 *West Briton & Cornwall Advertiser* 6 Jan 1972

73 *Journal of American-East Asian Relations* (1998), 212

74 IWM, Documents 22390 Sqdn Ldr R M Trevethan; Dorland House (18-20 Regent Street, London) was the operations centre for the SVP

75 TNA, DEFE 69/192, History of the Small Vessels Pool 1939-45 (linked to post-war Admiralty Ferry Crew Association) 4-page summary (1973)

76 Individual Narrative Report on RMT prepared by Family Historian, 21 Aug 2014

77 Falmouth Maritime Museum Library, World War2 file 442.032 'Falmouth in the war'

78 pers. comm. Charlotte New, 5 Apr 2017

79 Cornwall Polytechnic Society 'Our History', *http://thepoly.org/about-us/our-history*, accessed 30 Mar 2017

80 Michael Carver, *The Falmouth Observatories*, (unpublished)

81 Historic Cornwall, 'Cornwall & Scilly Urban Survey: Falmouth Report 32', *http://www.historic   cornwall.org.uk/csus/towns/falmouth/csus_falmouth_report_2005R003.pdf*, accessed 4 Feb 2017

82 pers. comm. Michael Carver 25 Mar 2017

83 *Oxford Mail*, 24 .01.1950

84 *The London Gazette*, 27 Apr 1954, 2508; 6 Nov 1956, 6279; 16 Feb 1965, 1698

85 pers. comm. Andrew Pool 4 Apr 2017

86 pers. comm. 21 Aug 2013

87 Ray Brough, *White Russian Awards to British & Commonwealth Servicemen during the Allied Intervention in Russia 1918-20* (1991) 97

88 WW2Talk Forum, 'Octogenarians with campaign stars', *http://ww2talk.com/index.php?threads/octogenarians-with-campaign-stars.33869/*, accessed 11 Mar 2018

Lucie Toller

The nurse: Lucie Toller

By her fine example she undoubtedly saved life

Lucie Toller's group of miniature medals (Royal Red Cross 1st Class, Military Medal, 1914 Star with '5th Aug.: 22nd Nov. 1914' bar, British War Medal 1914 – 20, Victory Medal with Mention in Dispatches Oak leaf) with France, *Médaille des Epidemies* separately on the right

Much has been written about 'Tommy Atkins' and his fighting experiences in the Great War, but relatively little has followed about his care when sick or wounded in battle. Nevertheless, there are some excellent accounts of nursing in the Great War, and some fascinating diaries that open our eyes to the physical, mental and practical aspects of caring for the sick and injured. I have quoted several in the pages that follow.

One of my 'five' was a nurse. Her name was Lucie Toller. Awarded the Royal Red Cross for her nursing professionalism in 1917, honoured by the French in 1919 for services to civilians, and decorated for her bravery and leadership in 1918, there are few front-line nurses to have achieved such recognition. But beyond that she is a mystery. I can chart her career, year by year, hospital by hospital. But of 'herself'? Nothing. The photograph that she sent to the Imperial War Museum aged around 40 gives little away. Timid, yet quietly steely? No ego or grandeur; possibly someone who did not want to be seen, or would prefer to be alone? Did she have a life outside her work; hobbies, lovers or close friends?

Recognising a limit to the conjecture that I can reasonably include in this story, I decided to treat her story differently from the other four. Instead, rather than focus completely on her and her invisible personal life, here is a story about the wider context of frontline nursing and the way in which Lucie Toller fitted into it. She was one of many fine women who dedicated themselves to tending the wounded, often in extremely difficult circumstances. She happens to have worked in just about all of the various foci of medical care where women were deployed, ranging from casualty clearing near the front line to the major hospitals on the French coast; an ideal framework on which to hang our glimpse into the world of frontline nursing in France as the war dragged on.

LMT in 1918 (IWM WWC D41-42)

Lucie Maud Mary Toller was one of that small band of professional nurses who joined Queen Alexandra's Imperial Military Nursing Service (QAIMNS) early in the 1900s. She served in France throughout the war.[1]

Her story begins when she was born on 8 November 1874 at Denny Abbey, close to Waterbeach, a small town halfway between Cambridge and Ely. Originally a Benedictine monastery, and well past its days as a religious haven, Denny Abbey was a fine building occupied by a succession of farmers. Today, the abbey is in the care of English Heritage and is dedicated to Cambridgeshire rural life.

Lucie's father, Richard Toller, was a wealthy man. He farmed some 600 acres nearby and was the scion of a long line of Huntingdonshire and Cambridgeshire farmers. His father, John Toller, was a successful landowner, running several farms including Anstey Hall Farm at Trumpington, Cambridge.[2]

Such was the world into which Lucie was born; a wonderful playground, with all the comforts that she could imagine. She was the third of four sisters. Her father employed a governess to educate her at home, and then sent her to a local private school.

Richard Toller died in 1884, aged 56. For some reason, his widow Sarah, the daughter of a St Ives watchmaker, tired of Waterbeach and moved to the coast at Lowestoft. This brought an end to Lucie's schooling. By 1891 – aged sixteen – she was apprenticed to a dressmaker, while her younger sister Mabel Rose went to school in the town.

It was a twist of fate that freed Lucie to turn to nursing as a career. Had she been the youngest child, she would have been required at home to look after her mother, as did Mabel Rose, who remained with her mother until she died in 1903. By that time, Lucie was 29 and her sister was 25.

Nursing calls

In January 1897 Lucie travelled to London to begin a three-year training programme as a probationer at the St Marylebone Infirmary, a hospital in the Ladbroke Grove area opened for the sick poor of St Marylebone in 1881. She was 24 years old and would have lived in the Nurses' Home there.

Her choice of hospital is interesting. The Nightingale Fund had chosen it as a training facility for nurses to serve in workhouse infirmaries, paying the probationers salaries, and providing gratuities for the medical staff in return for instructing the probationers.* Elizabeth Vincent, Lucie's matron, had herself trained at the Nightingale School of Nursing at St Thomas' Hospital, which proved to be the most successful of the Nightingale Fund's initiatives of this kind; by 1899 it was 'admitting between 20 and 30 probationers a year, many of whom in time became head nurses in other infirmaries.'[3] But, as devised by Nightingale, infirmary training was to a lower level than at general hospital schools, offering a professional career to less educated women. 'While educated "ladies" nursed in the prestigious teaching hospitals, infirmary nurses were from the lower social stratum', effecting a two-tier profession until the introduction of state registration in 1919.[4] How, or why Lucie would have chosen to train in this system? There can be little question that she was from the 'correct' social mix. Indeed, it is unlikely that the Army would have accepted her a few years later had she not been so. While her fellow probationers may have been less privileged than her, she probably learned much from them.

Completing her training as a Staff Nurse, she led a mobile life for the next few years, moving to the Royal Infirmary at Lauriston Place in Edinburgh as a 'Special Nurse' in March 1900 for fourteen months, followed by her first appointment as a Sister at St Bartholomew's Hospital, Rochester – one of the oldest hospitals in England. A year or so later, she returned to London as a Charge Nurse at the South Western Hospital in Stockwell, which specialised in the treatment of infectious diseases.

She remained there until April 1904, when she applied to join the QAIMNS. Lucie began her military career on 7 July 1904, when she reported for duty at the Queen Alexandra Hospital, Portsmouth. After nine months of probation, her appointment as Staff Nurse was confirmed. Five months later she achieved promotion to Sister, aged thirty-one.

---

* Care of the sick poor was an enduring concern for [Florence] Nightingale, who had been a lady visitor to the St Marylebone Workhouse in the 1840s

So began a career that took her far and wide, serving initially in the south of England in London and Aldershot, and including a seven-week stint doing 'duty on board' the transport S.S. *Plassey*, which took her to India. From Aldershot she moved in September 1909 to the 200-bed British Military Hospital at Bowen Road in Hong Kong. By all accounts, this was a magnificent, airy and modern building built on a hill that overlooked the harbour, run by RAMC, QAIMNS and Canadian army nursing personnel. After what must have been three very interesting and formative years, doubtless enlivened by the morning processions of sedan chairs carrying the sick up the hill from the lower levels, she returned to England. Stints at military hospitals at Tidworth and Netley then followed.[5]

August 1914 – a daunting prospect for front-line nursing

The medical resources available to the British Expeditionary Force at the outbreak of war in August 1914 comprised: RAMC – 1,279 officers and 3,811 Other Ranks (ORs); QAIMNS 293 less about 34 in Ireland, with a number of reservists; Territorial Force – 1,889 officers and 12,520 ORs.[6] The QAIMNS Reserve (QAIMNS(R)), willing to be drafted for active service within twenty-four hours' notice, numbered around 800, bringing the QAIMNS total to little more than 1,000 trained nurses. The Territorial Force Nursing Service was able to mobilise 2,784 nurses within a week of the declaration of war.[7] By the end of the year 1,791 trained nurses from all arms had been dispatched to the BEF in France.[8] Their task was a daunting one.

There was also a new source of support, although it was restricted to Home Front service until 1915. In 1909, following the example of Russian villagers who volunteered to tend the sick and wounded during the 1904-05 Russo-Japanese War, the War Office had introduced a system to harness volunteer assistance through Voluntary Aid Detachments (VAD). The British VAD were operated under the auspices of the British Red Cross.

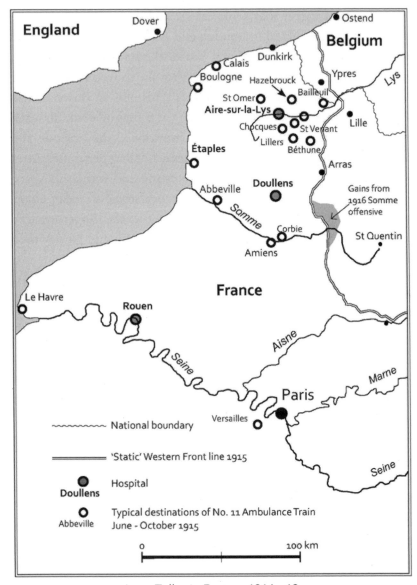

Lucy Toller in France, 1914 – 19

Such was their enthusiasm; over 1,700 female and 500 male detachments had been registered with the War Office by the beginning of 1914. Eventually, 'somewhere between 70,000 and 100,000 women served as VADs at some time during the war, some for very short periods, some for up to five years.' [9] While a relative few nurses served in France in 1914, it was not until mid-1915 that the serious need to reinforce the nursing effort led female VADs to be posted from Home Front service to military establishments in the war zones.

In spite of suspicion from the military establishment that VADs would put the sick and wounded at great risk due to a perceived lack of training and experience and corresponding VAD reaction to the military system, their numbers in military hospitals overseas reached around 8,000 by the end of the war.

Then aged 40, Sister Lucie Toller mobilised to join No. 12 General Hospital (12 GH).[†] She landed in France on 17 August – nine days before the bulk of her unit sailed from Southampton. Quite what she did in the meantime is unclear, but she must have travelled out with one of the other hospitals.[10] Dozens of QAIMNS nurses arrived in France early on, between 14 and 20 of August, and of those quite a number were unemployed and waited for orders for some weeks. It was a time of upheaval with hospitals opening, closing and moving remarkably frequently. While we do not know when she arrived at 12 GH, the unit's story in those early days, as set out in the hospital war diary is uncomfortably revealing.

This begins on 27 August on arrival at Rouen, where 12 GH set up on the Champs des Courses racetrack.[11] Uncertainty then spread as the German advance drew closer. Entire hospitals in Rouen including medical staff and patients evacuated down the Seine to the coastal bases before returning after a few weeks.[12] In the case of 12 GH, this involved navigating some 60km of the great meanders of the lower Seine to the harbour at Le Havre, and then following the coastline round to St Nazaire – a voyage of more than 700km. The constant movement of the hospitals, and consequent problems and muddles, are portrayed in the hospital diary:

---

† General Hospital – Top-level military hospital

27.8.14   Received orders to move out of standing camp to make room for incoming troops. Drew 5 marquees and encamped on aviation ground. Received orders to take over grandstand at racecourse. Drew 200 blankets and 200 mattresses.

29.8   Ordered to bring up all equipment and form a hospital as quickly as possible on aviation ground. Got four motor lorries from transport and removed about half the equipment to the camp. Pitched four additional tents (Marquees) for sick. Last load arrived after dark.

30.8   Received a letter... asking for a return showing strength of unit and weight of equipment. Replied '23 officers (including attached chaplains) and 143 men and about 100 tons of equipment.' 7.30 a.m. Received orders to remove patients – strike hospital and move equipment to Quay at once and report when able to move [evacuate]. Received three motor lorries to remove equipment. Each lorry took 1.5 hours to make journey and return. By 5.30 p.m. all equipment was removed from aviation camp. By 7.30 p.m. all equipment was removed from the grandstand and racecourse. The patients were placed on motor lorries and were placed on board the *St Patrick*. Men and officers slept on the quay... Ordered to embark on SS *Dominic*. Part of equipment loaded on SS *Basil* and part on the *Claremont*. Men worked smartly and were finished by 1.40 a.m.

31.8   On board SS *Dominic*. Owing to the hurry in which the equipment of six general hospitals was placed on the ships the equipment has got badly mixed up.

1 to 6.9   On SS *Dominic* and finally landed at St Nazaire.

15.9   After much muddle unloading/mix-ups/ entraining, left St N for Nantes, arrived there 16th and left at 12.30 p.m. for Rouen, ordered to set up hospital at the race course; 'sisters arriving tomorrow' [no further mention of Sisters]. Much effort to locate/transport correct stores/ organise water supply; latrines (RE); Issued a Union Jack to No. 8 GH on loan on 21 Sept! The secretary of the racecourse called. He objected to any drains being placed on the course itself.

30.9.   203 sick + 129 wounded, with 21 vacant beds.
           Converting rooms in the grandstand to offices stores,
           dispensary, etc. [13]

All in all, a tale of great frustration. How much did the hospital
staff know of what was going on?

12 GH was one of the first fourteen hospitals and convalescent
camps maintained by the BEF in the Rouen area. Between them
they provided some 25,000 beds. Olive Dent, a VAD nurse who
worked at the racecourse hospital at Rouen from September 1915
provides an intricate portrayal of the conditions in which these
medical personnel worked:

> For a bird's eye view of the camp would have revealed
> a forest of marquees and a webbing of tent-ropes. The
> marquees sometimes clustered so close that the ropes of two
> roofs on the adjoining side were not pegged to the ground,
> but were tied overhead, the one to the other, so supporting
> each other and saving space. Between such dual marquees
> was a tarpaulin passage, usually spoken of as a tunnel. Each
> row of marquees was known as a 'line' and named as letters
> in the alphabet. Thus 'A' line consisted of eight or nine tents,
> known as A1, A2, A3 and so on. All these marquees were
> exactly alike, and as we nurses passed from one to another
> several times in the morning, it was a little difficult to know
> whether one was in A1, A3 or A.5...
>
> I dreaded the thought of night duty with its tense
> anxieties, its stringent vigilance, its many sorrows... We
> have had nights when wind and rain have raged overhead,
> when our hurricanes [lamps] have blown out directly we
> lifted the tent flaps to go out, when we have been splashed
> to the knees with mud... when the rain has stung our cheeks
> like whipcord. [14]

The mud was everywhere...

By 5 October the hospital at Rouen was treating 428 patients, with 34 spare beds. Two days later orders were received to expand to 700 beds, all with continued reliance on tents; a risky strategy, as on 28 December 'a very severe gale blew during the night: several store tents blew down. Part of the roof of the operating theatre was blown off. The hospital marquees stood the gale very well. All day spent in repitching fallen tents.'

A day later came an order to expand to 730 beds; 760 if 100 blankets could be found. Thus ended 1914 for No. 12 General Hospital, Rouen.

To illustrate the enormity of the medical services' task, there were over 177,000 BEF casualties in the first five months of the war. Of these, almost 99,000 (56%) were battle injuries (dead, died of wounds, wounded, missing, or prisoners of war). The remaining 78,557 suffered from non-battle injuries such as tetanus, meningitis, dysentery, eye and ear infections, varicose veins, pneumonia, hernia, rheumatism, tonsillitis and venereal disease.[15] In contrast to these relatively common ailments, injuries from gunshot, shells, bombs, grenades and bayonets posed a drastically different challenge, and a very steep learning curve. And it was but a few months before the ghastly use of poison gas began when the Germans released more than 150 tons of lethal chlorine gas against two French colonial divisions north of Ypres in Belgium on 22 April 1915.

The base area hospitals, of which 12 GH was one, were part of the RAMC's chain of medical evacuation facilities that began at regimental aid posts at the front line and ended in military and war hospitals at home.[16] The overriding imperative was to get wounds treated as quickly as possible. Otherwise the chances of survival from a serious wound were slim. The regimental aid posts, typically in dugouts or trenches were the first link in the chain. There the wounded would receive first aid from RAMC doctors or stretcher-bearers. Those fit enough to return to the front would then do so, while those needing further treatment would begin a journey that would eventually take them – often by ambulance – to Casualty Clearing Stations (CCSs) close to the fighting. These provided the first encounters with female nurses and facilities for surgery. Those still requiring medical care would then be moved by ambulance train, road or barge to Stationary Hospitals or General Hospitals near major bases such as at Étaples or Boulogne. From there, those requiring specialist treatment, convalescence or too badly injured to remain in service would be taken by hospital ship for further care in England.

During her four years in France, Lucie Toller served in all three types of hospital and on an ambulance train.

Where specifically was Lucie Toller during those autumn months of 1914? The Bar fixed to the ribbon of the 1914 Star in her miniature medals group indicates that she was one of a very small band of QAIMNS personnel who qualified as being 'in range of the enemy's guns' during that brief period of crisis between 5 August and 22 November 1914. Perhaps she worked on one of the first ambulance trains that, along with barges, were used to evacuate casualties from the CCSs to hospital, or at one of the early CCSs? Some nurses are known to have accompanied senior officers to and from the bombardment zones.

But here lies an anomaly. While her entitlement to the 1914 Star is well documented, I can find no hard evidence of her entitlement to the Bar. (Of the 378,000 or so personnel to be awarded the 1914 Star, only 348 were from the QAIMNS and QAIMNS(R).[17] Relatively few of the 378,000 also met the qualifying conditions for the Bar. Of these only a *very* small number were women.)

Ambulance trains

Dame Maud McCarthy was Matron-in-Chief in France and Flanders for the duration of the war, throughout which she maintained an important diary. Following widespread initial reluctance to let nurses anywhere near the front line, she championed the value of her nurses in CCSs, and the ambulance trains and barges that were used to get the wounded back to hospitals.

Ambulance trains, introduced to ferry casualties from the front line to the base and other more fully resourced hospitals, were to become a key link in the RAMC's evacuation chain. Maud McCarthy reflected on their importance and the gradual progress towards deploying professional nurses on them that took place in 1914 when she wrote in 1919 that finally on 7 September 1914:

> A nurse was detailed to join one of these trains at Le Mans... There was a Medical Officer in charge of the train, on which there were about 115 wounded British Officers and 100 other ranks... On his return to Le Mans, the Medical Officer reported that the services of a Sister on the train were of inestimable value, and so it came about that on all trains arriving at Le Mans, two Sisters joined them for duty until its arrival at the Base... On September 16th two Nurses were sent on No.7 Ambulance Train to railhead [at the front] for the first time.[18]

And so, the nursing sisters joined the ambulance train crews. Without question they came 'within the range of the enemy's guns.'

Later on, Maud McCarthy got her nurses closer to the front line and noted with satisfaction 'one of the results of the presence of Sisters at Casualty Clearing Stations, which they joined in October and November 1914, was the very noticeable improvement in the condition of patients onto trains.'

The story of the ambulance trains is interesting. By 22 November ten ambulance trains had been established and were collecting wounded from the CCSs.‡ The nursing Sisters who worked on them were organised around a depot at Villeneuve St Georges, a railway complex just south east of Paris. In September 1914 they began to staff the seven ambulance trains on the basis of four Sisters per train.

---

‡   22 November was the end-date for qualification for the Bar to the 1914 Star

The first eleven trains were all adapted from French rolling stock. In his diary for No. 5 Ambulance Train (5 AmTr) Major Dennis RAMC noted that: 'the train has four large *fourgon* or luggage vans and nine bogey carriages which are *wagons lits*. There is a staff of 20 Frenchmen and one French officer.' The RAMC personnel numbered four officers, four senior NCOs and a crew of orderlies. The train could carry '136 lying down cases and 108 sitting up cases.' Also 'a small part of the restaurant car is shut off with glass doors as a small room for the English and French officers to dine in.' In comparison with less well-stocked trains, Dennis's steward listed – for a short while at least:

> ... the following food stuffs: Maconochie rations, corned beef, tinned chicken, fresh meat (where possible), bacon, potatoes, fresh vegetables, cheese, fresh bread (where possible), biscuits, butter, jam, arrowroot, sago, tapioca, eggs (when possible), tea, coffee, cocoa, milk (tinned), pea soup, lemon, brandy, whisky, red wine, white wine, beer, soda water, Vitel water, cider, champagne, rum.

Major Dennis also recorded that Sisters Woodhouse and Luard and Staff Nurses Cathels and Adler (all QAIMNS or QAIMNS(R)) had all joined the train by mid-October. By 22 November his train had run 17 round-trips to and from the front-line railheads.

These journeys involved a variety of hazards. Major B.B. Burke, CO of 3 AmTr, who had already been caught up with the evacuations from Rouen at the end of August noted early on 2 September:

> Shortly after passing Dammartin my ambulance train was stopped by a French engineering party and was told by their captain that he had just received information by aeroplane that parties of Uhlans were near, and that I could not proceed further. I insisted on proceeding & after some time he agreed to allow my train to proceed on condition that I

went personally on the engine accompanied by 2 of his men. Arrived at Le Plessins Belville at 0500. Could see British troops retiring on both sides of the Ry. [railway] Station. From roof of my carriage and by aid of glasses I saw field ambulances retiring also. Sent our bicycle orderly & message to OCs Field ambulances informing them of the position of AmTr. Took all their sick and wounded. Waited for as long as possible after main bodies of troops had retired in order to pick up any stragglers…

By 20 November his train had completed as many as 27 round-trips, carrying almost 6,000 cases – many from the Ypres salient.

One of the occupational hazards of working on the adapted French trains was that the carriages were not fitted with corridors. Each compartment – effectively a ward, staffed by two orderlies – was isolated from the others. Consequently, this necessitated 'constant

Red Cross train loading up at Casualty Clearing Station (Wikimedia Commons - *https://wellcomecollection.org/works/ y3bx26yy?query=red%20cross%20ambulance%20train* accessed 18 Mar 2019)

jumping up and down when the train is standing, in rain, snow, unspeakable mud, daylight or pitch-black night, or "foot boarding" from coach to coach.'[19] This practice – while absolutely forbidden – required some skill.

The war diaries for Trains 1 to 9 are complete for their operations in 1914. Collectively, they mention the deployment of 23 Nursing Sisters (ten of whom are named) and seven Staff Nurses (all named). Assuming that each train was staffed with its full quota of four nurses, at least six others were so deployed in the period to 22 November. Was Lucie Toller one of them?

We do know however that Lucie was the Sister-in-Charge of 11 AmTr from June to October 1915. This train was converted from ordinary French 3rd Class carriages in the first half of December 1914. It was 'one fitted up by the British Red Cross Society, and Order of St. John of Jerusalem' with nurses trained by the British Red Cross under the supervision of a Sister-in-Charge who was 'a member of the Regular Service.'[20] Adapted specifically to carry a large number of stretcher cases, it also was a non-communicating train.

The ambulance trains undoubtedly faced danger. The CO of 6 AmTr reported that his train was under fire on 6 October, while 7 AmTr was shelled at Ypres on 2 November (*q.v.*). Major Waring, CO of 4 AmTr recorded on 29 October that his train:

> ... arrived at Ypres at 3.30 a.m. At about 9.15 a.m. while waiting for patients to arrive a German airplane passed over the station and dropped several bombs one of these fell on the permanent way 50 yards from the end of No. 4 Ambulance Train but caused no damage. Entraining commenced at 10 a.m. taking in 18 officers and 240 OR [other ranks] including 2 Germans.[21]

What was life like for a nursing sister on an ambulance train? In her private papers, Sister Bickmore, who served on the trains between 1914 and 1917 gives stark insight:

Dashing at a high speed 'Empty' to a far advanced CCS to gather a 'Crisis load'; or returning at 10 miles an hour, bearing with it the shattered remnants of those who so proudly and bravely sallied forth against the foe on the battlefields a few short hours before. Sometimes under shellfire, sometimes under raiding or fighting aeroplanes, it serenely 'carries on'.

On arrival at the 'Rail Head' where the CCSs lie, the work for the staff begins.

The patients are brought to the train in ambulances or on little trolleys run on light rails. They lie on stretchers and are passed into the coaches or 'wards' of the train and are then transferred to the beds. The Sisters receive them and examine their medical cards, decide what diet they should have and arrange their shattered limbs, by means of bandages, pillows, sand bags etc., to travel with as little suffering as possible.

Mud, blood and sweat clothes them still, and the tormenting parasites accompany them unless they have been detained for a period at the CCS until fit to undertake the journey, in which case they have been cleansed and clothed afresh. No tongue can tell what these patients have been through, and none who have not at least seen them in their battlefield array can form any conception of it.

The Medical Officers [MOs] see each case personally, and order the treatment, which the Sisters carry out, while the orderlies attend to food, drink and general wants.

… The lights of the train are closely veiled. If an air raid takes place over and around it, all lights are extinguished and like a long dark snake it squats on the lines, waiting till the danger is passed. [22]

Reflecting too on the hazards of foot boarding, Sister Bickmore concluded that as 'the difficulties, fatigues and danger of the work on a "French" train are considerably added to by its construction, so also are the interest and the "thrill."'

But not even the 'thrill,' could mask the hideous reality of it all. Kate Luard, reflecting on the First Battle of Ypres, which seemed 'perhaps the most desperate of all', became overwhelmed by the carnage on 25 October when she wrote, after picking up 368 casualties, of whom more than 200 were dangerously and seriously wounded:

> ... one man with a huge compound fracture above the elbow had tied on a bit of string with a bullet in it as a tourniquet above the wound itself. When I cut off his soaked three layers of sleeve there was no dressing on it at all.
>
> They were bleeding faster than we could cope with it; and the agony of getting them off the stretchers onto the bunks is a thing to forget.[23]

Maud McCarthy had no doubts about the value of her nurses in those dreadful months of late 1914. She paid tribute to their professionalism and bravery in 1917, when she wrote:

> Great work was accomplished by the Sisters on Ambulance Trains in 1914. They worked under enormous difficulties, and with, for themselves, the barest necessities, and no comforts. The loads carried were heavy, and the journeys long. They worked too under dangerous conditions and there is no doubt that there were many examples of brave conduct which passed unrecorded.

One incident that McCarthy did mention was the occasion when 7 AmTr was caught up in heavy shelling early in November. While the train commander did not name any of the nurses serving with him in his diary for 1914, one who was with him on the night of that raid was Minnie Phillips, a reservist nurse. Recalling that the train was stranded at Ypres while its engine moved elsewhere to find water, she imagined with characteristic good humour what:

… feelings of great thankfulness and relief [as] she [the ambulance train] hooked herself on to her engine the next morning and gave him a graphic description of those horrid shells which had made holes in her sides and broken her windows, while he was away at Hazebrouck imbibing water. [24]

Perhaps she needed such distractions to shield her briefly from the grim reality of it all:

… patients were entrained with all the dirt, mud and blood of battle on them. All were fully dressed. Many had not had their boots off their feet for five or six weeks. Only those who have experienced it know what it means to undress a heavy man, badly wounded and lying on the narrow shelf of a railway carriage. Never before has it been brought home to me what a quantity of clothes a man has.[25]

Fortunately, as professional nurses joined the casualty clearing stations, they managed to begin to deliver their patients to the ambulance trains washed, fed and in pyjamas.

While work on the ambulance trains was undoubtedly stressful, Miss McCarthy recalled on 11 July 1915 'Miss Toller came about the Red Cross Train [No.11]. She is managing well under various difficulties, but she says her nursing staff are good and satisfactory in every way.' A report about a very unassuming lady?

Lucie's work on the ambulance trains did not go unnoticed: Sir John French included her name among those commended 'for gallant and distinguished service in the field' in his despatch of 30 November 1915. Her reward was a posting to 24 GH at Étaples on 21 October. She was soon appointed Acting-Matron, charged with the new Sick Sisters' Hospital at Villa Tino near Le Touquet, a 32-bed unit staffed by 24 GH that Miss McCarthy described as 'perfectly charming – most comfortable, well-furnished and luxurious.'[26] This became a facility for all sick sisters in the Étaples area.

Doullens – and casualty clearing

In May 1916, Lucie Toller transferred to the *Citadelle* at Doullens to take charge of two Casualty Clearing Stations – Nos. 11 and 35.

The CCSs were planned as rapid-turnaround units to treat wounded men sufficiently to enable them either to return to the line or, more usually, to be moved on to a Base Hospital. They simply were not intended for long-term stay.

There were 64 Casualty Clearing Stations on the Western Front. They moved from location to location as the armies advanced or retired.[27] Casualty Clearing Station No.1, for instance, was based at 11 different locations between November 1914 and November 1918.[28]

The small town of Doullens lies 35km southwest of Arras. It has a direct rail link to Amiens, 30km to the south. The *Citadelle* was a magnificent collection of fortified buildings and related tunnels on an immense 54ha site dating from the XVI Century when Doullens was a frontier town [with Spain]. Since then, it had functioned as garrison fort, prison for enemies of the state, prison for young women and – from 1914 to 1918 – a wartime hospital.

Not only was Doullens an important component of the medical evacuation chain, at least five British divisions had headquarters or other links with the town during the Somme operations. It provided extensive billeting facilities.

Originally established by the French Army, the British took over the hospital at the *Citadelle* on 11 June to establish No. 11 CCS, while No. 35 opened two weeks later.

The 4th Army had set up the two stations there as part of its preparations for the casualties anticipated from the Battle of the Somme which began on 1 July 1916: the ill-fated battlefields were just 20km to the east. The RAMC's preparations for the battle and related outcomes are well described by Sir W.G. MacPherson, noting the Fourth Army policy to set up CCSs in pairs. Each operated as a separate unit, but with wounded being brought to each in rotation in order to manage the numbers of wounded and their treatment more smoothly.[29] Describing their organisation and structure, Yvonne McEwen writes:

Casualty Clearing Stations were mobile miniature hospitals and, in the early days of the war, they were generally established in buildings. But by the late summer of 1915 it became standard practice to erect, in open ground, hospital tents which could then be moved forward or back. At 12,000 yards behind the lines, the Casualty Clearing Station was supposed to be beyond the range of artillery, but they were often shelled. To make casualty transportation easier, they were generally situated near the road or rail lines. Each Casualty Clearing Station had 100 staff comprising doctors, nurses, orderlies and technicians and had the capacity to deal with 1,000 patients per day. Operating theatres and wards for acute cases were sometimes housed in army Nissen huts. There were generally surgical teams, two of which were always on duty. Patients were classified into preferential wards such as those suffering from gas, fractures, gangrene, burns, enteric or trench fever. There was also a moribund tent. Here at the Casualty Clearing Stations sick and wounded had their first contact with the nurses, whose positive effect on the men's morale is described by the war correspondent Basil Clarke.

'They followed her [the sister] about with their eyes. She stood still when her work was done and spoke to the soldier in the bed nearest her. They chatted for three or four minutes, and one could see the interest of the wounded man in his steady gaze upon her.' ...

The Casualty Clearing Stations had to be ready to take in large numbers of casualties at very short notice, after which they were accommodated or re-classified for evacuation to the 'distribution zone.' Philip Gibbs presents a horrific picture of the wounded arriving at a zone in Lillers, Belgium.

'There were men with hunks of steel in their lungs and bowels vomiting great gobs of blood, men with legs and arms torn from their trunks, men without faces, or their brains throbbing through open scalps.'[30]

Unlike many other CCSs, the two at *Citadelle* were unable to clear their patients directly to ambulance trains. Initially motor ambulances transferred patients to Gezaincourt Station, some two kilometres to the south. Later on, arrangements were made with Third Army to drive them into Doullens and the railway station there.

The military disaster at the Somme is well chronicled. Not only were countless British soldiers killed, but also the number of wounded far exceeded predictions. The extra load on the casualty clearing stations was exacerbated by two events: firstly, the arrangements for evacuating the wounded to the CCSs by ambulance worked so well that casualties reached the CCSs faster than expected; secondly many casualties were brought directly to Gezaincourt by light rail, adding to the total numbers to be evacuated by ambulance train. Finally, there were only three ambulance trains in the Fourth Army area when the battle commenced. As a result, there was an acute shortage of space in the casualty clearing stations during the night of 1st/ 2nd July.

A nursing sister attending to gassed men on an ambulance train in France during the 1918 German offensive (Wikimedia Commons - Nederlands Archief: Fotocollectie Eerste Wereldoorlog, 158-0146)

In the event, 14,416 of the 23,993 Fourth Army wounded who had been brought to field ambulances during the first 24 hours of the battle had reached one of the 14 casualty clearing stations. This was way more than the available accommodation: Fourth Army planners had reckoned before the battle on dealing with 24,000 wounded in a day, with 10,000 in field ambulances, up to 9,500 at the casualty clearing stations, and 4,900 on ambulance trains at any one time. Had it not been for contingency provision for additional ambulance trains and evacuation by barge or road (for 'sitting-up' wounded) the CCSs would have been seriously over-congested. And so, by 3 July when Fourth Army evacuated 14,930 wounded by rail, road and barge, the casualty clearing stations had been cleared; affording some relief to the over-stretched RAMC and nursing staff there. [31]

As far as the two hospitals at the *Citadelle* were concerned, 11 Casualty Clearing Station received 154 patients on 29 June. A further 108 arrived on 1 July, including many stretcher cases. No. 35 Casualty Clearing Station received 220 casualties on its first day. The following day brought 220, and 130 more on the day after that. On 2 July, the second day of the battle, 400 more arrived, followed by a further 500 on 5th. The numbers of new casualties only began to decrease from 7 July. (Many of the early Somme casualties to reach Doullens were from a diversionary attack on the Gommecourt salient on 1st July.)

By this time, Lucie had been nursing battlefield casualties for almost two years. But how many of her nurses were that seasoned – probably very few? It is hard to imagine the impact of such horrors as amputations, gross deformities and the stench of gangrene on inexperienced personnel. There was little or no time for rehearsal. Keeping her staff focussed and calm during such horrifying and exhausting times must have been a struggle. Judging by Maud McCarthy's later comments, she succeeded admirably.

Lucie Toller continued to make her mark at Doullens. The Matron-in-Chief visited her twice, noting on 17 July that 'This place [11 and 35 stations] in the short time has become a most magnificent unit, more like a General Hospital than a Casualty Clearing Station in every respect. Miss Toller who is in charge of both units is managing most excellently.' A month later she 'spent the night with Miss Toller and her Staff in this wonderful old fort, their quarters being perched on the top of a huge high arch on top of a large rock, all most historic and grand. This unit has improved enormously since my last visit, Miss Toller managing most excellently.'

In the five months of operations that marked that phase of the Battle of the Somme, the field ambulances of the Third, Fourth and Fifth (Reserve) armies collected 316,073 wounded – a forbidding load on the medical services.[32] By then No. 35 Casualty Clearing Station's arduous job was done: the Canadian Army Medical Corps took over the *Citadelle* in November and remained there until the end of the war. Sister Toller stayed on to facilitate the handover and reported back to QAIMNS headquarters at Abbeville on 29 November 1916.

Her respite was short. On Boxing Day, she was notified of her re-appointment as Acting-Matron and posting back to Rouen, to 9 General Hospital this time. She moved two days later. Her predecessor at 9 GH appears to have struggled, as Lucie's briefing stressed 'the importance of keeping all the regulations and having all her report books and messing accounts in good order.'

1916 had been a challenging year for Lucie. But 1917 began well for her, as signalled by her award of the Royal Red Cross (RRC) 1st Class in recognition of her 'valuable services with the armies in the field.'[33,34] Lucie was the 709th person to be awarded the RRC in the Great War. One can assume that well over half of these would have been Second Class awards, which were instituted in November 1915.

Having returned to Rouen, the first five months of 1917 passed smoothly. Then she and a few key nursing sisters were instructed to facilitate the handover of 9 GH to an American hospital that arrived at Boulogne in May, which they duly did.

Aire-sur-la-Lys and new challenges

On 14 June 1917 Lucie Toller reported for duty as matron of the newly established 39 Stationary Hospital at Aire-sur-la-Lys – a town between St Omer and Bethune; famous – since 2005 when it was classified as a World Heritage Site by UNESCO – for its medieval bell-tower. An active but otherwise quiet town during peacetime, it provided the headquarters for the British First Army in 1915 and 1916,[35] and during Lucie's time, the headquarters for Portuguese troops who arrived in France in February 1917.

The hospital had been set up in a prison, adapted and maintained by the Royal Engineers who had built huts, wards, latrines, dugouts for shelling and bomb protection and provided 'heating arrangements for the Sisters' bath house.'

In its description of the chain of evacuation and the roles of the various establishments involved, the RAMC provides the following clarification in its website *RAMC in the Great War*:

> [the title] 'Stationary Hospital' was a bit of a misnomer as these units could move easier than the CCSs. There were two Stationary Hospitals to every Division and each one was designed to hold up to 400 casualties. There was, however, a tendency to use these as specialist hospitals, i.e.: sick; VD; gas victims, neurasthenia cases, epidemics, etc. [Stationary hospitals] were normally found occupying a civilian hospital in large cities or towns but were equipped for fieldwork if necessary. [36]

As the front line ran around 30km to the east, Aire was well within range of German long-range guns. Soon after Lucie's arrival, the townsfolk suffered heavy shelling and numerous air raids that took place in the area during July.[37] She and her staff spent many tense hours treating those injured.

There were frequent influxes of casualties from casualty clearing stations, arriving by ambulance or train at all times of the day and night.

The hospital had close links with French civilians and the town administration. Amusingly, Lt Col T.B. Unwin RAMC, the main diarist, noted in the hospital War Diary for 12 July:

> ... the receipt on 12 July of 'sanction from DMS for two nursing sisters to attend at operation on the wife of the

Commandant of Police, Aire'; received [exoneration] certificate from the husband [Commandant] that the British Government would accept no responsibility for accident or complications during or after operation.

The nursing staff now had faced fresh challenges: new approaches to the treatment of gassed cases; increasing awareness of shell shock, and a focus (albeit confused) on 'Not Yet Diagnosed Nervous' (NYDN) cases which reflected the on-going denial of the realities of shellshock and what is now recognised as post-traumatic stress disorder.

The question of NYDN cases came to a head following the 1916 fighting on the Somme when, as the author Taylor Downing observed, 'the incidence of shell shock had reached epidemic proportions and was totally unacceptable.'[38] He concluded 'the huge number [of psychiatric casualties] equated to the loss of three whole divisions from shell shock in one six-month period.' To make things worse, from the military point of view, it became clear that the majority of shell shock cases that were evacuated to the UK were unlikely to return to France.

It fell to Charles Myers, an RAMC officer appointed as consultant psychologist to the British armies in France, to persuade Sir Arthur Sloggett, the Director-General of Medical Services, that NYDN cases could be treated effectively in forward areas, rather than be evacuated to the rear. This was an approach that the French Army had adopted with some success. Myers argued that specialist units should be set up 'as remote from the sounds of warfare as is compatible with the preservation of the "atmosphere" of the front.' In November 1916, Sloggett permitted Myers to open a 'small number of specialist units either as casualty clearing stations or stationary hospitals situated about ten miles from the trenches.'[39] The overall approach was to take soldiers directly from a battle environment and replace this with a brief period of rest. Men at one such centre opened northwest of Ypres for the Fifth Army were 'fed, allowed to rest and then put on a programme of graduated exercise, ending with route marches,'[40] A Canadian study of 132 NYDN cases treated in August 1917 found that 73% returned to active service, with 'only 27% going back to base:' a complete reversal of the situation a year earlier.[41]

On 17 July 39 Stationary took 169 such cases, and in the autumn there were discussions at the Aire *Mairie* about billeting convalescent NYDN cases for farm work.

Excepting a short break in September, Lucie Toller ran her hospital throughout this period. Once again, her work did not go un-noticed. Following her visit on 29 November, the Matron-in-Chief noted that:

> The work and arrangements seem excellent in every respect and the accommodation and comfort of the nursing staff has enormously improved since Miss Toller took over. There is a thorough atmosphere of happiness and order throughout the whole establishment. In addition to the large number of soldiers and officers, there was a tiny baby of six months only, as a patient, suffering from shell shock, from Armentieres. The COs of the various Departments in the district are inviting a certain number of Nursing Sisters to dinner on Christmas night and the Matron [Lucie Toller] asked me if I approved. I agreed and hoped they would have a nice time. The Matron makes a point of the extreme kindness of the Heads of Departments in the district, both to the nursing staff and their great interest in the welfare of the patients in hospital.

How she managed to foster 'a thorough atmosphere of happiness and order' in such difficult circumstances defies imagination. Reflecting too, the contribution that the hospital made to the civilian population in Aire, the French Army awarded her the *Médaille d'Honneur des Epidemies en Vermeil* [gilt] *in 1919*.[42] She was one of only four QAIMNS staff to be so honoured during the whole war.

Étaples: a jigsaw of hospitals

Just before Christmas 1917, missing the Christmas dinner that she had secured for her staff, Lucie Toller left Aire to take up the post of Acting-matron of 26 GH at Étaples. She had already spent eight months there in 1915/1916, at 24 GH. In addition to the decorations already bestowed on her, she was about to join that select band of just 138 women who were awarded the Military Medal (MM) for 'Bravery in the Field' in the First World War, of whom just eight were from the Regular QAIMNS.

The Military Medal had been instituted by Royal Warrant on 25 March 1916, as 'a silver medal to be awarded to non-commissioned officers and men for individual or associated acts of bravery on recommendation of a Commander-in-Chief in the field.' During the Great War period it was awarded to 115,577 individuals for services in the field. Norman Gooding, keenly interested in decorations to women, has written of the story of the move to award the medal to women in some depth, along with comprehensive profiles of the 138 women so honoured.[43]

Located on the north bank of the River Canche, some 25km south of Boulogne, Étaples begun the war as a relatively sleepy fishing port. Its prosperity had been greatly enhanced in earlier days by the building of the coastal railway between Boulogne and Amiens, 55km to the southeast. By 1914 there was a population of between 5,000 and 6,000, a working fishing community with its associated cottage industries, and a flourishing holiday resort to the west of the river known then as Paris Plage. The combination of warm light, unspoilt fishing communities and relatively cheap accommodation attracted a number of English-speaking painters from around the world. As the author Jane Quigley wrote in 1907:

> Étaples has been called – and not without reason – a dirty
> little town, but it is healthy for all that, and endears itself
> to many who work there. The artistic sense finds pleasure
> in its winding cobbled streets, and mellow old houses, and
> in the dark-complexioned southern looking people. Models

are plentiful and pose well for a small payment either in the studio, or in the picturesque gardens that lie hidden behind the street doors.

A great source of interest is the fishing fleet that comes up the estuary of the Canche to the quays where the fisher people and shrimpers live in a colony of their own. There is constant work for the sketchbook, especially on Monday, when the boats go off for several days, the whole family helping the men and boys to start. [44]

Sadly, this little community can have had no idea of what was about to hit it. The war began and jerked it remorselessly into rapid and traumatic change. Almost overnight the town became a major depot and transit camp for the BEF and, crucially, a focal point for treating wounded from the front before shipping them home to England. In the process, the population grew to around 80,000.

By 1917, Étaples had developed an important strategic role: its proximity to Boulogne and ready rail access to both north and south made it a favoured choice for a major transit station for troops on their way to the front, and for refresher-training for those rested from the front. The railway and its siding also made the town a natural destination for ambulance trains. These could handle both the movement of the sick and wounded away from the front and the repatriation of severely wounded and convalescent personnel back to England from the Étaples hospitals.

The railway from Boulogne approaches Étaples directly from the north-northwest. All that separates it from the right bank of the Canche is a belt of sand dunes and an occasional small copse. Close by to the west, the main road from Boulogne follows into the town. Once at Étaples Station, the line veers southwest for about 1,500m – through the town – before heading due south again across the river towards Abbeville. By 1918, an area approaching 100ha sandwiched between the main town to the south and a vast training encampment to the north had become home to eleven hospitals of one kind or another, equipped to treat over 20,000 sick or wounded. The town and area further south to the river — the southern half of the sandwich — was largely taken over by troop camps.

The hospitals were a confusing mixture of design and construction. Elinor Meynell paints a detailed picture of these complexities when writing of Lucie's hospital.

> No. 26 hospital consisted of a main building of corrugated iron, divided into four surgical wards of 23 beds each, two operating theatres and an X-ray room, with kitchen, administrative block, laboratory, stores, dispensary, latrines and wash houses in outbuildings of similar construction. There were 31 wards of 27 beds in freestanding wooden huts 120ft long with tarred canvas roofs. They [the wards] were barrack huts only 15ft wide, and could accommodate only a single row of 21 beds, the extra 6 being placed lengthwise along the opposite wall… Heating was by stoves, two to a ward. Electricity and a piped water supply came across the river from Paris Plage, with standpipes between the lines of huts and taps in the theatre block, kitchens, dispensary and laboratory. The latrines and bathhouses were at some distance from the wards. There was no drainage system, solid material was incinerated, and liquids, of whatever source, were run through gullies into soak pits driven 7-8ft into the chalk.[45]

She also noted that the staff quarters lay in the area between the railway line and the main road running north to Boulogne immediately to the west of the hospital (as were quarters for other hospitals.)

Yvonne McEwen adds more in *In the Company of Nurses*:

> By 1917 the work and patients at No. 26 were extremely diverse. Apart from the usual medical and surgical wards, a Skin Department was established as well as a special centre for the management of fractured femurs. The effectiveness

of the Carrel-Dakin continuous wound irrigation treatment was monitored at a special Observation Unit and a 'shell shock' centre was developed... According to Colonel Cree [OC] 'No.26 GH was made thoroughly International and Cosmopolitan with many and varied centres of interest. It has become a centre for Portuguese and Australians, sick and wounded and we constantly have Indian, Japanese, Maoris and men of many nationalities with many languages being spoken in the wards.'[46]

Marquees and other tents used for wards, Nissen huts and other corrugated iron buildings, and Alwyn huts (wooden accommodation with canvas-skinned roofs) were common throughout the complex of hospitals. Meynell noted however that the St John Ambulance Brigade hospital on the northern corner was 'considered by all who knew it as the best designed and equipped military hospital in France.' Regardless of all this, there was precious little protection from aerial bombardment.

The pressure put on the town and population through the overall military build-up was immense. The diary of the Australian nursing sister Elsie Tranter who worked at 26 GH gives us insight to the comings and goings within this vibrant community:

2.3.1917: The streets are very narrow, indeed in one part so narrow that you could touch the walls on either side from the car. We passed through the village, along past some farms, under a railway bridge, past the motor ambulance depot (which, we are told, is called 'Thumbs Up Corner') to the Land of Hospitals. Here before us was a stretch of six kilometres of hospitals. This district, Camiers and Étaples, takes 6,500 patients. This hospital, No. 26, takes 2,600. The nursing staff, including VADs and special military probationers, number eighty-five. It is a regular city of huts and tents. Hospitals on one side of the road, officers' and sisters' quarters on the other...

26.3.1917: We have large training camps round us here for Australian, New Zealand, English and Scotch troops. Thousands of men pass by every day. Day after day we say 'Goodbye and good luck' to lads with their full kit on, on their way to that well-known place 'up the line.' There is a continual tramp, tramp all day long. Each morning just after breakfast, we see hundreds of soldiers passing on their way to the 'Bull Ring' for drill.§ They are usually headed by the Australian band...[47]

Strategically, it is hardly surprising that the Germans focused on the town; the railway link between Boulogne and Amiens was a prime target, as was the bridge over the Canche. The thousands of troops billeted there must have been even more tempting. And amid all this lay the hospitals.

Air raid of 19 May

On the evening of 19 May 1918, 27-year-old *Leutnant* Ernst Schmitz took off from the German airfield at Lille in his twin-engined Friedrichshafen, G III bomber to attack Étaples. His aircraft was loaded with four 100kg, four 50kg and eight 25kg bombs: altogether 700kg of high explosive. He and his two crew-mates were part of an attacking force of about 20 aircraft from Squadrons BG06 and BG07, which approached Étaples along four separate routes chosen following reconnaissance flights over the preceding ten days.

At around 11.30 p.m. his and the five other aircraft in his flight approached the town. There was clear moonlight. That, with the searchlights and anti-aircraft defences around the town, exacerbated the crew's vulnerability – even at a height of around 2,500m. The raid had begun almost an hour earlier. *Leutnant* Max Ziervogel, the observer, aimed a burst or two of machine gun fire at the searchlights in a futile gesture of defiance. Then,

---

§   Bull ring: British Army training ground at Étaples which was infamous for its severe discipline

over the railway bridge, the aircraft was hit twice by anti-aircraft fire. Schmitz lost control, but managed to crash land in trees near Villiers, a village just south of Étaples. Fortunately, Ziervogel had managed to drop the eight heaviest of his bombs from between 300 and 400m, knowing that they would not explode.

British soldiers arrived at the crash site just in time to see an uninjured Ziervogel and *Oberleutnant* Kurt Jentzer, the slightly wounded nose gunner, drag the badly wounded Schmitz from the plane.

While the three were taken into custody, the air raid continued, and the attacking aircraft bombed a large area in a raid that finally ended around 12.30 a.m. More than two thirds of the bombs fell on the hospitals area, causing serious damage and injury. As the Commandant of Étaples Administrative District noted in his War Diary:

> ... attacked by Enemy Aircraft. Casualties – 1 officer, 1 Nursing Sister, 167 ORs killed; 27 officers, 11 Nursing Sisters, 584 ORs wounded; 18 ORs missing; 1 enemy aeroplane brought down. Crew of 3 officers captured.

The many flimsy buildings in the hospitals area offered little protection: there were many casualties; damage to property was extensive.

Eighteen year's old Theodore Fox, on 16 AmTr that offloaded at Étaples the morning after the raid, recorded that some of the bombs fell on the siding used by the ambulance trains, and that four had been hit. 'Number 35 had an aerial torpedo through the stores, No. 37 had two men wounded; No. 2 had a fair amount of damage, and No. 4 had many windows smashed and was scarred along the side with fragments of small explosive bombs.'[48]

Amid all this, the medical staff defended their patients and their own staff with great fortitude; a challenge exacerbated by the vulnerability of their buildings and facilities and lack of preparedness for such an event. While not forgetting the courage and resourcefulness of the RAMC personnel, the announcement in the *London Gazette* of 26 July 1918 for the award of the Military Medal to thirty-eight British women flagged their remarkable contribution. Twenty-three of these were recognised for their courage and devotion to duty at Étaples; twelve for the night of 19/20 May and eleven for a raid that followed on 31 May/1 June. The other fifteen decorations were for bravery during air raids at St Omer. Recognition for eight Canadian Army Medical Corps (CAMC) women followed in the *London Gazettes* of 24 September (four at 1 Canadian General Hospital, Étaples and one at 3 Canadian General Hospital, Dannes Carnier) and of 29 January 1919 (two at 7 Canadian General Hospital, Étaples.)

Those honoured for the first raid on Étaples included one CAMC matron, one QAIMNS acting-matron (Lucie Toller), one QAIMNS and five CAMC nursing sisters, two QAIMNS staff nurses, three VADs, one British Red Cross Society (BRCS) nurse and four BRCS ambulance staff.

Their MM citations reflect coolness, resilience and leadership during the raid; continued treatment of the sick and wounded regardless of personal safety, saving life, rescue, evacuation and treatment of bomb victims. Lucie Toller's reads:

> For gallantry and devotion to duty during an enemy air raid. When the Sister's quarters were wrecked and nurses wounded, Sister Toller collected the staff and placed them in comparative safety. By her fine example she undoubtedly saved life.

While attesting to Lucie's courage and leadership, this matter-of-fact account barely scratches the frightening reality of it all. While other hospitals suffered direct hits to their working infrastructure, including several wards, 26 GH's damage was confined to two blocks of the Sister's quarters. Many of the Sisters would have sheltered amid the distinctive noise of the aircraft engines, the crash of bombs falling and the explosions that followed. There was machine gun fire from the air (reported to have caused some of the casualties at No. 7 Canadian Hospital). Fires blazed from the four marquees that made up one of the wards at No. 7 Canadian 'that lit up the whole of my hospital grounds,' which was almost opposite the 26 GH Sisters' quarters. [49] More bombs fell on the blazing tents, all of which were visible from the Sisters' quarters, jammed between the road to Boulogne and the railway line. The direction to safety was far from obvious when the three bombs fell on 26 GH. To have calmed, organised and then led her frightened staff from the damaged buildings must have required all the clear thinking, direction and confidence that Lucie could muster.

There was controversy in some quarters about the fact that nursing sisters were regarded as officers and therefore thought to be entitled to receive the Military Cross as opposed to the Military Medal. I discuss the correspondence and related comment on this topic that took place in 1918 and 1919 at the end of this story.

Here is a summary of the bombing effort on the hospitals on the night of 19/20 May 1918. The data vary slightly from the initial reports, and presumably reflect greater accuracy, including the sadness that some initially reported as wounded had since died, including one Canadian nursing sister. More than 720 persons had been injured during the raid, including almost 106 dead and 276 injured in the hospitals area.

Bomb casualties at Étaples – 19/20 May 1918

Hospital	Bombs dropped 19/20 May	Men k	Men w	Women k	Women w	MMs to women[50]
24 General	1					
26 General	3	1	1		2	4
46 Stationary	3	17	68		2	3
51 General	1	3	1			
56 General	1	3	19			1
1 Canadian General	9	60	86	2	6	4
7 Canadian General	19	13	58			2
9 Canadian Stationary	9	2	13			
St Johns Ambulance Brigade,	7	5	15			
6 Convalescent Camp	2		9			
Sub-total – hospitals	55 (41%)	104	270	2	10*	
To north, south, west of hospitals	78 (59%)	75	265 **			4
Overall total – Étaples Administrative District	133	179	531	2	10	18

* Six nursing sisters and four VADs

** Includes 4 staff from 24 GH wounded outside the hospital area

Source: Appendix 'A' to General Asser's Report of 19 June 1918.[51]

The Étaples hospitals were no longer a safe haven. Thirty-five more were to die including one nursing sister in a follow-up raid in the hospitals area on the night of 31 May/ 1 June; four nursing sisters were among 79 wounded.

In the aftermath, the question 'why were the hospitals bombed?' was hotly debated. The topic gained major political traction following an article in the *Times* of 25 August 1918 headlined 'German Savagery at its Worst', which whipped up indignation ('rivalling the sinking of hospital ships or the Lusitania'), and commented that [the size of the hospital area]:

> ... makes it a mark no airman could possibly miss. An airman blind and drunk could let bombs fall from any height in any wind and weather, and they must land somewhere among the attendants' quarters or on the tents where the nursing

sisters move among the rows of cots with their helpless occupants.

Consequently, the War Office wrote to warn GHQ France that the three shot-down 'prisoners... may be brought to trial. Before their despatch to this country please make all necessary enquiries to establish their guilt and knowledge of what they were doing.'

Under interrogation, the three German airmen completely denied any instruction to bomb the hospitals and all expressed surprise that the hospitals were so near an important railway line. Lt Jentzer 'claimed that the primary object was to bomb the railway and the reinforcement camps. They knew hospitals were there, but from their photographs, no Red Crosses were visible, nor any indications which helped them to distinguish them from purely military buildings.'

Ziervogel said, 'It is very sad. I had orders to come and bomb Étaples. I could not tell the hospitals from ordinary buildings.' He had been able to see Étaples in the distance and saw a large chessboard-like arrangement of huts and square and bell tents, but 'absolutely no sign of a red cross anywhere.'

Schmitz died of his wounds at Étaples on 29 May and is buried there.

In contrast to the public rhetoric and the opinion of Sir Douglas Haig, the RAF concluded following its own investigations that the bombing of the hospitals was 'not intentional.' This led the Director of Military Operations to advise the Deputy Chief of the Imperial General Staff that while it did not seem possible to arrive at a definite conclusion on the matter:

> We have no right to have hospitals mixed up with reinforcement camps, and close to main railways and important bombing objectives, and until we remove the hospitals from the vicinity of these objectives, and place them a region where there are no important objectives, I do not think we can reasonably accuse the Germans. [52]

By May 1918 the German bombing campaign had in fact become a steady feature of the war in France. Mabel Peel of the Women's Army Auxiliary Corps at St Omer recalled 'we had to count on raids whenever there was a moon. Sometimes we would have as many as three in one night, visits from three different squadrons of *Gothas*' [German heavy bombers that began service in 1917] adding ruefully that by the spring of 1918 they had become 'capable of carrying very heavy bombs.'[53]

Having narrowly escaped from an air raid at Abbeville, young Theodore Fox was keenly aware of the bombing threat. He heard, one week before the 19 May raid, that a German aircraft had dropped a message warning of the risk to hospitals if the hospitals were not separated from the camps. He also had the impression that Étaples 'did not have the anti-aircraft defences that such a base deserved.' And 'I do not think there were any dugouts.'[54]

True or false, the raids on Étaples were 'accidents' waiting to happen.

Lucie remained at Étaples for the rest of the war. By this time the influenza pandemic that stole so many lives had taken hold, stretching the medical services in France even further.

And so, the war ended. As Yvonne McEwen lamented in *It's a Long Way to Tipperary* 'There were many innovations and inventions by nurses throughout the period of the war, but sadly they were given little credit for them.' She concludes:

> nevertheless, during the Great War, the nursing profession came into its own and the women of that time were, by any standards, quite exceptional. They were modest and unassuming about their contribution to the war, they did not seek plaudits and they nursed because heart and conscience denied any other action.

LMT's letter to the widow of Private Fred Hawkins, March 1918
(courtesy of 'Hollytree' of the Great War Forum)

They also made sacrifices. Two QAIMNS nurses are buried in Belgium; one killed by shellfire at a casualty clearing station in 1917, and one who died of influenza. As we have already seen, three nurses were killed in the Étaples air raids, as were others in air raids on hospitals elsewhere in France. The Commonwealth War Graves Commission has details of 373 nurses (including 132 QAIMNS women) who died in the period 1914 to 1921, along with some 30 for whom information is sketchy. Of these 11 died as a result of enemy action on land; others died from disease or accidents. At sea, 24 Canadians and New Zealanders drowned when their hospital ships were torpedoed and a further 31 nurses were lost at sea.[55] Altogether, some 1,500 nurses from many countries are thought to have died in the Great War.[56]

A modest woman

After four and a half years in France, Lucie Toller returned to England and reported for duty at York Military Hospital on 13 February 1919. Later that year she holidayed in Norway. Perhaps she was able to join her QAIMNS colleagues at the London Peace Parade in May? On 20 December the *British Journal of Nursing* was able to report that she had been decorated with the Royal Red Cross (First Class) and the Military Medal at a ceremony at Buckingham Palace on 11 December 1919 held to honour British women associated with nursing.

There is a quaint side-story to the end of Lucie's war. In August 1918, the Woman's Work Sub-Committee at the Imperial War Museum set out to gather photographs of the army nurses who had received the Military Medal and wrote to her, requesting one. Lucie, busy at Étaples at the time, replied that while she would be happy to provide information but that 'publication of a photograph is quite another matter, especially for one in the Regular Service.'

The IWM quickly clarified the position, assuring Lucie that there was no objection to this from the military authorities. On 10 January 1919 she replied:

> At last I have time to think about my own affairs and correspondence.
>
> I send you a recent photograph of myself. I never have any taken in uniform, but this one is considered to be a very good one.
>
> If you want any information, I will give you a short description. I joined the QAIMNS on July 7th, 1904. Emb

[arked] for France Aug 1914. Was mentioned in Sir J French's dispatches 1916. Given the 1st Class R.R.C. for work on the Somme 1917. Awarded the MM as an 'Immediate' award at Étaples during the severe bombing – 1918.

I think this is all I can claim. [What an unassuming woman.]

Lucie's photograph differs from the majority of the other 363 women in the collection, as almost all of them are formally posed, and in uniform. We see an unpretentious, straightforward woman. She is perhaps shy, yet comfortable on her own? She is confident enough not to be compelled to conform to the dress code that we can imagine was expected. She conceals what must have been considerable inner strength. We see someone who is definitely her own person.

Such are the weird machinations of the military that, although she had performed such duties for several years, it was only in June 1922 that Lucie was officially gazetted as Acting Matron.

While the war was over, her overseas travels continued. Following a posting to No. 336 CCS at Cologne in Germany in September 1921, she then moved on to Constantinople in Turkey a year or so later. Brought back to Tidworth Military Hospital in Hampshire in June 1923, she finally transferred to Belfast late in the autumn of 1924. There – having acted in this role for eight years – Lucie finally achieved the formal rank of Matron on 31 October 1924. This was the equivalent to the Army rank of Major.

'Likely to have thick personal file?' (meaning 'likely to be a trouble maker?') may not be such a prominent comment in end-of-interview notes these days, but it was not unusual a century ago. Up until this time, her personal file would have been an exemplar 'thin one' but, as we will see, almost overnight it swelled to such an extent that she must have read like a Queen of the Awkward Squad.

A shameful affair

In Belfast Matron Toller fell victim to a series of events that led to the state of despair and disgust that resulted in her resignation from the QAIMNS. It all began with an accident which resulted in a comminute fracture of the right tibia and fibula, and which necessitated an operation to plate the tibia together. This precipitated a process during which the British Army, which she had served so well, effectively discarded her in her own hour of need.

Formal proceedings followed: at a Court of Enquiry held at Belfast on 1 March 1926 to enquire 'into the circumstance under which Matron Miss L.M. Toller, RRC, MM, QAIMNS, received an injury on 27 February 1926' her driver, L.J. Pick, stated that:

> On 27th February 1926, at 5.30 p.m. I proceeded to the Sister's Quarters to convey the Matron to Hollywood. While placing a chair in the back of the Ambulance I heard a shout and on looking around I saw the Matron lying on the ground at the bottom of the steps, leading into the house. I called for assistance and some Sisters came – having bandaged her leg we placed her on a stretcher and conveyed inside the house.

Lucie's statement read simply:

> At approximately 5.30 p.m. on the 27th February 1926, I was proceeding on duty by Motor Ambulance to the Military Hospital Hollywood, for the purpose of examining candidates for the forthcoming Nursing Orderlies Examination R.A.M.C. While I was closing the Hall Door of the Sisters Quarters against a very strong wind the door handle came away in my hand and I was precipitated down the steps.

Captain H. E. M. Douglas RAMC, the President of the Court of Enquiry, concluded that:

> Having carefully considered the evidence, I am of the opinion that Matron L.M. Toller, RRC, MM, QAIMNS met with

this accident through no fault of her own and that she was
on duty at the time.

Major General F.F. Ready, the CO of Northern Ireland District
concurred on 16 March. Her injuries began to heal, and a 'Special'
Medical Board held in London on 29 June concluded that:

> The bones are now in good position as shown by X-Ray
> plate. She still has some thickening at the head of fracture
> and swelling above the ankle. The movements at the ankle-
> joint are slightly restricted especially inversion and eversion.
> The condition of her leg will probably improve with further
> treatment by exercise.

On 23 October 1926 she wrote to Florence Hodgins, her Matron-
in-Chief to tell her that she had managed to pass the [Medical]
Board the previous Friday and travel arrangements had been made
for her to return to Belfast on the 28th, the date when her sick
leave expired. This she duly did.

Her return to duty was not a signal that she was completely
fit. A note on her file records that: 'It would appear that the lady
in question is not at the present fit for foreign service. On 5 April
1927 an RAMC surgical specialist wrote:

> ... [she] is due to have the plate removed from her right leg
> next week. She will be confined to bed probably 3 weeks, and
> will not be fit for foreign service for at least three months from
> the date of operation. She is suffering from periodic attacks of
> Urticaria since she fractured her leg, and in my opinion these
> attacks would be aggravated by service abroad. [57]

She still had not recovered fully and was naturally mindful of
possible long-term impacts. On 13 September she formally asked
her CO at Belfast 'whether the disability consequent on this
accident is regarded as 'in and by military service.' Her CO duly

forwarded her query to the Assistant Director of Medical Services (ADMS), Northern Ireland District, who promptly forwarded it to the War Office. And this is where the gross injustice began. Her personal file, open to all to see as WO 399/8376 at the National Archives at Kew, did indeed begin to bulge.

The way in which the Army dealt with the whole saga is clear to see from the extensive communications and related minutes contained in the file. There were those who supported Lucie's plight, and those who were determined to wash their hands of it. The minutes, written not long after the Court of Enquiry of 1st March (which found in Lucie's favour), document the way in which the military establishment tried to duck the issue of responsibility for the accident. They include:

Minute 9:   This Matron was injured when trying to close the door of the Sisters' Quarters against a strong wind, when the door handle became suddenly detached, causing her to fall from the steps. The Lady was proceeding to carry out an examination of candidates at the time. How should the injury be regarded, please? 20.3.26.

[Then, following up the question of whether the accident was 'in and by military service' that had already been raised and related reluctance to agree to 'by military service' – presumably to limit any liability for compensation.] Minute 10: 'In not by'

Minute 14:   It seems to me that Min.10 is a hard ruling in this case – in view of the evidence at the court of enquiry. The immediate cause of the accident was a defective door-handle on a quarter kept in repair by a Military Authority – and Miss Toller was undoubtedly proceeding to duty. I think the correct ruling is 'in and by.' Concur? 28.8.26.

[But while some were clearly sympathetic to her plight] Minute 16: that 'she was certainly not on duty

– has been laid down time after time – if that were the only argument the case would fail. Going to duty isn't duty. The point in my opinion is whether the door handle in a *public* quarter differentiates the case from that of a door handle in a *private* lodging – always assuming in this case that there was negligence in the handle being defective.

Minute 20: Previous knowledge might mean negligence. Otherwise it is a pure accident and there is no responsibility [of the Royal Engineers who were responsible for maintenance]. The question here is whether there would be a common law liability apart from the Crown exemption and the answer is that there would not as there was no negligence. The housemaid in your house would get compensation under the Workmen's Compensation Act on the ground of her incurring an accident in the course of her employment; her employment being continuous. [X] Miss Toller at the time was that of a tenant, not an employee, and our only question is whether we have a liability in the capacity of landlord. '& we have not' [written in blue].

Minute 22: I cannot quite see the force of the argument at [X] in Minute 20. Miss Toller did not merely occupy the quarters. As a Matron she is responsible for the charge of the Sisters' quarters. In these circumstances I consider that she was an employee of the department when the accident occurred. [Followed by a note that I don't think the DG, AMS minute is really relevant.']

Minute 24: DGAMS. As it appears that had she been a civilian she would have had no claim, I do not think we can press it. DPS.

Minute 25: DPS/ Very well. Let us drop it. 23.10.27.

Altogether a shameful affair. There is nothing in the file to suggest that Lucie had any legal support.

Eventually a reply was drafted to the ADMS in September 1927 that reads '... it has been decided that the injury sustained by Matron Toller... shall be regarded as incurred "in and not by" the service.' Hand-written corrections to the draft amended it to read '... it has been decided that *any disability resulting from* the injury sustained by Matron Toller.... ~~shall~~ *cannot* be regarded as ~~incurred~~ ~~'In and not By' the~~ *attributable to military* service.' The amended draft was adopted formally on 26 September.

The ADMS had no alternative but to relay this response to Lucie Toller, which he did on 28 September 1927. Not surprisingly this was distressing for her. Having no doubt thought about this carefully, she wrote to her CO on 25 October stating simply:

> I cannot understand why it has been decided that any disability resulting from the injury sustained by me cannot be regarded as attributable to Military Service.
>
> My duties necessitated that I should leave my quarters, and by leaving my quarters to perform my duties I met with the accident.
>
> I therefore wish to appeal against the decision given.

The Under Secretary of State at the War Office informed the GOC Northern Ireland on 26 November 1927 that the Army Council was unable to alter the decision of 26 September 1927.

And so, the Army shamelessly closed the door on any hopes that Lucie Toller might have had regarding compensation for her injury. At the same time, she knew that she was no longer as mobile as the Army would have liked. Such treatment after such exemplary service must have broken her, for some three months later she wrote to the Matron-in-Chief 'Dear Miss Hodgins, would you kindly tell me if I am correct in thinking that by the end of July 1928 [my pension] will be £162pa? I would like to be sure, so would be very glad if you would verify it for me.' On 13 March 1928 she was informed that as long as she continued to serve until 7 August 1928, she would be eligible for retired pay at £162pa.

She duly asked to be allowed to resign on 19 August 1929. This she did. Ironically the name of the house to which she retired was called 'DunRomin.'

A few days later the Matron-in-Chief wrote to her giving permission to retain her QAIMNS badge 'in recognition of your over 25 years' Service and good work during the Great War.'

Lucie Toller began life as a pensioner with an income of £170pa. She was 54. After a few pension increases and the award of a Retired Pay Hardship Addition in 1947, her final pension (in 1959) reached £295. 14s.

In 1922 she had successfully applied to be registered with the General Nursing Council for England and Wales. I have no idea whether she continued with any nursing-related work after she left the Army.

What of her private life or interests? There is precious little to tell us. Serving members of QAIMNS were not permitted to marry, and she remained single after her retirement.

She had returned from Hong Kong in 1913 with a dog. Did her love of dogs continue? Did she keep in touch with her QAIMNS colleagues and friends? Or, determined to forget their grim wartime experiences, did they have an unspoken agreement to keep themselves to themselves?

She settled in Christchurch in Hampshire to be near two of her sisters who lived nearby. Mabel, widowed in 1918 not long after her marriage, lived in Bournemouth and died in 1955. Sarah, a spinster who died in 1956 also lived at Christchurch.

Lucie died at 8 Beresford Road, Southbourne near Bournemouth on 15 March 1962 at the age of 87. She left £3,917: if you assume that this sum included the value of her home, she was just 'getting by.'

Not for want of trying, I am sad not to have found anything concrete relating to her post-Army life. Her sister Mabel had five stepchildren, the last of whom died in 1976. One of them had a grand daughter, born in 1944, who lives in Spain. It would give me enormous pleasure to meet her and share what we know of Lucie Toller – surely one of the most highly decorated nurses of the Great War.

As Alison Fell, reflecting on what she sees as the complex and sometimes conflicting roles for those women who witnessed the war as a nurse, concludes: 'Nurses were observers of suffering, active participants in the war effort, professional carers, and stand-ins for a male patient's mother, sister of lover.'[58] We will never know how Lucie Toller may or may not have struggled in carrying out these multiple roles, but I strongly suspect that this quiet, brave, caring and thoroughly professional woman never flinched. We see some of this in a letter that she wrote from 12 GH, Rouen on 4 February 1915 to the widow of Cpl Walter Drake of the 2nd Battalion Duke of Wellington's Regiment; he fought at Ypres and died of typhoid:

Dear Mrs. Drake. I received your letter this morning. I am so very sorry for you. Your poor husband passed away at 4.30 p.m. on Feb 1, and about two hours before he died he said, 'It is finished.' We did all we possibly could.

Every man to me is a single person, and although I have many under my care, each one and each one's home people I hear about, and if anything, the married get my first and best consideration. I cannot tell you I sympathise with you, but I know what it is to lose one's all. Your little ones I hope will be a comfort to you, but such a word as comfort seems a mockery at such a time, when the love and glow of your life has gone. Yes, Mrs Drake, you have my hearts sorrow, and that is all I can give you now

The funeral was yesterday. I gave some violets in your name. The grave is in the English military cemetery in

Rouen. He had full military honours, with three officers in attendance. I enclose to you the money he had on him when he came into hospital, and I think you will need all you have. There are a few papers and a photograph of a little child, which will be sent on to you by the officer in charge. Good-bye Mrs Drake, and try and bear up for your little one's sake. Yours in sincere sympathy. L M Toller (Sister)[59]

Who better to represent front-line nursing in the Great War?

Médaille d'honneur des Epidemies

During the Great War, it was customary for Allied nations to bestow their honours and awards on personnel from their partners. The British for example awarded 2,218 Distinguished Conduct Medals to the French Army, 878 to the Italians, and 327 to the Belgians.[60] In the same spirit, the French Government honoured individuals from the British Empire.

Many, but not all of these awards were gazetted in the UK. (Those to British citizens in France who worked directly for French organisations, such as Emily Kemp *q.v.*, and whose awards were made personally in France, were not.) I have identified 17 issues of the *London Gazette* that mention the award of the *Médaille d'honneur des Epidemies* to British Empire personnel. These begin in 1919, and altogether list 155 awards, 85 to men and 70 to women. From my analysis Lucie Toller, named in the fourth issue, was one of four QAIMNS nurses (including Maud McCarthy, her commandant) to receive the medal in *vermeil* [gilt]. Only one other QAIMNS nurse received a medal – hers was in *argent* [silver]. Not surprisingly, the large majority of the male recipients were from the RAMC and the women from the several army nursing services.

What is not clear is how many of these awards were the result of personal recommendations by the French, and how many were allocated by the authorities in London. We know from Miss McCarthy's diary of 15 December 1918 that she:

> … forwarded to DGMS in accordance with his instructions for recommendations for the award of French Decorations for members of the Nursing Staff. Submitted 4 names for the award of the *Médaille des Epidemies en Vermeil*: and 10 names for the award of the *Médaille des Epidemies en argent* for valuable services rendered to the French sick and wounded, both soldiers and civilians, in forward Areas.

It would make complete sense if Lucie Toller was one of those whom she recommended.

The *Médaille d'honneur des Epidemies* was instituted in 1885, following the consequences of the serious epidemic of cholera of the year 1884.[61] Originally, this medal was awarded by the Ministry of Commerce, followed by the Ministry of the Interior and finally by the Ministry of Hygiene.

The criteria for the award *Médaille des Epidemies* required that people distinguished themselves during times of epidemic disease:

- by exposing themselves to the dangers of contamination, by caring for patients suffering from contagious diseases;
- by preserving a territory or locality from the invasion of an epidemic disease by personal intervention;
- by helping to disseminate the practice of disinfection or by participating in disinfection operations during an epidemic.

The medal was issued in four levels: bronze, *argent*, *vermeil*, and, highest, gold.

Apart from the three ministries, the *Médaille des Epidemies* was awarded [*inter alia*] by the Minister of War (from a decree in 1892), on the recommendation of the chiefs of corps or of the service, subject to approval by the military governors or the corps commanders. Interestingly, to qualify for the *Vermeil* or Gold medals it was necessary either to hold the Bronze or *Argent* medal or to belong to the Legion of Honour.

It seems unlikely that many Allied medical staff would have met these criteria. But, bearing in mind the overall spirit of the exchange of awards, and the undeniable contribution that many made to the treatment and well-being of both French servicemen and civilians, it is not surprising that strict compliance was not required, particularly as we know that selection was often made by the British.

Lucie's *London Gazette* listing for this award clearly mentions No. 39 Stationary Hospital, where she was acting-matron from June to December 1917. Remembering too the extensive medical needs of French civilians at Aire-sur-la-Lys while she was there, this fits squarely with Maud McCarthy's target of 'for valuable services rendered to the French sick and wounded, both soldiers and civilians, in forward areas.' Later awards may well have been for work during the influenza epidemic of 1918, which Lucie and her nurses would inevitably have faced at Étaples in 1918.

Military Medal to Women

The introduction of the award of the Military Medal to women is interesting in the wider context of public recognition of women. In *The Order of the British Empire*, Peter Galloway reflects that with the exception of the Order of the Crown of India, Order of Merit, Imperial Service Order, Royal Red Cross and the Order of St John, women were not eligible for any Decoration prior to 1917. That year, the Order of the British Empire (OBE) was established to address this and many other shortcomings of the existing honours system and also to recognise the wide level of service during the Great War.

In the period 1914 to 1920, 138 MMs were awarded to women for gallantry. Of these, eight (6%) went to QAIMNS staff and 29 (21%) to the QAIMNS Reserve.[62]

For men, the Military Medal was a decoration for bravery in the field awarded to non-commissioned officers and private soldiers. The comparable third-tier bravery award for commissioned army officers – and some warrant officers – was the Military Cross. It was not until 1993 that the MM was discontinued, and the MC retained for personal of all ranks.[63]

Military nursing sisters, including those of the QAIMNS, were classed as officers. Consequently, there were those who protested that nursing sisters who had been awarded the MM should by rights have received MCs. The editor of the *Nursing Mirror* raised this formally when he wrote to the Secretary to the War Office early in 1917:

> With regard to the Military Medal, which has been awarded to two more Nursing Sisters this week; we have on two occasions drawn attention in our columns to the incongruity that they should appear in the lists together with non-commissioned

officers and privates. Members of the Nursing Force, as you are aware are recognised in the Army as officers, and as such, should rightfully be awarded the Military Cross, which, we understand is the same reward as the Military Medal, but the former is reserved for officers and the latter for men. If we are wrong in this statement, perhaps you will kindly correct us.[64]

Clearly wishing to twist the knife, and probably with a little impudence (but also ahead of his time) he added 'we should be much indebted to you if you could give us any information as to how we should proceed to get this matter adjusted. You will, we are sure, at once recognise the anomaly of the present state of affairs.' The Establishment's response, though lacking in logic, was swift. It took but a week for them to reply:

I am commanded by the Army Council to acknowledge receipt of your letter of 26 January 1917 relative to what you say is an incongruity, from the fact that Nurses are eligible and receive the Military Medal, which is a decoration reserved for Non-Commissioned officers and men.

It is noticed by the Council that it is claimed that Nurses should be awarded the Military Cross by virtue of their status. In reply I would point out that the Military Medal is not awarded to Ladies by virtue of their holding positions as Nurses, but is awarded by reason of the fact that, as a mark of Royal favour, His Majesty was pleased to approve an extension dated 21st June 1916 of the warrant of the Military Medal, which extension ordained that 'the Military Medal may under exceptional circumstances, on the special recommendation of the Commander-in-Chief in the Field, be awarded to women, whether subjects or foreign persons, who have shown bravery and devotion under fire.'

The question of the position of Nurses in relation to other ranks does not, therefore, arise so far as the award of the Military Medal is concerned.

While clearly intended as a shut-up bid, this did not quite work. The discontent rumbled on. In the following April, no less a personage than Sir F.E.G. Ponsonby, Keeper of the Privy Purse, wrote to Major General Sir F.J. Davies at the War Office to say that:

> Quite unofficially I heard by chance that there was some dissatisfaction expressed amongst the nurses at the Military Medal being given to them, instead of the Military Cross. They argued that this was tantamount to treating them as private soldiers, and that as they were supposed to have the rank of an officer [this is very demeaning] they should, therefore be given the Military Cross...

Anticipating concern that this might be discussed in the press, he clearly wished the War Office to be prepared for this if and when it occurred. He concluded 'naturally, when women become eligible for the Order of the British Empire, and understand better the different grades, they will certainly be dissatisfied with medals instead of the Orders.' [65] This was clearly a matter of concern to the Palace.

Davies replied by return, stating 'the Medal is only conferred on nurses for acts of bravery apart from their professional duties, in fact it is won in their capacity as *women*.' He went on to observe, 'the Military Cross won by a combatant officer in respect to combatant duties has, as an equivalent, the Royal Red Cross conferred on a Nurse for professional duties.'

But he also had other worries: would extending the Military Cross to nurses open the door for a similar claim to the Distinguished Service Order? And would this then lead to a mismatch between officer ranks and related conditions between men and senior nurses?

Lacking a response to the War Office's reply to the *Nursing Mirror* letter of January 26 and any other subsequent public comment, Davies appears to have anticipated that the problem would go away, concluding that 'so long as the Military Medal is awarded to women for specific acts of gallantry, and the Royal Red Cross to Nurses for professional duties, I suggest that our position is secure, and that no injustice is being done.'

A couple of days later Ponsonby replied to advise 'His Majesty quite agrees with the view taken by yourself and Sir Alfred Keogh [whom Davies had previously consulted].'

End of story? No. It was now the Canadians' turn to stir the pot, writing to the War Office on 21 December 1917 to draw their attention to the fact that 'Matrons and Nursing Sisters of the Overseas Military Forces of Canada [OMFC] hold commissioned rank' and enquiring 'whether such Matrons and Nursing Sisters would be eligible for the award of the Military Cross.'

The writer referred particularly to the recent bombing raids on casualty clearing stations and hospitals behind the lines, where 'these [Canadian] Nursing Sisters have shown great courage and devotion to duty.' (As we have seen, eight CANS nurses won the MM during the Great War.)

It seems that the Army Council rolled the dice for the final time early in January 1918, almost a year after the opening salvo from the *Nursing Times*. Writing to the OMFC it announced:

...

2. In reply I am to state that the Royal Warrant of the Military Cross does not allow for the award of this decoration to women nor is the Army Council of opinion that circumstances justify consideration of the extension of the Terms of the Royal Warrant.

3. I am to point out that the Military Cross awarded to an officer for service in the field is considered as the equivalent of the Royal Red Cross conferred on a nurse in recognition of her professional services as a nurse.

4. The Military medal can be awarded to both men and women and when conferred on a nurse 'For bravery in the Field' such award is for bravery, apart from professional duties and is therefore won in her capacity as 'woman' not necessarily because she is a nurse.

5. The Army Council is fully cognisant of and thoroughly appreciates the great courage and devotion to duty displayed by nurses during raids on Casualty Clearing Stations and Hospitals behind the lines.

At the same time the Council is thoroughly satisfied that the Field Marshal Commanding-in-Chief, the British Armies in France will in all cases use his discretionary powers in regarding deserving services.

The final paragraph could mean anything. Indeed, that was the story in 1918. Since then, the role of women in battle and recognition of their courage has grown steadily.

Almost a century later, Michelle Norris of the RAMC won the MC for her gallantry in Iraq on 11 June 2006 in support of the Princess of Wales's Royal Regiment; the first woman to do so. This came about following a review of the gallantry awards system in 1993, following which other ranks could receive the Military Cross (and the equivalent RN and RAF awards) as well as officers. This change coincided with the-then prime minister John Major's introduction of changes to address social class differences and make it easier for the public to make nominations for honours. As Lord Wakeham announced to the House of Lords on 4 March 1993 'at present, except for the Victoria Cross, awards for gallantry are linked to the rank of the recipient.

Officers are eligible to receive crosses or equivalent decorations, but non-commissioned ranks are eligible only for medals. The time has come to end this distinction. In future, the level of award will be determined by the part played by the individuals concerned and the courage they displayed, without regard to their rank.' (Hansard, 'The Honours System', *https://api.parliament.uk/historic-hansard/lords/1993/mar/04/the-honours-system*, accessed 13 Aug 2018)

Norris was a Private Soldier at the time. Since then three female medics have received MCs for bravery in Afghanistan. Two were RAMC Lance Corporals and one a Royal Navy Able Seaman Class 1.

Notes

1 The QAIMNS – which formally became a corps of the British Army as Queen Alexandra's Royal Army Nursing Corps (QARANC) in 1947 – was formed from the Army Nursing Service in 1901. This followed the earlier formation of the Royal Army Medical Corps (RAMC) in 1898 and placement of the nursing sisters of the Army Nursing Services onto the war establishment in 1901. This in turn resulted from the successful deployment of Army Nursing Service members in both Boer wars and campaigns in Egypt and the Sudan, and evolved from the pioneering work of Florence Nightingale that stemmed from the Crimean War

2 Michelle Bullivant, 'Toller Family Tree Notes – all over Cambs', *www. michellebullivant.com/2/category/1871/1.html*, accessed 1 Feb. 2014

3 National Archives summary of documents held at London Metropolitan Archive from *http://discovery.nationalarchives.gov.uk/details/r/79f42398-c022-4689-a2ec-660a2c904d8b)*, accessed 2 Aug. 2017

4 N. McCrae & K. Kuzminska, *The Origins of a Two-tier Profession: Nursing School at a Poor Law Infirmary* (2017) 266

5 Cited in Juliet Piggott, *Queen Alexandra's Royal Army Nursing Corps* (1990) 42

6 Yvonne McEwen, *It's a Long Way to Tipperary* (2017) 45

7 Christine Hallett, *Veiled Warriors: Allied Nurses in the First World War* (2014) 20-21

8 Members of the QAIMNS, *Reminiscent Sketches of 1914-1919* (1922) iii

9 Sue Light, 'Voluntary Aid Detachments' in Scarlett Finders blog, *http://www. scarletfinders.co.uk/183.html*, accessed 22 Aug 2017

10 pers. comm. Sue Light 7 Feb 2014

11 TNA, WO 95/4081, War Diary of 12 General Hospital, Rouen

12 pers. comm. Sue Light 7 Feb 2014

13 TNA, WO/95/4081 …

14 Anne Powell, *Women in the War Zone* (2013) 123-124, 126

15 Yvonne McEwen, *In the Company of Nurses: The History of the British Army Nursing Service in the Great War* (2014) 65

16 RAMC in the Great War 'The Chain of Evacuation of The Royal Army Medical Corps', *http://www.ramc-ww1.com/chain_of_evacuation.php*, accessed 5 June 2017

17 Hayward, Birch & Bishop, *British Battles and Medals* (2006) 498-500

18 WO 222/2134, Reports on various Army nursing services in France 1914-1918 (The work of the nursing services with British ambulance trains and station units in France, in 1914)

19 Miss Bickmore, *Life on an Ambulance Train in France, 1914-1917*, Documents 3814, Imperial War Museum, London; also, Anne Powell, *Women in the War Zone* (2013) 91

20 Maud McCarthy's note on ambulance trains, 1917 (WO 222/2134, Reports on various Army nursing services in France 1914-1918)

21 TNA WO95/4131/1, Lines of Communication Troops 4 Ambulance Train

22 Bickmore, *Life on,* / Powell *Women in ...*, 88-89, 91

23 Anon, *Diary of a Nursing Sister ...* / Powell *Women in ...* 96

24 Members of the QAIMNS, *Reminiscent Sketches 1914 to 1919* (1922) 42

25 ibid 43

26 WO 95/3988/7, War Diaries, Headquarters Branches and Services. Matron in Chief, (Dame E.M. McCarthy, 'War Diary: Matron-In-Chief, British Expeditionary Force, France and Flanders', *http://www.scarletfinders.co.uk/42. html, entry for 6 Dec. 1915*, accessed 14 Jan. 2014)

27 McEwen, *It's a long way ...*, 105-106

28 The Long, Long Trail, 'The CCS's in France and Flanders' sourced through *http://www.longlongtrail.co.uk/army/regiments-and-corps/locations-of-british-casualty-clearing-stations,/* accessed 26 Aug. 2017

29 Sir W.G. MacPherson, *History of the Great War: Medical Services, General History Vol. III* (1924) 27-31

30 McEwen, *It's a long way ...*, 104-105

31 MacPherson, *Medical Services*, 46-47

32 MacPherson, *Medical Services*, 50

33 *London Gazette* 2 January 1917

34 RRC: A decoration created by Queen Victoria in 1883 to recognise army nurses for exceptional services, devotion to duty and professional competence in British military nursing. See *http://www.qaranc.co.uk/ royalredcross.php*

35 The Long, Long Trail, 'The British First Army 1914-1918' accessed 20 Sep 2017

36 RAMC in the Great War, 'The RAMC Chain of Evacuation', *http://www. ramc-ww1.com/chain_of_evacuation.html*, accessed Jan 2014

37 TNA, WO 95/4107 War Diary of 39 Stationary Hospital, months of June to December 1917

38 Taylor Downing, *Breakdown: The crisis of shell shock on the Somme, 1916*, 2016 eBook ref. 647.6/803 accessed 01 Oct 2017

39 Edgar Jones & Simon Wessely, *Shell shock to PTSD: Military psychiatry from 1900 to the Gulf War* (2005) 21

40 ibid 22

41 ibid 24

42 *London Gazette* 28 January 1919

43 Norman Gooding, *Honours and Awards to Women: The Military Medal*, (2013) 17

44 Jane Quigley, 'Picardy: A Quiet, Simple Land of Dreamy Beauty where Artists Find Much to Paint', *The Craftsman* (June 1907) 255-62, *https://www. scribd.com/document/162106722/The-Craftsman-1907-06-June-pdf*, accessed 29 May 2017

45 E.W. Meynell, *Some account of the British Army Military Hospitals of World War I at Étaples (*1996) 45

46 McEwen, *In the Company of Nurses ...*, 141-2

47 'Elsie Tranter's Diary', National Library of Australia, *http://throughtheselines.com.au/research/etaples#elsie* accessed 05 Dec 2107

48 IWM: Documents 15735. Private papers of Sir Theodore Fox; 'A boy with the BEF – Recollection of 1918' signed by him April (1979) 34

49 Report from Major G.E. Kidd, CAMC (from WO32/5189, German Air Raids on Hospitals in France)

50 *London Gazettes* (30 July 1918) 8999-9001, (20 Sept. 1918) 11339, (28 Jan. 1919) 1448

51 TNA, WO32/5189 German Air Raids on Hospitals in France

52 TNA, WO32/5189: File note from Sir P de B Radcliffe, Director of Military Operations, 29 June 1918

53 IWM, Documents 16722: Private letters of Miss M D Peel; Self-published pamphlet (1921) 19

54 IWM: Documents 15735, 36

55 Data in McEwen, *It's a long way ...,* 200-208

56 'List of Nurses who Died in World War 1', Wikipedia, *https://en.wikipedia.org/wiki/List_of_nurses_who_died_in_World_War_I* accessed 06 Dec 2017

57 Letter of 7.4.1927 from Major General Commanding Northern Ireland District to Undersecretary of State for War in respect of proposed posting to Malta (from TNA, WO 399/8376, Nursing Service Records, First World War, Queen Alexandra's Imperial Military Nursing Service, Toller, Lucy)

58 Alison Fell & Christine Hallett (eds), *First World War nursing: New perspectives* (2013) 188-9

59 Posted by 'DaveC' (David Cochrane) on the Great War Forum on 17 May 2016

60 Howard Williamson, *The Distinguished Conduct Medal Awarded to the Allied Armies by the British Government during the Great War 1914 to 1918* (2018) 18-19

61 France-Phaleristique 'Médaille d'Honneur des Épidémies', *http://www.france-phaleristique.com/medaille_honneur_epidemies.htm*, accessed 21 Sep 2017

62 Analysis of data in Gooding, Honours and awards to women ... 17

63 After the Victoria Cross (first tier) followed by the Distinguished Service Order/ Distinguished Conduct Medal (second tier)

64 This and related follow-up correspondence are in: WO 32/4965, 'Decision Regarding Award of Military Cross to Nurses'

65 The reference to the OBE is interesting. Roger Willoughby (pers. comm.18 Apr 2016) observes that 'the Order of the British Empire (all classes including medals) was certainly intended to be awarded to women and men alike and as such it was distinguished from other orders. Its class structure reflected social, military and political ranks or classes and inevitably reinforced these. With 612 (or roughly 30%) of the British and Imperial *medal awards* going to women, they were certainly represented. How this percentage relates to women's relative involvement in the war effort is unclear, though I would say it was a significant step forward over the previous situation. In terms of the 612 awards, this figure relates purely to

the 'medal of the OBE', what we would later call the BEM. In total 2,015 first type BEMs were awarded to British and Imperial recipients during the period of its existence (1917-1922). A further 900 or so were awarded to foreign nationals (men and women). [The 2,015 BEMs compare with the 25,419 (11,646 Military & 13,773 Civil) awards of the various grades of the OBE above the Medals of the Order for approximately the same period; (see A Winton Thorpe *Handbook to the Most Excellent Order of the British Empire*, 1921, 12) 11,369 of the 25,419 were at Officer grade and 10,246 at Member grade. The numbers awarded to women are as yet unknown]. Going back to the opening point, we can see the Order of the British Empire as a more egalitarian, reformed and inclusive award (though within it, we will likely find ongoing evidence of patriarchy, imperialism, etc.). As a *new* order, it opened up wider social recognition (including to women, working classes on the Home Front, etc.), while at the same time maintaining social exclusion from the traditional preserves of power (including, for our purposes, all the other 'old' orders; the Garter, Merit, Thistle, Bath, St Michael & St George, etc.). On this reading, the awards to women may be seen as moderately progressive, in so far as they challenged existing social inequalities, yet at the same time the Order itself could be regarded as something of a sop.' Regardless of language in the correspondence that reads with such arrogance, the move to make women eligible for the MM should probably be seen in the same light.

Gerald Andrewes

The volunteer:
Gerald Andrewes

Just a very nice, kind grandfather

Gerald Andrewes's group of miniature medals (Queen's South Africa Medal with 'CAPE COLONY', 'ORANGE FREE STATE' 'TRANSVAAL', 'SOUTH AFRICA 1901' and 'SOUTH AFRICA 1902' clasps, 1914 Star with '5ᵀᴴAug.: 22ᴺᴰ Nov. 1914' bar, British War Medal 1914-20, Victory Medal (British issue), France: *Croix de Guerre*, 1914-18 reverse with single star) together with his early full-sized ribbons and a Silver War Badge

The maelstrom of the Great War sucked people from all walks of life into the chaos that it spawned. While those in uniform were prominent in their structured way, civilians caught in the fighting watched as their lives were torn apart, many as refugees; others further from the front line were sucked up into the great machinery that grew inexorably to keep the armies in action.

Untold numbers looked for ways that they could contribute – as volunteers. Many sought ways to help the sick and wounded. Some financed medical services or related equipment. Others used their organisational or manual skills, sometimes both, to provide help, often having to learn from scratch. We have already read of the contribution of the Voluntary Aid Detachments in Lucie Toller's story. When we read of Emily Kemp, we will learn something of the British civilian initiatives to assist casualties in the French Army.

But we should not forget that many of those in uniform were also volunteers. Some were ex-soldiers who joined up when the war broke out, often as non-combatants. Others, too old for military service, were accepted by other organisations that gave them access to active service.

Voluntary service brought people way outside their comfort zones. While some relished the occasional excitement that came with the unfamiliar and often uncomfortable world that they encountered, many ran great risks, as did a group of volunteer ambulance drivers of *Section Sanitaire Anglaise* No. 16 working with the French Army in 1917:

> During September Section 16 was moved down the Meuse, beyond Verdun, and took up the duty of transporting the wounded from Bras and Mont Grignon. Bras is a ruined village, which lay close to the German lines, exposed to machine-gun fire. Not a light could be shown, not a sound must be made, in moving the wounded from the *Poste de Secours*. Stretcher-bearers took the wounded on handcarts down to the bank of the Meuse Canal at Bras; then they were put on barges and towed to Mont Grignon. The ambulances were stationed in that suburb of Verdun and drove them thence to hospital.

Section 17 continued at its post at Esnes, under Hill 304, and its duty was one of constant danger. The stretch of road from one ruined village to another was much exposed to shell-fire, and during the midnight hours, when the supply and ammunition carts were moving up, the enemy guns were always particularly punctual and attentive. The road itself was not only pitted with holes, but encumbered with wreckage of wagons,

Among the broken wheels lay dead and putrefying horses. It was difficult enough to steer the cars among these obstacles; but at night the confusion was thrice confounded. Endless transport columns moved up and down continuously, and among them pack-trains of donkeys, used to carry material of all sorts right up to the front lines, strayed across the road, in their wayward fashion; and all the while the shells were screaming and exploding in the darkness. The cars were often struck by flying fragments, but so skilfully were they driven that no serious accident befell them.[1]

On 11 August 1914, a tall, handsome, forty-year-old man volunteered to join the army as a private soldier. A few days later he stepped onto French soil to drive trucks with the Army Service Corps (ASC) – an integral cog in the machinery that engaged as a result of Great Britain's declaration of war on Germany on 4 August. He was a well-educated, successful professional. We can only speculate as to what drove him to resist the lure of rank and authority that welcomed countless such as he into the officer classes. How much his previous military experience influenced him is debatable, but by 1914 he was no longer a youngster.

Our story begins earlier when, on 28 May 1886, a young widow of private means named Annie Louise Andrewes registered her two sons Gerald and Charles for entry to King Edward the Sixth's Grammar School in Berkhamsted, Hertfordshire. Gerald, born at Lower Norwood in London on 18 April 1874, was just 12. His brother was eighteen months older.[2]

GSA in his late 40s - around the time of his marriage
(© Martin Wyer)

Charles quickly shone at school. In little over a year, he proved himself as a strong runner, won Second Eleven colours as a footballer, and played a minor role in Twelfth Night. Two years later he captained the Second Eleven and was a competent musician.

Gerald however was not notably sporty beyond some skill on the Fives court. He was interested in music, and sang glees (those English part songs, generally unaccompanied, which were popular among Victorians).

But Charles contracted diphtheria. He died at home in Berkhamsted on 11 December 1889, aged 17. Gerald, aged only 15, was with him at the time. Only a few days before, the two had been competing in Fives matches.

The health statistics for Berkhamsted Regional District record only two deaths from diphtheria in the 15 to 19 years' age group for the whole of the 1880s: Charles was incredibly unlucky; little consolation to his mother and brother. The boys' father, a wine merchant, had died late in 1874 when they were very young. Gerald must have struggled, both with the sudden loss of his brother and also with the added responsibility of supporting his mother. It was he who registered his brother's death.

Gerald completed his schooling – just a short walk away from his home at Bridge House in Chapel Street, where he and his mother continued to live. They were comfortably off – Annie reported herself in the 1891 census as 'living on private means' – and employed a servant. She could also draw on support from four siblings and five sisters-in-law: her niece Kathleen, two years younger than Gerald, lived with them for a while. Today, Bridge House is Grade II-listed, and lies within what is now the Berkhamsted Conservation Area; harking back to Victorian prosperity in the town.

Sixty years later Gerald, by then senior partner in the successful firm of insurance brokers that bore his name, encouraged his stepdaughter Edna Wyer to send her son Martin to the same school.

What happened in the years after Gerald left school? There is a hint in pages 6 to 8 of the *Berkhamstedian* (Berkhamsted School magazine) of 1919, which contains a section called 'War Distinctions.' It lists 73 soldiers, sailors and airmen who won awards in the Great War ranging from Mentions in Despatches to the Victoria Cross, with honours also from France, Italy and Imperial Russia.

Alongside one major general, 15 colonels, 18 majors and 36 subalterns appear three enlisted men. Of these three, Gerald (included for his award of the French *Croix de Guerre*) was the most junior. * While his entry lists him as a corporal in the Royal Army Service Corps, he spent most of his time in France and Belgium as a private soldier. More to the point, he won the *Croix de Guerre* for his work with the French medical services, having been previously discharged from the (then) Army Service Corps as unfit for military service.

Gerald was not alone in that band of well-educated and privileged young men who foreswore status and rank while serving their country, accepting grimness of war at the bottom of the military pile. But it is interesting to conjecture why he did. Was this an escape from the anguish of his brother's death and related responsibility that was thrust on him? How much had he sheltered behind his elder brother's success and popularity? Had this forced him to grow up fast? How much had he learned from what must have been his mother's lone struggle to raise him and his brother? Or had he become philosophical about suffering and privilege, and simply wanted to break away from the comforts of genteel Berkhamsted?

Rifleman volunteer

Whatever drove him, he did not wait long. On 15 February 1892, aged 17, Gerald enlisted as Private G.S. Andrewes with the 1st London Volunteer Rifle Corps, with which he served as a part-time soldier until June 1898.[3] (In the 1890s there were more than 200,000 volunteer soldiers of all disciplines in England, Wales and Scotland. This force was the forerunner of today's Army Reserve – formerly the Territorial Army.) Based at Bunhill Row, in Islington, Gerald's service would have involved a number of days training, often on a Saturday, and attending a fortnight's camp every year.[4] He would have become proficient at drill and musketry.

---

* *Croix de Guerre* – French medal (Cross of War) instituted in 1915 to recognise mentions in despatches

In the meantime, his mother, who did not remarry, died at Streatham, Surrey on 12 March 1895. She left an estate that would have been worth around £200,000 today, which must have gone a long way to helping her son to establish himself.

By the time that Gerald left the London Rifle Brigade, he had served well, being 'returned as Efficient' for seven successive years. During the working week he progressed as an insurance clerk. He then had a change of heart, and on 28 August 1898 attested as Trooper Andrewes with the Royal Horse Guards at Hyde Park Barracks.[5]

His move from part-time soldiering to the Regular Army marked a distinct career change. But evidently life with the cavalry did not suit him; less than seven weeks later he bought his way out of the army, which he was entitled to do within his first three months. This cost him £10 – about £1,000 at today's prices. At the time of his discharge he was described as 5' 11" tall (well above the average male height), 'of fair complexion with hazel eyes and brown hair.'

Nevertheless, his enthusiasm for matters military endured; a month later he re-enlisted as a volunteer with the London Rifle Brigade. He remained on their Muster Roll until 31 October 1902, some four years later.

The second Anglo-Boer War broke out on 11 October 1899 – the very day that Gerald finalised his release from the Royal Horse Guards. As the war progressed, it was agreed that volunteers should be allowed to serve overseas for a period of one year to overcome shortages in the regular troops.[6] Consequently the London Rifle Brigade provided a Volunteer Service Company to reinforce the Royal Fusiliers. Gerald seized the opportunity to participate and on 23 February 1900 attested at Hounslow for one year's short service as a private soldier.[7]

Interestingly, apart from the usual physical description in his attestation papers, these record a 'circle on left forearm and V.I. in blue ink.' The Royal Horse Guards had noted this mark four months earlier, and it was recorded once again in mid-1902. Who was 'V.I.' – an early girlfriend perhaps?

By 1900 Gerald had more than eight years of volunteer experience, and so it is perhaps not surprising that he was promoted to corporal within two weeks – a rank that he held for the remainder of his time with the fusiliers.

To the Veld...

On 3 April 1900 Gerald Andrewes arrived in South Africa as a member of the 2nd Battalion, Royal Fusiliers (2RF), where he remained for thirteen months. His battalion had reached South Africa the previous November, and by the time of Gerald's arrival had been involved in the Battle of Colenso and Relief of Ladysmith. It had then moved on support the relief of Mafeking.

In theory, the Voluntary Service Companies acted as second-line forces employed in the rear, but some were engaged in front-line actions such as the 15 militiamen with the Royal Welsh Fusiliers who fought alongside 2RF at Rooidam in early May. This criterion was flimsy in South Africa, where the concept of 'rear areas' in the wide, open spaces of the veld was rather shaky: Boer horsemen, who were excellent marksmen, might strike anywhere at any time that suited them. 'Consequently, any British soldier was liable to find himself in action or required to march quickly to aid comrades under attack.'[8] Consequently those militiamen deployed to safeguard the railways and escort baggage convoys that stretched out over such vast distances were under threat. Poor logistics, food and water shortages and disease added to their discomfort.

In June 1900, 2RF moved to Eastern Transvaal, where it took part in many operations, including the occupation of Brokhorst Spruit, east of Pretoria. The following February, the battalion moved by rail to Rosemead in Cape Colony, 'where rebels and raiders were then causing Lord Kitchener no little anxiety. Here they had a worrying life, not very fruitful of glory. The enemy was more elusive than ever.'[9] Three months later, Gerald's time was up.

Having returned from South Africa and completed his period of engagement with 2RF on 1 July 1901 he returned to the London

Rifle Brigade, with which he continued to serve until 31 October 1902; over ten years since he first joined. He continued to perform well, being steadily returned as 'Efficient' for 1899, 1900 and 1901. I have a strong suspicion that he returned to South Africa during this period, this time with the 1st Battalion, Imperial Yeomanry.[10]

Gerald was now 28, still listed by the army as a 'clerk' in civilian life and living in London; it was now time for him to focus on a professional career. This led him to Birmingham, his home for almost the rest of his life. By 1910 he had established himself as an insurance broker, with an office on the second floor of Temple Courts, at 55 Temple Row.[11] This was a grand building with offices shared by lawyers, accountants, architects, dentists and other professionals, along with three firms of whisky merchants in the basement. He had clearly 'arrived.' At some point he brought in a partner – Howard Bradley. The firm became known as Andrewes and Bradley. He became involved in freemasonry, becoming a member of the First Lodge of Light in Birmingham in December 1913. He was a lodge master for a while.

Around this time, he lodged at 8 Sunnyside in Berkswell, half way between Solihull and Coventry; he was still single, and a youngster compared with his 94-year-old landlady and her two stepdaughters. He remained there until August 1914, all the while building up his practice and earning prominence in the Birmingham business community.

August 1914: In retreat

And then came the start of the Great War, bringing tumult in Europe on a scale never seen before. Britain's military response, reportedly slow at first, was to mobilise a small army called the British Expeditionary Force and commission the Royal Navy to ferry it across the channel to Belgium and France and support those two countries.[12]

Amid a widespread surge of patriotic fervour, Gerald travelled to Avonmouth where he enlisted with the Army Service Corps as a private soldier on 11 August.[13] As someone with previous military

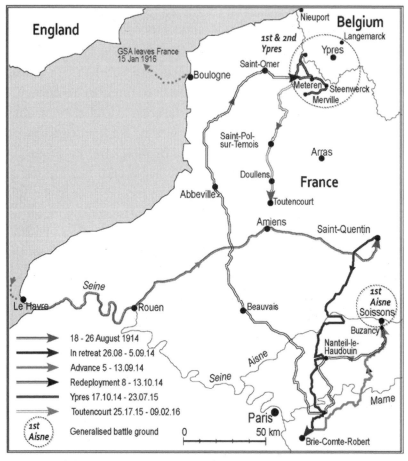

England

Belgium

France

Nieuport

1st & 2nd Ypres

Langemarck

Ypres

GSA leaves France 15 Jan 1916

Boulogne

Saint-Omer

Meteren
Steenwerck
Merville

Saint-Pol-sur-Temois

Arras

Doullens

Abbeville

Toutencourt

Amiens

Saint-Quentin

Seine

Le Havre

Rouen

Beauvais

1st Aisne Soissons

Buzancy

Nanteil-le-Haudouin

Aisne

18 - 26 August 1914
In retreat 26.08 - 5.09.14
Advance 5 - 13.09.14
Redeployment 8 - 13.10.14
Ypres 17.10.14 - 23.07.15
Toutencourt 25.17.15 - 09.02.16
Generalised battle ground

Seine

Marne

Paris

Brie-Comte-Robert

1st Aisne

0   50 km

4th Division Ammunition Column Aug 1914 – Jan 1916

service, and probably as an experienced driver, he was fast-tracked through the enlistment process. He sailed for France just four days later without the usual initial training – they probably overlooked his age in order to deploy him quickly. While at Avonmouth, Gerald joined an ASC unit that supported the artillery brigades of the Fourth Division – part of the BEF's Third Army.

Many regard the ASC – insalubriously dubbed 'Alley Sloper's Cavalry' – as unsung heroes of the Great War. As Napoleon observed 'an army marches on its stomach' it was the ASC's task to provision the British Army and ensure that it *could* march – and indeed fight. By the end of October 1914 the ASC had more than doubled in size, to around 33,000 men.[14] By the end of the war, the ASC is reported to have numbered 10,547 officers and 315,334 men together with tens of thousands of Indian, Egyptian, Chinese and other native labourers, carriers and stores men under its control.[15] The headstones in the many Commonwealth War Graves Commission cemeteries in France remind us poignantly that many ASC personnel were killed in action or died of wounds.

The BEF began its mobilisation to France on 12 August. In less than one week some 80,000 men had landed from passenger and cargo ships at French ports under the watchful eye of the Royal Navy and French ships. Gerald's unit sailed from Avonmouth on the cargo ship SS *Muriel Coverdale* just before midnight on 15 August. The ship spent 16 and 17 August just off Le Havre, and early on the 18th sailed up the River Seine to Rouen. There the unit disembarked, albeit somewhat shambolically, leaving one lorry completely smashed on the quay. [16] It then made its way to St Quentin where it linked up with the 4th Division's ammunition column (IV DAC) on 26 August. Gerald was to join the group of ASC drivers seconded to work within this unit.

His arrival at St Quentin collided with the German's rapid advance towards Paris. For the next ten days IV DAC moved south to escape German forces immediately to the east. Sometimes the enemy was uncomfortably close, particularly on 1 September when the column was engaged in cat-and-mouse movement with German cavalry in the area around Nanteuil-le-Haudouin, just east of the Ermenonville Forest. Gerald was caught in this as reported in his letters home:

> On the evening of 31 August, we were encamped in a glorious estate belonging to Prince Radziwill, and news was brought in that the Germans were approaching. The next day, our ammunition column, consisting of about 100 lorries, was going along at anything from fifteen to twenty miles per hour, each car being about fifteen to twenty yards from the rear of the one before it, when we got the order

to reverse. At the same time shots were heard somewhere about the front lorries. Each lorry turned in the space at its disposal, although the road was only an ordinary country one, which was a wonderful performance, and we were exceedingly lucky in leaving only seven in the hands of the *Uhlans*.[†] During the next few days they were all recovered.[17]

Not far away was Douglas Croom, a 26-year-old mechanical engineer who had enlisted with Gerald at Avonmouth and accompanied him to France. Another ASC driver, he was attached to the Fourth Division's ammunition park – the unit that supplied IV DAC with ammunition. On 31 August, when Gerald was at St Sauveur, some 30km to the south, Croom had gone to sleep on the grass by his lorry at Ermenonville. Recalling his awakening on 1 September:[18]

Woke up with a start and fright by someone kicking me. It was not Germans but the sentry, who said it was 3 o'clock and time I was about. I fetched some tea and had a huge breakfast consisting of bread and marmalade and cheese, then took the opportunity of taking a stroll around this place. It was evidently in the hands of a wealthy man, as there were swings, tennis courts, bandstand, a fine stream for fishing, stag running around and hunting stables and kennels, in fact everything money could get.

Anyway, while looking around I hear short repeated blasts on a whistle which means every man stand by his lorry and I began to think of the rumour of last night and especially when I, with 50 others were marched off with loaded rifles and fifty rounds or more in our pouches, we went out scouting in the neighbouring woods, as Germans were expected in the vicinity, but we did not see any and returned to camp and soon after started to move off. We toured around for about 15 miles and came back to the same

---

† *Uhlans* – German cavalry

village, but on entering it we were attacked by the enemy who were occupying the village.

'Men bivouacking in rain under mackintosh sheets'
(Morris Meredith Williams/ © Phyllida Shaw)

After much confusion and rifle fire we were able to turn our lorries round and retreat quickly. The lorries in front suffered very badly and we lost some men and our Captain Bell and Lieutenant Humphries. ... When about five miles away, [we] had to get our rifles and lay down in a mangel field waiting for the enemy to come. We waited there for about three hours but they did not come after us, so we started off again with only one Lieutenant about 10 at night and no lights and no grub either and no smokes. We kept on going until about 2 a.m. when we made a halt in a village and we were able to get a few biscuits and a wee bit of bully beef and get a wink of sleep.

Feeding the guns - 1st and 2nd Ypres

IV DAC's 160km retreat south ended on 5 September 1914, when it reached Brie-Comte-Robert, a town southeast of Paris. This coincided with the beginning of the First Battle of the Marne, when the French Army held the German drive towards Paris and brought about the German withdrawal north to the River Aisne. On 6 September the BEF began to engage, advancing north towards this river, crossing on the night of 13 September. IV DAC was not far behind, and established itself that day at Buzancy, just south of Soissons, remaining there until 8th October. As Gerald recalled:

On 13 September we arrived in the neighbourhood of Soissons and were engaged there until 8 October. We were particularly pleased to see Winston Churchill out here, and he seemed very pleased with himself and everything he saw.[19]

In another newspaper report captioned 'More German Trickery – Birmingham Motor-Drivers Experiences' he had written:

Sometimes at a halt I get talking to some of the peasants, and everywhere they tell you how the Germans have taken everything. We heard in one town of a trick of theirs. When a regiment was about to enter a town, they would send on a man speaking excellent English, and he would see the Mayor and say that the English cavalry were coming, and would they get buckets of water and food for the troops, for which they would pay – then of course they came along and never paid at all.[20]

And now the column began to fulfil its proper role, supplying ammunition to three of Fourth Division's artillery brigades.

In 1914, Fourth Division consisted of 10th, 11th and 12th infantry brigades, a cavalry squadron and a cyclist company, four brigades of the Royal Field Artillery, No. 31 Heavy Battery of the Royal Garrison Artillery and two companies of Royal Engineers.[21]

At full strength, three of the four RFA brigades would each have three batteries of six 18-pounder field guns. The three batteries of the fourth brigade would each have been equipped with six 4.5-inch howitzers. The RGA battery was equipped with four 60-pounder (5-inch) guns. Altogether, Gerald's unit was responsible for supplying 54 field guns, 18 howitzers and four heavy guns as well as small arms ammunition for the infantry brigades.

Each of the artillery brigades had an ammunition column which brought up shells from refilling points located behind the lines, generally using horse-drawn carts. It was the divisional ammunition column's job to collect ammunition from the divisional ammunition park and transport this by lorry to replenish the refilling points. The ammunition parks, run by the ASC, maintained stocks of ammunition that they collected from nearby railheads that were supplied from the rear. Sometimes ammunition column trucks collected directly from the railheads, and also delivered directly to the gun batteries.

While at Buzancy, IV DAC's work at last began in earnest; collecting ammunition from a railhead at Fere-en-Tardenois and other locations and carrying it to refilling points. The team also distributed small arms ammunition, blankets and field dressings, moved limbered vehicles and water carts and supplied the cavalry with pompom ammunition for anti-aircraft protection. And then the line stabilised and operational pressure began to ease.

But that was all to change, due to pressing concerns about the vulnerability of the channel ports and a new urgency to relocate the BEF from the Aisne to the Belgian coast. Between 8 and 13 October IV DAC moved 370km north from Buzancy to Meteren, east of Saint-Omer.

Then followed a German 'rush for the channel' which was halted by French, British and Belgian troops defending a precarious line from Arras in France to Nieuport on the Belgian coast. This lasted from 10 October to mid-November. The First Battle of Ypres, a Belgian town that the Germans failed to take, was decisive. This began with a German attack at Langemarck, north of Ypres, on 20 October and ended indecisively in mid-November. During this time IV DAC moved a few kilometres west from Meteren to Steenwerck on 2 November, remaining there until 28 November.

Not surprisingly these operations required large quantities of materiel to sustain them. Here we see a summary of the numbers of rounds of ammunition that the unit distributed to brigade refilling points from September to December 1914. The data for September reflects the demands of the fighting on the Aisne, and the battling around Ypres in October and November.[22]

Ammunition supplied by IV DAC in 1914

Nature of ammunition	September	October	November	December
18-pdr shrapnel	3,368	20,418	16,565	11,796
18-pdr high explosive (HE)	0		3,000	724
4.5-in howitzer shrapnel	1,963	3,822	3,671	2,440
4.5-in howitzer lyddite (HE)	1,419	3,470	1,725	304
60-pdr shrapnel	694	1,477	1,970	0
60-pdr lyddite (HE)	449	480	848	0
Small arms ammunition	1,104,800	3,121,500	2,386,350	400,000

Source: Analysis of data in TNA, WO 95/1468

These data show a heavy use of shrapnel shells – packed with small metal balls and designed to burst in the air to ravage the 'beaten' zone below. This was a frightening weapon, particularly to infantry advancing or retiring over open ground *en masse*, and for whom the importance of steel helmets had not yet been recognised.

In the wider context, IV Division was but a small part of the overall deployment around Ypres.[‡] Casualties among German and British forces numbered around 80,000 and 54,000 respectively alongside heavy Belgian and French losses, as well as civilians caught in the midst of it all.[23]

That the tempo of the battle had turned by mid-November is evident from IV DAC's activities. There was an acute shortage

---

‡   The BEF deployed seven British, two Indian divisions and a cavalry corps at the First Battle of Ypres alongside the French Eighth Army (*https://en.wikipedia.org/wiki/First_Battle_of_Ypres_order_of_battle*, accessed 15 Feb 2018)

of artillery ammunition, and little was available for 18-pounders in particular for the rest of the year. But there was a surge in demand for barbed wire, sand bags, picks, shovels, Very (flare) pistols and rifle grenades – all symptomatic of establishing the trench systems that were to dominate the Western Front for the next four years.

The weather deteriorated as well – heavy rain, hard frosts, snow and the muddy thaw that followed added to general discomfort and operational constraint. Lorry loads were lowered to 200 rounds of 18-pounder shell to reduce skid risk. Non-paved roads became impassable and keeping lorry engines going in sub-zero conditions was challenging.

The column moved to Merville on 28 November, and King George V inspected parties on 2 December. A few of the officers and NCOs were granted leave. In mid-December a more regular rhythm to ammunition supply resumed and a (possibly humourless) higher command chose Christmas Eve for the column to return to Meteren, where it remained for the rest of the year. Christmas day brought a hard frost, a church parade and distribution of the King's Christmas cards and Princess Mary's gifts.

And so, Gerald Andrewes' 1914 came to a close. In four and a half months he had experienced the retreat to the Marne, advance to the Aisne and the rush back to Belgium, covering over 800km in the process. As he had spent the majority of this time uncomfortably in range of the enemy's guns during this time he would later qualify for the '5TH Aug. – 22ND Nov 1914' 'Mons' bar to the 1914 Star medal.§ He had slept in all manner of places, gone hungry and unwashed, endured operational life in sunshine, rain and snow, struggled to drive on impassable roads and wrestled with frozen radiators and lorry breakdowns. He had also witnessed the onset of trench warfare.

---

§ Bar to the 1914 Star; authorised by the Army in 1917, the 1914 Star was the first campaign service medal to be struck for the First World War and was issued to those who served in France and/ or Belgium between 5th August and 22 November 1914. The bronze bar awarded to those who had been under fire during this period was authorised in 1919.

He remained in France and Belgium for the whole of 1915, including 4th Division's heavy engagement in the 2nd battle of Ypres from April to May 1915. He even had a five-month spell as a lance corporal but, true to form, reverted to private at the end of the year.

Out to graze

On 16 January 1916 Gerald Andrewes returned to England for general ASC duties. These included spells at Catterick and, in 1917, the reserve motor transport depot at Grove Park, a centre for training courses in motor vehicles maintenance. Eventually he was discharged from Woolwich Dockyards as 'unfit' on 1 August 1917. His Army Character Reference records that 'he has been employed lorry driving in France and Belgium; a sober, reliable and intelligent man.'[24] There is a prominent stamp in his papers that simply states 'Discharged – No longer fit for War Service. Para.392 (xvi) K.R.'

Further elaborations reveal that his unfitness was 'not of recent origin; not a result of, but aggravated by ordinary military service. Permanent. No incapacity.' So, no disabilities pension… A further caveat states 'this man's capacity is lessened 5% temporary.' But he did qualify for a gratuity of £48. 15s. and the assessors *did* take into account his two months of service with the Horse Guards in 1898.

By then he had been a full-time soldier for over three years, and a part-time volunteer for more than eight. For his early Great War service, he earned the 1914 Star with date bar, and – on discharge – Silver War Badge No. 125926 (which recognised his army service and subsequent discharge as 'unfit'); enough for any self-respecting man to call it a day.[25]

Driving ambulances for the French

So, did he grab an easy way out of the army or was he pushed? Quite possibly the latter, because we find him among the names of more than 7,400 British volunteers listed as having 'gone abroad on Red Cross and kindred war-work for the French' up to

December 1917.[26] So, it did not take him long to return to France. From his *Croix de Guerre* citation we learn that he was driving ambulances for the French Red Cross with a unit called *Section Sanitaire Anglaise* No. 1 (SSA 1), established under the auspices of the British Ambulance Committee (BAC), an organisation set up in 1914 'to make up the deficiency in the number of motor-cars available for ambulance work in France.'[27]

The development of British volunteer support to the army medical services in 1914 is remarkable. In her books *Life Class* and later in *Toby's Room* the novelist Pat Barker gives canny insight to the practical, social and military influences on the transition from peace to war in London, and the grim realities of life as a volunteer front line hospital assistant and as an ambulance driver in France; the letters from Paul (in France) to Elinor (in England) are harrowing, particularly as they chart the worsening plight of the wounded, and gradual creep of destruction into hitherto peaceful towns and villages.

The story of specific support to the French is well told, even if a little flamboyantly, in Laurence Binyon's book *For Dauntless France*, written for the British Committee of the French Red Cross. Its origins date from the perilous days in the autumn of 1914 when a ground swell of support in Britain for the French was paralleled with an overwhelming wish to 'do something' in some way.

This help manifested itself in many ways. Binyon's lists of individuals and organisations that sprang up to fund, organise and drive this movement at high level read like pages from 'Who's Who.' Many volunteered, including men who were too old for military service, and others who were younger but did not believe in fighting. Many young women (often from well-off families who wanted to help, but were not permitted to enrol in the army) joined in.

What is even more impressive is the wide variety of skills and trades that the volunteers who served overseas brought with them – some professionally trained, others simply willing to learn. Frequently they found themselves in very difficult and often dangerous circumstances. Of those Britons who had volunteered for service with the French by the end of 1917 perhaps 55% were women, of whom almost 20% were married.[28]

To elaborate further, here is an alphabetical list of 'ranks' of those listed in the British Committee, French Red Cross: Medal Rolls who, through their service overseas, qualified for the British War Medal 1914-20 and Victory Medal 1914-19.[29] There are 42 covering all seniorities ranging from VAD to Surgeon, Canteener to Cook, Masseuse to Matron, and Orderly to Orderly Chaplain. Broadly this diverse and skilled band of individuals fitted into three main strands of civilian-driven support to the French: hospitals, convoys and canteens. Gerald and his colleagues in SSA 1 were part of the convoys.

The early focus on ambulance services, which evolved into the ambulance convoys, developed in part from two private initiatives to help Belgium in 1914. These were the Monro Motor Ambulance Corps (MAC) founded by Dr Hector Monro, and the Friends' Ambulance Unit (FAU) which, starting out as the Anglo-Belgian Ambulance Unit, was founded by members of the Quaker movement. These – and other groups and individuals who made their way to France, sometimes with their own vehicles – all helped to bolster the French ambulance services. What started out as a more *ad hoc* form of support was gradually formalised within the French systems between 1914 and 1916.

The convoys (equipped with British ambulance cars provided from donations raised and managed through the British Ambulance Committee) were designed around the French Army's own *Sections Sanitaires* and integrated into their structure. Typically, they were staffed by British volunteers.[30] While remaining civilians, they wore British khaki uniforms with French badges, contrasting with the blue-grey worn by their French colleagues. Some, perhaps Gerald himself, will have had some knowledge of French.

Laurence Binyon noted that it was the BAC that provided the first five complete British convoys attached to the French Army.

They became *Sections Sanitaires Anglaises* numbered 1 to 5. The first two were mobilised in January 1915 – SSA 1, the first, to the Vosges, near the Swiss border, and SSA 2 (the second) to the St Mihiel Salient, around Commercy in the centre of the French line. Binyon also reported an early reluctance from the French authorities to accept the *Sections* for anything other than 'a mild routine of evacuations.' Yet the sympathetic and understanding French staff officers controlling SSA 1 listened to the frustration from what they probably saw as a random bunch of gung-ho 'gentlemen' civilians and let them have their way.

The *Sections* soon won their spurs; performing courageously and effectively and integrating with the French with a mixture of affection and shared purpose. This won great respect.

While no women drove with the *Sections*, they certainly drove ambulances on the Western Front in other guises. Women volunteers with the First Aid Nursing Yeomanry for example drove for the French Army in the *Sections Sanitaire Yeomanry* (SSY). One of these units (SSY 3, otherwise known as the Hacket-Lowther Unit) was allowed to do front line work, following secondment to the French 3rd Army in 1918.[31]

Lady Dorothie Feilding, a volunteer working in the British sector, was prominent in the list of the first five women to be awarded the Military Medal for her work driving ambulances and tending wounded in the field with the MAC in 1914.[32] Other volunteer women drivers were decorated later on in the war: Ellen Russell, a driver with SSY 2 who worked with the French 4th and 5th Armies, won a Military Medal in 1918 for evacuating both British and French wounded while under heavy shellfire. She also received the *Croix de Guerre* from the French.[33]

A key feature of the *Sections* was that they were intended to carry French wounded – not from behind the lines, but directly from the front. French acceptance of this role stemmed from lengthy negotiation and, eventually, their clear appreciation of the valuable work that the *Sections* were doing. Laurence Binyon describes the *modus operandi* at the front:

Regimental stretcher-bearers carry the wounded from the trenches, or the places where they have fallen, to the *Postes de Secours*. These are placed as close behind the line as is practicable; it may be two or three hundred, or as much as two or three thousand yards. There, the wounds are roughly dressed. The wounded are then sent on to a *Poste de Triage*, where they are sorted out, and, if necessary, have their hurts re-dressed. The lightly wounded are sent from the *Triage* to a Field Dressing Station, whence they can return to the front as soon as they are well enough: more severely wounded are sent to the nearest Casualty Clearing Station; the very badly hurt are sent to a Field Dressing Station till well enough to travel farther.

From the *Poste de Triage* backwards all the work is done by the *Section Sanitaire* of the division. And now the ambulances of the section almost always work the whole way back from the *Poste de Secours*. It has been told how at the time of the first gas attack in the Second Battle of Ypres, the service of horse ambulances which brought the wounded from the *Poste de Secours* broke down; and a section of the FAU was among the first to replace the horse ambulances, and the '*brouettes*' or light hand-carts which were also used, with the far swifter automobiles. The roads are not always practicable for these; but the English sections have shown a fine spirit of enterprise in pushing up their motor service as near the firing line as possible, as during the last of the Verdun battles; and in the difficult mountain-paths of the Vosges, by starting a section of motorcycles.

As the drivers of English sections rank as privates in the French Army, they receive the regular pay of five *sous* a day and army rations, which are supplemented out of mess funds. Cooking is done in the roomy and well-equipped *camion cuisine* or kitchen lorry.

The workshop cars are fitted up with lathes and a variety of machines which enable them to tackle any kind of repair.

New BAC ambulances in France, presented by the Explorers of Great Britain (© Paul Handford)

Billets are found in huts, tents, dilapidated cottages, or ruined farms. Though many of the volunteers are men of middle age, there has been remarkably little illness among them. And in spite of a number of casualties, the good fortune of the sections has often seemed almost miraculous. More than once or twice a post or billet just vacated has been blown to pieces; and the story we have told is testimony to the storms of shellfire through which they have worked for days and nights and survived. [34]

This is the environment in which Gerald Andrewes elected to serve towards the end of 1917. While he may have spent much of his earlier time in France and Belgium marginally behind the front line, this all changed when he joined SSA 1. This unit, with a distinguished record dating back to early 1915, had survived many hazards. As one of the first two of twenty such units, it cut its teeth in the Vosges Mountains, supporting the very costly fighting on the French right flank in Alsace-Lorraine. Then, at the end of 1915, SSA 1 began the first of two arduous tours aiding the dreadful fighting at Verdun, which continued over ten months of German assault in 1916 at a total cost of around 700,000 casualties. In between tours, while the unit spent five months further to the west during the second battle of Champagne between Rheims and Suippes, the French rewarded the convoy as a unit with the *Croix de Guerre* for its distinguished service at Verdun. [35]

The philosopher Olaf Stapledon, a Friends Ambulance Unit volunteer with SSA 13 helps us to imagine more of the Section's work: writing in 1917 when aged 31:

The Convoy took up its position at the foot of the Montagne de Reims. For many days we had little more than ordinary routine work, but our village was fairly constantly shelled. From the Montagne we could watch an immense stretch of the front undergoing a preliminary bombardment. At last the attack began. All our cars were now continuously in service; but though two French motor sections had come up to help us, it was quite impossible to cope with the multitude of wounded. Crowds of them had to drag themselves along the heavily shelled road on foot. Wounded Germans also came pouring in, their grey coats covered with blood.

A single narrow road served our sector. Along it swarmed troops, guns, limbers, tanks and ambulances. There was one particularly bad stretch where the road passed a [German] battery concealed in a wood. Here horses were put to the gallop and ambulances floundered hurriedly among the shell-holes regardless of the cries of their suffering cargo. Once when I was on this stretch, following a galloping limber [two-wheeled cart], a shell landed on the limber and the road was immediately blocked with a confusion of splintered wood and the bodies of horses and men. Our people had to clear the way for the cars, thereby inadvertently assisting the French Army. We were now beginning to have our own casualties and losing cars. After twenty-four hours of this sort of thing nerves began to give out. At least, I speak for myself. Everybody else seemed so damnably calm. I began to wonder how much more I could stand. Yet deep down in my mind, and difficult to introspect, was a strange quietness, an aloof delight. Odd, to be terrified and yet at peace! [36]

A year later, Stapledon's young colleague Romney Fox wrote of the death of their comrade Colin Priestman, a fellow Quaker who had died of wounds. He reckoned that around two-thirds of the *Section's* ambulances had been hit by shellfire and shrapnel, including his own. Setting aside new hazards such as booby traps, he did find moments of relief:

The wild flowers amongst the trenches & shell holes are beautiful. Great splashes of red & yellow & white & blue – poppies, ox-eyed daisies, vetches, blue & yellow, borage, cornflower, larkspur & many whose names I do not know. They are a pleasant sight. [37]

We learn from the citation for the award of Gerald's *Croix de Guerre* in December 1918 that SSA 1 worked in support of the French 39th Infantry Division, led by General Pougin and took part in some critical and dangerous engagements. This document translates charmingly:

'Released from all obligation in the English Army with which he served for the main part of the campaign [Gerald's ASC service], he at once joined the service of France in the SSA No.1 where he was always notable for his courage and devotion, notably at Verdun (April 1918), Kemmel [Fourth Ypres](April, May 1918) and the Battle of the Marne [Battle of Reims] (July 1918).'

General Pougin with members of SSA1 at Metz November 1918 following their presentation of the *Croix de Guerre*; GSA is probably third from left, front row (IWM HU 82732/ © IWM)

What this tells us is that Gerald witnessed some particularly perilous moments of the war, providing crucial assistance during the German's final and desperate assault known as the 'spring offensive.'¶Response to which finally brought about the unification of all allied forces under a supreme commander, General Foch. One result was that French reinforcements were brought in to reinforce British troops in the Ypres Salient. This was to counter the German assault in April 1918 in the River Lys sector called 'Georgette', which aimed to drive the British to the sea. The 39th French Division relieved British defenders at Kemmelburg just north of Ypres and fought there at the Second Battle of Kemmel.[38] Gerald and his SSA 1 colleagues were engaged there; by then a fully integrated unit of the French Army, the *Section* had quickly moved 350km from the Verdun sector.

He must have had an overwhelming feeling of *déjà vu*, having been present at that equally dangerous moment there three and a half years earlier at the First Battle of Ypres. Just about everything

¶ See '*Kaiserschlacht*' in Jack Nunn's story

had changed. The landscape must have been unrecognisable – hardly a building untouched, the maze of trench networks, broken infrastructure, fields with no livestock or trees, and endless clusters of burial crosses. He could not have failed to wonder 'when will this ever end?'

The last action listed in Gerald's *Croix de Guerre* document is the second battle of the Marne, which marked the repulsion of a

Citation for GSA's *Croix de Guerre* award

German attack on 15 August 1918 in the Reims area that stalled two days later. The counter-attack that followed, where French divisions were supported by American and later British troops, followed through to the armistice of 11 November.

By the end of hostilities, SSA 1 had operated virtually along the whole length of the Western Front, from the Belgian coast to the Swiss border. Gerald had seen all of the northern half of it, and probably more. He remained in France with BAC until 1919 supporting the huge post-war humanitarian effort there.

What would he have thought at the end of it all? He had begun his war moving shells towards the guns; in effect facilitating a process of death and mutilation. He ended it helping to relieve the suffering of those afflicted by German weaponry amid harrowing circumstances. It is hard to imagine that this would not have seemed very ironic.

More than thirty members of the SSAs were killed or died during their service in France.[39] Only 19 of these along with seven other volunteers who drove ambulances appear in the list of those commemorated by the Commonwealth War Graves Commission – unsung heroes indeed.[40]

Back to Birmingham

By the time he came home he was 45 years old, and still single. He returned to his old office premises at 55 Temple Row and continued to build his business. In spite of this relative stability, his adjustment to post-war life back in Birmingham must have been strange. He also returned to live in the same lodgings in Berkswell and stayed there until 1922.

He and his partner Bradley had maintained their office throughout the war; he carried on until the 1950s when he died – still practising. By then he had taken on a younger partner called Taylor. The firm rejoiced with the slightly esoteric telegram address of 'Average, Birmingham' – fitting for a firm of insurance brokers?

He changed his digs, and so met his future wife, his landlady at 237 Hagley Road in Edgbaston. They married in 1923. Her name was Ethel Marion Chavasse. She was ten years younger than him, and relatively tiny. She had been married into a well-known family called Chavasse. Noel Chavasse, the double-VC was a relative. Her first husband James was an inventor, describing himself in his 1911 census return as 'Commercial Traveller Machinery.'

Ethel Marion and James had married in 1903 and lived then at 122 Hagley Road. They had two children – Edna and Phillip (born two years later). James Chavasse died, aged just 42, when Edna was eight. His career had been somewhat precarious, and his widow found it useful to take in lodgers. Edna's son Martin recalls, 'Mother was born in 1904. He [James] died in 1912. I think that Ethel Marion was on her own for a while. She used to come up to London to the theatre with various boyfriends, and often referred to the various stars she had met over the years. I think she had quite a notable and sociable life. She lived to 101. It's thanks to Gerald that she had a better life at the end, because when her first husband died, she had no money.'[41]

In 1928 Ethel's daughter Edna married John Wyer. Their children Judith and Martin were born in 1934 and 1938. Martin's wife Margaret recalls Gerald as 'a very good-looking man' who was 'charming – from what I heard, he'd call Granny (he used to ring her up from the offices at lunchtime) and ask if 'my lovely lady would like to come to lunch today'; he was obviously a kind and generous man. Granny used to talk about him a lot.'

Martin Wyer speaks very warmly of his grandfather, noting that 'he was working right up to the last – he was in hospital for very short time. I know he did have a problem with his hands – because he was a pianist – I imagine that it was arthritis; he had to give up because his fingers were stiff... I think he paid the boarding part of my fees [at Berkhamsted School]. He was a very kind man. I suspect that he helped to pay for the little extras when he and Ethel used to join us on our annual summer holidays. For his 25-years' wedding anniversary we all stayed at the Cumberland Hotel, at Marble Arch, soon after we moved to London.'

Gerald gained considerable driving experience in the army. This ties in with an enthusiasm for cars and driving that Martin remembers from car rides in a large Austin when he stayed with his grandparents. Gerald was particularly keen on courtesy on the roads – something 'entirely in keeping with his character.'

In describing Ethel, Martin explains, 'what did she do? While they had no children of their own, they lived a life of luxury. He made a lot of money from his broking business. They built their house at 340 Lordswood Road, which in those days [1934] was a very nice, modern house – had two or three bathrooms. My sister and I used to visit them when very young. They had a maid who used to bring us breakfast – 'what would you like Miss Judith and Master Martin?' – those were the days! Granny loved life. She loved giving things. She gave us our start in life. She rang us up after we got engaged, and said, 'I've seen a house in Woking – I think you should go and see it'. She always had the upper hand.' As Margaret Wyer added, 'yes, she always liked to be the boss! She liked giving people things. It had to be what she liked. She enjoyed life. She was very generous.'

Gerald Andrewes died on 28 October 1955, aged 81. Later, Martin Wyer tried unsuccessfully to get his grandmother into a masonic home, and so she left Lordswood Road to join her family in Surrey. As Martin explains, 'she lived to a ripe old age and was very active up until when she was 99. She only went into a home at 100.' She died in 1986, aged 101.

So, there we have Gerald Andrewes. A gentle, capable, modest and generous man – 'just a very nice, kind grandfather.' He carved out a successful career and served his country well – with his framed *Croix de Guerre* citation on the wall to remind him of days that he probably did not discuss as he grew older. He loved the family he gained with his wife. As Margaret Wyer commented 'we have a lot to be thankful to Gerald for.'

And what about Second World War service? He was 65 and, judging from a photograph of him in 1939, still fit enough when war broke out, and it is difficult to imagine that his sense of duty

Postcard showing Gerald and Marion
Andrewes at Bournemouth, 1939
(© Martin Wyer)

did not stir once more. While he may well not have been a dead ringer for Corporal Jones of 'Dad's Army', it is not hard to imagine him donning a tin hat once more for, say, fire watch duty on one of Edgbaston's roofs; more of a Sergeant Wilson perhaps? After all, he had a complete set of five mounted medal ribbons, which does suggest that he wore uniform again at some point after 1919 …

South Africa 1902?

The first in the group of miniature medals worn by Gerald Andrewes is the Queen's South Africa Medal (QSA) with 'CAPE COLONY', 'ORANGE FREE STATE' 'TRANSVAAL', 'SOUTH AFRICA 1901' and 'SOUTH AFRICA 1902' clasps

His QSA and the first three of the five clasps are listed in the medal roll for the 2nd Battalion, Royal Fusiliers. His 'SOUTH AFRICA 1901' is also verified in the roll for the 2nd Battalion, Royal Fusiliers, but *not* the 'SOUTH AFRICA 1902' clasp. I have been unable to verify the 'SOUTH AFRICA 1902' clasp definitively.

What is tantalising is that his attestation papers for the ASC list 'London Rifle Brigade Volunteer', 'Royal Horse Guards', 'Royal Fusiliers', 'London Rifle Brigade again', '1st City of London Yeomanry' as his answer to the question 'Have you ever served ...'

His service with the first three units is clear from the original documentation. But what is this reference to the 1st City of London Yeomanry? A City of London Yeomanry had been created in 1900 as the 20th Battalion, Imperial Yeomanry, nicknamed 'The Rough Riders.' They served in South Africa and were disbanded following return home in April 1901. That year, a new unit, the 1st County City of London Yeomanry (Rough Riders) was formed with veterans of the Boer War campaign. In April 1902 it was renamed as the 1st City of London Imperial Yeomanry (Rough Riders).[42] While I have not found a medal roll for the '1st City of London Imperial Yeomanry', there is a roll for the '1st Battalion Imperial Yeomanry' that confirms the entitlement to both the 'SOUTH AFRICA 1901' and 'SOUTH AFRICA 1902' clasps for one 20416 Trooper G Andrews. Remembering that spelling mistakes do find their way into the medal rolls, and that we have seen that 'Andrewes' is frequently misspelt 'Andrews,' I am prepared to bet that he re-enlisted and returned to South Africa, and that this explains the mystery 'SOUTH AFRICA 1902' clasp.

Notes

1 Laurence Binyon, For Dauntless France: An account of Britain's aid to the French wounded and victims of the war (1918) 90, 91

2 pers. comm. Lesley Koulouris 27 Nov 2013

3 Discharge certificate of an Enrolled Volunteer dated 29.6.1898. Andrewes' service number was 6091 (courtesy M Wyer)

4 Shropshire Regimental Museum, 'The Shropshire Rifle Volunteers: Outline History', http://www.shropshireregimentalmuseum.co.uk/regimental-history/ volunteers-territorial-and-militia/the-shropshire-rifle-volunteers-outline-history/, accessed 15.05.2017

5 Parchment Certificate of Discharge dated 11.10.1898 (courtesy M Wyer). His service number was 703

6 'Volunteer Force', Wikipedia, https://en.wikipedia.org/wiki/Volunteer_Force_ (Great_Britain), accessed 15.05.2017

7 His service number was RF8965

8 Victorian Military Society, 'Militiamen in the Second Anglo-Boer War', http://www.victorianmilitarysociety.org.uk/reserach/2012-09-09-11-20-22/ archive/60-militiamen-in-the-second-anglo-boer-war, accessed 15.05.2017

9 The British Empire, 'Royal Fusiliers, City of London Regiment', http:// www.britishempire.co.uk/forces/armyunits/britishinfantry/fusiliers.htm, accessed 15.05.2017

10 As 20416 Trooper G Andrews

11 BT Archives; London, England; British Phone Books 1880-1984 – Birmingham Area, 1910

12 Max Hastings, Catastrophe: Europe Goes to War 1914 (2013) 40

13 TNA, WO 364/55, Soldiers Documents from Pension Claims, First World War, (No. 527 Private G S Andrewes)

14 pers. comm. 'ss002d6252' in Great War Forum thread 'Call-up criteria 1914?', 8 Dec 2013

15 The Long, Long Trail, 'The Army Service Corps in the First World War', http://www.longlongtrail.co.uk/army/regiments-and-corps/the-army-service-corps- in-the-first-world-war/, accessed 22.01.2014

16 TNA, WO 95/1468/1, War Diary of IV Divisional Ammunition Column

17 Evening Despatch, 05 December 1914

18 TNA, WO 95/1468/1, War Diary of IV Divisional Ammunition Park (unnumbered appendix)

19 Evening Despatch, 05 December 1914

20 Birmingham Daily News, 20 October 1914

21 '4th Infantry Division (United Kingdom)', Wikipedia, https://en.wikipedia. org/wiki/4th_Infantry_Division_(United_Kingdom)#First_World_War, accessed 11 Jun 2018

22 Data from WO 95/1468/1, IV DAC War Diary

23 Hastings, Catastrophe, 485

24 Character Certificate issued at ASC, Woolwich dated 28.7.1916 (courtesy M Wyer)

25 TNA, WO 329/3211 Royal Army Service Corps (Woolwich) list RASC 1251-1500. Silver War Badge

26 Binyon, *For Dauntless France*, 337

27 The Spectator Archive, '28 November 1914, Page 4 – The British Ambulance Committee', *http://archive.spectator.co.uk/article/28th-november-1914/14/the-british-ambulance-committee*, accessed 17.01.2014

28 Rough analysis of the names listed between pp. 337 and 369 of *For Dauntless France* …

29 WO 329/2323, British Committee, French Red Cross: medal rolls FRX/101B; FRX/101B1; FRX/101B2; FRX/101B3; FRX/101B4; FRX/101B5; FRX/101B6. Pages 1-306. British War Medal and Victory Medal

30 Fiona Reid, *Medicine in First World War Europe: Soldiers, Medics, Pacifists* (2017) 171

31 pers. comm. Paul Handford, 3 Jan 2014

32 London Gazette, 1 September 1916, 8653.

33 Bonhams auction catalogue, 27 March 2013, *http://www.bonhams.com/auctions/20807/lot/188/*, accessed 12.07.2018

34 Binyon, *For Dauntless France*, 97-99

35 *Ibid* 104

36 Olaf Stapledon, 'Experiences in the Friends' Ambulance Unit' from *We Did Not Fight 1914-18: Experiences of War Resisters* (1935) 359-374

37 Unpublished letters from George Romney Fox (1898-1968) to Theodore Fox; pers. comm. Harry Bott, 6 February 2019

38 C.B. Davies, J.E. Edmonds, R.G.B. Maxwell-Hyslop, *Military Operations France and Belgium, 1918 March–April: Continuation of the German Offensive* (1995) 409-428

39 pers. comm. Paul Handford, 3 Jan 2014

40 Analysis of CWGC online records for the 106 persons buried or commemorated in France 1914-18 who did not serve in the Army, Navy , Air Force or Merchant Navy, *https://www.cwgc.org/search-results?tab=wardead&fq_warliteral=1&fq_country=France&fq_servedinliteral=Miscellaneous*, accessed 27.06.2019

41 Conversations with Martin and Margaret Wyer 31 Jul 2013 and subsequent correspondence

42 Gentleman's Military Interest Club, 'The 1st City of London Yeomanry (Rough Riders)' (post by Leigh Kitchen. 7 Dec 2007), http://gmic.co.uk/topic/23715-the-1st-city-of-london-yeomanry-rough-riders/, accessed 11 Jun 2018

Emily Kemp

The philanthropist:
Emily Kemp

*Not at all sure that Kashgar is a
suitable tourist resort for ladies*[*]

Emily Kemp's group of miniature medals (British War Medal 1914-20,
Allied Victory Medal, France: *Médaille d'Honneur des Epidemies,
Médaille de la Reconnaissance Française, Médaille d'Honneur
pour Actes de Courage et de Dévouement*) together with her Gold
Medal from the French Geographic Society (courtesy of *www.
aberdeenmedals.com*)

---

[*] From a British Foreign Office file labelled 'Chinese travel of Miss Emily G Kemp and
Mary M MacDougall' dated 16.10.1912

Early in 2011 Tessa Morris-Suzuki, a historian of modern Japan and Korea, wrote about 'a remarkable but almost completely forgotten woman traveller named Emily Georgiana Kemp' who journeyed extensively in Asia in the early 1900s. Ninety years earlier, in June 1922 the *Dundee Courier* had noted similarly:

> A woman traveller of whom one hears very little, though her achievements are great as those of others in the limelight, is Lord Rochdale's sister Miss Emily Kemp.

The writer then reported that Miss Kemp had recently become the first woman to address the French Geographical Society in Paris.

So, who was this woman, what else did she do, and why is she of particular interest in relation to the Great War?

Emily Georgiana Kemp was born on 20 May 1860 in Rochdale, Lancashire – the youngest of five sisters. The oldest, Emily Jessie, was nine years older.

Their brother George, the youngest of them all, was born in 1865. Her family was wealthy – her father George Tawk Kemp being a prominent entrepreneur and industrialist.

Rochdale, now part of Greater Manchester, became an important hub in the weaving industry during the industrial revolution of the 19th Century. As a well-known wool merchant, George Tawk Kemp was one of Rochdale's movers and shakers. He flourished while those in the cotton industry suffered in the early 1860s in the wake of the American Civil War: this stopped imports of raw cotton, forcing mill operatives and their families out of work and into poverty.[1] This prompted public action to provide relief, as had happened twenty years earlier when people in Rochdale inspired the Co-operative Movement in the 1840s; this grew in the wake of the suffering within a weaving community whose livelihoods had been overturned by the introduction of mechanisation.[2] One way and another, the Rochdale in which Emily Kemp grew up had demonstrated a social conscience.

EGK – self-portrait (from the frontispiece of the *Face of China*)

George Kemp was also a devout man. Emily Lydia, his wife, personally gave the children religious instruction, with bible lessons on Sundays at which they were expected to pray with little or no preparation. In parallel, both her parents were keen that the children become good linguists; they started with French very early on, and later progressed to German and Italian. Emily was clearly disappointed that Latin was not on the list – it was not considered necessary for girls.[3]

Their parents and grandparents were keen politicians, and the girls grew up in a world of much political comment, accompanied by enthusiasm for English and French history. In turn, underpinned by strong parental passion, they learned about foreign missions. It must have been both exciting and stimulating to learn of the adventures described by missionaries who visited their home.

Their grandparents were also strong missionary supporters. Every year they hosted a grand dinner to coincide with the annual missionary meetings, and Emily cannot have missed their determination to involve ministers of all denominations as part of their promotion of Christian unity. She recalls the preparations for the dinner; 'the beautiful mahogany table, with its cut glass and silver reflected in the shining surface, and above all, the noble decanters of sherry and port, of which no small amount was consumed.' After the dinners, the whole party would adjourn to West Street Baptist Chapel in Rochdale for the missionary meetings, which the young Emily Kemp regarded as the most interesting services of the time.

Emily's early formal schooling came from a Swiss governess, who looked after the three younger sisters. As well as fostering lively and sometimes controversial debate – Emily describes her as a 'rabid man-hater' – she clearly let the girls' imaginations flourish.

They grew up in an idyllic world: large gardens, pets and ponies; a motherless lamb to rear by hand each spring; long walks and awareness of nature, its beauty and needs. In parallel, they learned about sorrow and human suffering. Their parents took them to visit the sick; they 'pricked texts for the blind every Sunday' and often visited schools for the poor.

In time, the governess made way for a private school in Camberwell in the London outskirts run by a Mr Danesfield.[4] This was an intolerant establishment, run by governesses bent on curbing any natural freedoms, and certainly on quashing any unladylike traits or related ambition. Amid this impersonal and stifling environment, Emily excelled in Italian and German, revelling in fluent and gleeful conversation with her peers that the governesses could not understand. Further escape from the oppressive regulation came though participation in services at the Metropolitan Tabernacle at the Elephant and Castle in South London, and the Moody and Sankey evangelical meetings that began in London in 1875. As Emily herself observed that 'there was a painfully exotic spiritual atmosphere, and religious experiences were almost *de rigueur* among the pupils the whole time I was at the school.'

Late in 1874, Emily travelled abroad for the first time, when the whole family wintered at Cannes. The 'gloriously strange and vivid' environment and people fascinated the girls, who 'walked, drove, picnicked and sketched', and catalysed ideas. The elder sisters decided to do something for the 'ragamuffins who haunted the streets' and set about hiring a room and giving them classes in the evenings. Back in Rochdale, this progressed further with a service for the slum children who otherwise disrupted the services at West Street Chapel. Regardless of the overall good that these activities may or may not have achieved, the unruly audiences provided excellent training for the budding teachers and organisers.

In 1877, Emily accompanied her sister Florence to the Fraulein Aliele Cannstadt School at Wurstemburg [Wurzburg] in Germany – one of several schools for girls in the town. She stayed as a border, living in the Principal's house. Florence had been there for six months the previous year together with her sister Lydia. The two had worked hard and enjoyed their time there, earning the admiration of their German professors who clearly thought that they were quite exceptional for English girls. Emily did not rate herself as highly as her sisters, but she felt unswerving loyalty to them.

1881-1892 The scholar

So, what do we see in the young woman who then went up to Oxford in 1881? Privileged; well if not unusually educated; religious with a social conscience; of above-average exposure to the world outside Britain; a politically astute and competent communicator; a fledgling rebel perhaps – probably sticking to her guns when crossed, and well capable of looking after herself.

Aged 21, Emily Kemp became one of the earliest undergraduates to study at Somerville College, Oxford.[5] She is number 28 in the College Register. In so doing she joined an elite group of young women that outstripped the intellect of the vast majority of her sex. Somerville had opened in 1879, and in the college's own records:

> ... was founded to include the excluded. It was created for women when universities refused them entry, and for people of diverse beliefs when the establishment religion was widely demanded.' [6]

Somerville was also the first Oxford College to be non-denominational, and remains religiously non-aligned to this day.[7]

This ethos and environment must have seemed tailor-made for Emily. In *Somerville for Women*, Pauline Adams writes of the confusing impact of women undergraduates on Oxford life, quoting Kemp's own description of 'how some of the men attending Dean Kitchin's lectures at Christ Church were so terrified when the first women students came in (by a different door) that they ran away,' and how 'attending Bright's lectures on English History at Queen's College, we were taken through all manner of dark and dingy passages and through his house... and when we got into the hall we sat at one end and the men the other.' [8]

Emily also recalled that Madeleine Shaw Lefevre, the first Principal of Somerville, liked her students to dress tastefully, and had an eagle eye for any apparel that she deemed conspicuous. She herself [Kemp] was told 'if she wishes to go to a garden party in a white flannel tennis dress, carrying a racquet and shoes (which was considered to be aping the men) she must drive and not walk through the streets.'

These remarks may well have been made when two feisty septuagenarians – Emily Kemp and Margaret Roberts – spoke at a dinner for current members of the college as part of the 1929 Jubilee celebrations, recalling student life in Somerville's earliest days.[9]

Past and present Somerville students at a reunion - probably in 1886; EGK is 2nd from left in the middle row and her friend Margaret Roberts is behind her, to the left (PI/0007/ © Somerville College)

Beyond recording that she had received tuition from a Mr Wilson and that she had not sat any exams, the College Register provides no record of her academic progress up to the time she left Oxford in June 1883. Nevertheless, as strongly demonstrated later in life, her experiences while at Somerville proved a strong and life-long influence.

Two years later she joined the Women's Committee of the Baptist Missionary Society and became preoccupied with the idea of Christian missionary work.[10] This led her to begin studies in London at the London School of Medicine for Women in 1888. Then part of the Royal Free Hospital, the school is now part of the medical school at University College London. The Register of Students lists her as one of 28 young women who entered for the winter session 1888-89: she was the 225th to enrol. During this time, she lived at College Hall in Byng Place, Bloomsbury. The only comment alongside her name in the register is 'Given up.' Four of the remaining 27 also 'gave up' without further explanation. Others went on to qualify as doctors.

Many years later, she confided to her friend Margaret Roberts (one of the very first Somerville cohort) that her health had not been good enough to enable her to complete her medical studies and continue on to become a medical missionary.[11] This is surprising, considering the intrepid and risky nature of the travels she undertook later on.

Her next step was to study Fine Arts at the Slade School of Drawing, Painting and Sculpture, joining the intake for 1890-91. The Slade is the internationally renowned art school of University College London. The syllabus revolved around six courses: Drawing from the Antique and Life, Painting from the Antique and Life, Sculpture, Etching, Composition, and the Study of Animals.[12] In her second year, she won a Third-Class prize for landscape painting. Early in that year, Alphonse Legros, Slade Professor for 1892-93, sketched one of the few images that we have of Emily.

She had registered for her third year, 1893-94, at the time that Frederick Brown succeeded Legros as Slade Professor. At this point Brown introduced Henry Tonks to the Slade as his assistant, and Emily would have met him at this time. Tonks was a qualified surgeon as well as an artist, and he would later work with her in France in 1915 as a physician.

First steps in China

In the autumn of 1893, she received a request from China, and she left the Slade without completing her studies. By then her talent was sufficiently well recognised that she exhibited an original etching 'Study of a Head' at the World's Colombian Exposition at Chicago in 1893. Margaret Roberts recalled Emily's deep affection for her art training at the Slade such that 'all through, wherever she travelled, she made sketches. Her sketches of China, so vivid and colourful are wonderful – they make the scene real.'

Two of her sisters – Jesse and Florence – were by now well established in China at a medical mission at Taiyuan, the capital city of Shanxi Province.[13] Florence was married to Eben Edwards, a doctor who ran the mission hospital. They had a young family. To this day, missionaries almost invariably serve for several years at a time, and then return home for a year or so on furlough.[†] Emily had agreed to act as nursery governess to Florence's children while their parents returned to England on furlough, and so, in the autumn of 1893, she travelled to China for the first time.

Emily sailed for Shanghai on 25 August. Shanghai at the time was a cosmopolitan port that had thrived in the wake of the First China War (1840-42) when the British named Shanghai a treaty port that came to be controlled by the British, French, and Americans, all of whom acted independently of Chinese law.[14] Each colonial presence had introduced its particular culture and architecture thus creating a vibrant and exciting city.

At Shanghai she met one of her sisters and her husband, and together they ventured on to Taiyuan. Their journey lasted two weeks, and involved travel by houseboat to Tianjin, and then on by mule litter. It was cold and full of surprises – not always pleasant. She later wrote of sleeping in wretched inns on brick bedsteads that were heated from underneath by a fire that was invariably poorly regulated. As for the journey 'sometimes we had to be carried across [rivers] on men's backs, and it is not altogether a pleasant experience to cling on to a bare, greasy back in a kneeling position,

---

† Furlough – home leave

194

Shanghai, 1893
(E.G. Kemp/ © Ashmolean Museum, University of Oxford)

with your arms around an unwashed neck!'[15] Yet there were more entertaining moments:

> One day we met six mandarins in four-bearer chairs, carrying an important document from the Emperor at Peking into Szechwan. They were received everywhere ceremoniously, and crackers set off in their honour; they were accompanied by a military escort and gorgeous banners.[16]

What a vivid new world for a relatively sheltered young lady from Rochdale!

Emily worked hard in Taiyuan. Apart from her immediate charges, she ran a Sunday school class for the 14 English children in the mission. In *Reminiscences of a Sister* she records an unhappy incident when she took the boys out to fly their kites on waste ground near the hospital. There they annoyed some Chinese kite fliers who proceeded to cut their kite loose mid-flight. There followed a scuffle from which she and the children beat a hasty retreat. There

Chinese opium den, 1893/4
(E.G. Kemp/ © Ashmolean Museum, University of Oxford)

were also irritating conflicts among the members of the China Inland Mission (CIM), an organisation founded in 1865, of which the Taiyuan mission was part.

Taiyuan at that time was free of western influences and related detrimental impacts on culture and the way of life. It is not surprising then that Emily was wary of disaffection towards foreigners as demonstrated, for example, by the kite-flying incident. Among other differences, she worried about opium smoking and its impact on Chinese society.

In the autumn of 1894 she returned home, earlier than planned, as the Sino-Japanese War of 1894-5 had broken out. This cut her overlap with her sister Florence was cut short to just eleven days. Little did she know that many of the youngsters that she taught were to die with their parents, at the hands of the Boxer rebels a few years later.

In the late 19th century, the University of Oxford was one of the founders of the so-called 'extension' movement, through which universities began to offer educational opportunities to adult learners outside of the traditional student base. This meshed with an awakening social awareness in the 19th Century of working-class people and their needs. Oxford University signalled an educational responsibility to the general community by sending lecturers into towns and cities across Victorian England, bringing university culture to a diverse adult audience. The first of the early Oxford Extension Lectures was delivered in 1878; by 1894, Oxford University Extension centres were bringing adult education to much of England and a few cities in Wales. Following her return from China, Kemp did secretarial and other work for this organisation.

Not so long afterwards, Emily's own writing began to attract critical review. The *Morning Post* of 8 June 1897 for example reported:

In Temple Bar [January 1897] Emily G. Kemp makes 'A plea for the Study of Sonnets' arguing that their brevity should have a special charm in this age of hurry, and that many of the greatest minds have expressed high thoughts in this musically condensed form. In her many well-chosen quotations she brings to bear an acute and critical poetic facility.' (Temple Bar – A London Magazine for Town and Country Readers, was a literary periodical of the mid and late 19th and very early 20th centuries).

1900 Boxer Uprising

The Boxer Uprising was a rebellion by violent anti-foreign and anti-Christian supporters of the Militia United in Righteousness (*Yihetuan*) who opposed imperialist expansion in China and associated Christian missionary activities. The uprising began in 1889 and continued to 1901, when an eight-country alliance eventually defeated it with a force of over 20,000 troops. On 20 June 1900 the Boxers, supported by the Chinese Army, laid siege to the Legations Quarter in Peking (today Beijing). This lasted until its relief 55 days later. In the meantime, violence broke out against Christian missionaries, and many were killed. Among these were Emily's sister Jesse and family, murdered with 50 others in Taiyuan on 9 July 1900. In all the chaos it was not until September 1900 that Emily learned that Jessie, her husband and son had perished along with many other friends.

Among the dead was Edith Coombs, Emily's friend from Somerville, who ran the girls' school at Taiyuan. She died on 27 June 1900, when it was said that she had been thrust into one of the burning mission buildings and burnt alive [a view disputed by Lau Anshi in 1997 who claimed that Coombs was killed after brandishing a pistol].[17]

Fortunately, Emily's brother-in-law Dr Edwards and his family had been on furlough from Taiyuan during the uprising. He had the grim task of returning to China as an interpreter to German members of an official mission to investigate the uprising. He later wrote *Fire and Sword in Shansi: The Story of the Martyrdom of Foreigners and Anti-Chinese Christians* to which Emily Kemp referred later in *The Face of China*.

1907-1908 Back to China ...

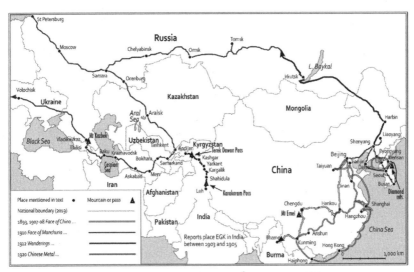

Emily Kemp's travels in Asia, 1907 – 1920

Details of Emily's life between her 1900 and her second visit to China in 1907 are sketchy at best. We do know however that her support to missionary work broadened, particularly towards women in Asia. As early as 1895 she had been an honorary member of the Baptist Zenana Mission, an organisation directed and financed by women, established in 1867 to send women missionaries to India. Their mission was to convert women to Christianity, and help them escape from the hard and oppressive lives that they suffered at the time, along with their subservience to men. The mission's work soon expanded from purely evangelical work to education and medical care.

Emily visited India at least twice. She spoke at a Baptist meeting in Holborn in April 1903 following one visit to India. In 1904, she was a member of a BZM deputation, taking a special interest in training facilities for women.[18] Then in January 1905, the *Burnley Express* reported that she had once again left for India in connection with the BZM. She maintained her connection with the mission for almost the rest of her life and gave financial support to a missionary training college for Bengali women at Calcutta that had opened in 1908. Even in 1931 she still sat on two of its committees.[19]

In late 1907, she returned to China by sea, landing at Shanghai in August. Accompanied by May MacDougall, a 32-year old Scot, she began a six-month journey through the provinces of Shandong, Hebei, Hubei, Sichuan and Yunnan.

Here the fog thins dramatically, thanks to her revelations in *The Face of China*. As she journeyed, her friend the theologian Marcus Dods, to whom she dedicated her book, wrote to her perceptively in October 1907:

> I try to think of you there surrounded by yellow faces and invaded by incredible and unconquerable odours; but I hope you are not too uncomfortable and that your companion's equable and cheery temper is not too severely tried. Be sure you write up your diary day by day, and don't disappoint your publisher and the public. Any tit-bits that you can spare for so hungry a mortal as I am will be highly prized, if you can find time to select what you think will specially suit a taste you know [Dods himself]. I have an impression your travels are going to be note-worthy and will afford an opportunity for the utilisation of your gift of drawing and painting. And what fun you two will have. It is so useless going to even the funniest scenes if you have no one to wink to, or to the most beautiful, if you can't see your admiration reflected in another face. Hoping to hear from you, and commending my spirit to you as a frequent third in your small party, I remain... [20]

By any account, Emily and May shared experiences that few Britons would have dared to contemplate. They travelled some 8,000km by steamer, houseboat, train, barrow, sedan chair, foot and, finally, by car. Some journeys, such as the 1,100km by train from Beijing to Hankou or navigating the Yangtze and Yellow rivers by boat may not sound particularly gruelling. But travel by road and across country by chair was another matter. Describing the descent from Mount Emei [formerly Mt Omi] in Sichuan Province, Emily wrote:

> The descent of the mountain we found extremely arduous, despite our being shod with straw sandals and having to [rely on] support of our pilgrim sticks; it was dreadfully slippery, and for six and a half hours we toiled steadily down flights of steps or glissaded down them on our backs. We calculated the distance as not less than 12 miles. Then you see the coolies pick up the chairs and carry you for another three hours after you are dead beat as if they had done nothing.[21]

By the time the pair crossed into Burma at the end of their travels, Kemp reckoned that they had been carried 1,900km by chair, each carried by four men. For their final trek, they and their entourage numbered 24 for the 33 travelling days it took to walk from Yunnan to Bhamo, in Burma.‡ They paid the 18 coolies £34 for the full 33-day period.

'A deck washer on the Irrawaddy' (E.G. Kemp/ © Ashmolean Museum, University of Oxford)

What had they judged as suitable garb for such a journey? Emily answers this herself, telling us that her self-portrait at the beginning of her book shows 'our complete travelling costume, together with the Buddhist pilgrim stick and the horn spectacles which were formerly a distinctive mark of the scholar.'§

---

‡ Including an interpreter, servant, porters and guards

§ Her choice of clothes reflects her cultural awareness: the Chinese regarded the European fashion for relatively tight-fitting clothes as the equivalent of standing naked. Her sensitivity in this regard goes a long way to explaining why the Chinese received her so well.

In contrast to the unspoilt nature of the Chinese and their customs and traditions that she had found in her travels of 1893/84, Emily Kemp was now struck by what she saw as the universal impact of foreigners, their practices and their culture; in her words, she 'found no village untouched by the great awakening.'

A further change – and all this after little more than ten years – was the transition from earlier [Chinese] suspicion and possible hostility towards foreigners to the warmth that she experienced during her travels. In *The Face of China,* she wrote:

> Considering the behaviour of many travellers towards the Chinese, this [reversal of behaviour] seems to me really astonishing; but they are very sensitive in their appreciations of mental attitude, and they responded unhesitatingly to the call we made on their chivalry by placing ourselves unreservedly in their hands. We were repeatedly warned not to do this, but our confidence was justified by the event. In no European country could we have been more courteously treated, and in very few have I travelled so happily and so free from care.[22]

Emily Kemp at last gathered her diaries and put pen to paper, resulting in *The Face of China* published in 1909. This covered both her 1893/94 and 1907 experiences. In her sub-title to the book, which reads '*travels in east, north, central and western China – with some account of the new schools, universities, missions, and the old religious sacred places of Confucianism, Buddhism, and Taoism*' she sets out the agenda for all her subsequent writing. While she does not specifically list girls' education or political and social change in China, these became important foci for her.

The book is also a showcase for her watercolours and ink sketches, which far from just illustrating the text provide an insightful record of both places and people. Given her concerns about westernisation and the changing face of China, these images – all 71 of them – have even more importance.

Her purpose is clear. 'If anyone is induced by reading this book to make personal acquaintance with China, it will not have been written in vain.'

The expedition certainly left its mark on the intrepid pair. In the preface to *The Face of China* Emily Kemp wrote: 'the journey was one long series of pleasant surprises, as my friend [May MacDougall] expressed the feelings of both of us when, on crossing the border into Burma, she exclaimed: 'if only we could turn round and go all the way back again!'' What spirit!

The book was not widely appreciated. One unfavourable review published in the *Burlington Magazine* in 1909 (which might have been more positive through the lens of today), states:

> Slightly attached to sundry evangelising bodies, she shows a moderate interest in the Christianising of the Chinese, and a much livelier interest in their country, manners and customs. On these she chatters shrewdly and agreeably, according to her own fancies.

In the years that followed Emily reinforced her keen interest in China, the change process there and the related geopolitical manoeuvres. She recognised that the European and other western powers appeared to have relaxed and perhaps muted their commercial and political jockeying with the Chinese Government in the wake of the Boxer Uprising, while nevertheless remaining vigilant and hungry. In contrast both Russia and Japan steadily increased their grip on the borders, most notably in Manchuria and Korea. Such was Kemp's intense interest in these borders and her frustration with the rapid rate of change and related inability to keep up to date, that she resolved to see for herself.

1910 Manchuria and Korea

'Taking heart of grace by the kind reception' of her former book on China, she 'determined to visit Manchuria and Korea, and to try and describe them by pen and brush' as she had described in the *Face of China*. [23] For this, she turned once more to May MacDougall, her trusted travel companion, who was 'willing and eager to repeat our wanderings.' Emily sets the scene herself in her introduction to *The Face of Manchuria, Korea & Russian Turkestan*, published in 1910.

> Less than three years ago I made a journey with a friend, Miss MacDougall, across the Chinese Empire from north-east to south-west, and while my interests in the changes going on there was intensified, a profound anxiety took possession of my mind as to the effect these changes would produce in the national life. The European and other Powers who had wrangled over the possibility of commercial and political advantages to be obtained from the Chinese Government (after the Boxer troubles) have withdrawn to a certain extent, but like snarling dogs dragged from their prey, they still keep covetous eyes upon it, and both Russia and Japan continue steadily but silently to strengthen their hold upon its borders. These borders are Manchuria and Korea, and it is in this direction that fresh developments must be expected. I read all the available literature bearing on the subject, but so rapidly had the changes occurred that books were already out of date, and they failed to make me see the country as it now is. [24]

Her concern lay in the wake of the Russo-Japanese war and continued Japanese interest in Manchuria. Emily was fearful of the threat of invasion if the Japanese were not allowed to settle there. She therefore determined to provide a record before such an event.

The two set off on 1 February 1910 to join the Trans-Siberia Express at St Petersburg, travelling the long journey to Manchuria, and passing through Siberian towns with exotic names such as Omsk, Tomsk and Irkutsk. They finally left the train at Harbin

– 8,400km and some ten days later. Lamenting what she saw as the inadequacies of the *Baedeker* guide, Emily resolved to devote at least part of the book she would write to remedy this.

Why they decided to travel early in the year – bitterly cold and wintry – is strange. Nevertheless, as with all her journeys, Emily had planned well: arranging welcoming links with missionaries; securing assistance and guidance from British diplomats at home and on the way; and making the most of introductions and good local connections.

From Harbin they moved on by train to visit medical missionaries at Shenyang (formerly Mukden).

Shenyang at that time reflected strong Russian and Japanese influences, which were to be enhanced by Russian émigrés following the revolution of 1917. Their hosts there ran an excellent hospital – rebuilt since its destruction during the Boxer terror. Through the British Consul they visited the mausoleum of Nurhaci, the founding emperor of the Manchu dynasty and his wife, Empress Xiaocigao. Even at the end of March the extreme cold persisted, adding to the discomfort of local travel by sleigh.

Having found time for a flying visit by train to Taiyuan[¶] via Beijing, they returned to Manchuria to visit an Irish Presbyterian mission with a girls' boarding school near Shenyang before moving on to Liaoyang; this was the site in 1904 of the first major battle of the Russo-Japanese War, which ended in a Russian retreat.

Once back at Shenyang, they began the long train journey to Korea. Having crossed the Yalu River at Uiju they reached Pyongyang, swapping trains for chairs and rickshaws and little trolleys on tramlines. They explored the city with great interest. The Pyongyang water carriers, their culture and role in society, particularly fascinated Emily. Trains took them further south to Seoul (where she broke rules to sketch the Empress's tomb) and then on to Busan. The pair had determined to explore the Diamond Mountains – now the Mt Kumgong National Park in the southeast corner of what is now North Korea. To reach

---

[¶] Emily's destination in 1893 and the scene of her sister's murder in 1900.

them they sailed up the east coast to Wonsan. Then followed an eight-day, 360km trek back to Seoul by pony, following part of the mountain range that runs down the eastern coast of Korea, inspecting visit an important monastery on the way. Their journey was not without discomfort:

> My guide insisted I should ride with a foot on each side of my good beast's neck, but that brought disaster, for it meant nothing to cling to, so a sudden spring forward of the beast, result of a prod in the back, landed me promptly in the dust. [25]

Safely back in Seoul, travelling discomforts finally got the better of them and they took a luxurious steamer to Dalian to avoid repeating the slow and uncomfortable rail journey back to Manchuria. There, before setting off to return to Harbin, they stayed at a Russian-owned hotel and relished travel in a 'comfortable little carriage with India-Rubber tyres.'

Their final stop in China was a mission at Asiho, just southeast of Harbin, sited rather unwelcomely near the public execution ground. They found a fascinating mix of Buddhist and Moslem temples there. When it came to leaving, their friends fortunately knew how to deal with the challenges of getting on to the trans-Siberian train to Irkutsk, stopped at Harbin for just half a minute. Having dodged through crowds to get to the station, each hurled one piece of luggage into the carriage while the travellers scrambled onto the train!

They travelled on the Russian State Express, which they found less comfortable than the Chinese 'International' that had brought them on their way in to Harbin. Emily devoted an amusing chapter in *The Face of Manchuria...* to her travel guide for the train journey, traversing Lake Baikal – Irkutsk – Tomsk – Omsk – (where she learned by telegram of the death of the King) and Chelyabinsk. On the ninth day from Harbin they reached Kinel, a western suburb of Samara on the left bank of the Volga, from where the railway line to what was formerly Russian Turkestan begins.

There they bought 2nd class tickets to journey on to Tashkent; £2. 10s. 3d to travel 2,100km. Their route took them to Orenburg, on to Aralsk and then round the northern shores of the Aral Sea and across the Syr Daria River. Having crossed expanses of desolate territory, they reached Tashkent ten days after leaving Harbin. Now the capital of Uzbekistan, the city was then the capital of the Russian territory of Russian Turkestan. Here for the first time they were without an interpreter and, not speaking any Russian, even took to sketching their requests in an attempt to order food. After briefly exploring the city and its welcome greenery, they moved on by train across barren desert that led to Samarkand. They were following one of the primary paths of the network of tracks that constituted the Silk Road, the ancient and oft perilous trade routes that linked East to West across some 8,000km.

Samarkand lies at a trade crossroads and has been a Silk Road town for over 2,000 years.[26] The two travellers' imaginations must have been bombarded by visions of past camel trains, their exotic cargos and plucky caravaneers and merchants, whose journeys were long and arduous; a fully loaded camel typically covered 40km a day.

Billeted at the Grand Hotel Samarkand, Emily and May toured the city by *droshky* (a low, four-wheeled, open horse-drawn carriage), visiting Tamerlane's tomb and many mosques. They relished the history and mystique of the city while musing over the widespread excesses of the Moghuls – extravagance, ruthlessness, opulent and exquisite buildings, and art. Then came a train to Bokhara from where they travelled on into modern-day Turkmenistan through Merv and Askabad. They reached the shores of the Caspian Sea at a 'miserable little sun-baked village called Krasnovodsk' [today Türkmenbaşy]. From there they took a steamer to Baku on the western shore of the Caspian. Emily found the countryside around Baku 'hideous – a sort of eruption of oil derricks...'

After Baku they started for Vienna by train, stopping off at Tbilisi in Georgia, from where they experienced a terrifying car journey to Vladikavkaz via Mt Kazbek and its narrow roads.

Offshore view of Baku, 1910 (E.G. Kemp/ © Ashmolean Museum, University of Oxford)

Vladikavkaz is the current capital of the Russian Republic of North Ossetia-Alania. There, they boarded a train to Vienna, and were back in London a week later. Their journey had covered more than 22,000km.

Before this last step, they had to leave Russia. Their train took them some 2,250km through Russia via Rostov-on-Don, into what is now Ukraine. There they reached the border town of Volochysk on the east bank of the River Zbruch. On the west bank lay Pidvolochysk – then in Austria. At Volochysk the two travellers were taken off their train, where they were delayed for what they were warned would be three or four days waiting for their passports to be endorsed to leave the country – something they thought had been arranged for them in Tbilisi. Emily's last words in her book were:

> At last the night ended, and we saw with pity a group of emigrants trying to breakfast under a dull drizzling sky opposite the station. A friendly porter gave us the news we were longing for – a telegram had arrived [from Tbilisi]. No words can express our delight, for we seemed to know every stone of that railway platform, and we rushed to the office to demand our passports, of which the officials had taken

possession. Our detention had lasted 24 hours, and as we shook the dust from our feet we failed not to be thankful for the Providence, which caused us to be citizens of a land of liberty instead of tyranny. It is only in Russia that one thoroughly realises it; and the irksomeness of it becomes intolerable. Implicit obedience, silent subjugation, and the irresistible power of despotism are here brought home effectively to the stranger. But this impression remains with the traveller throughout the entire journey -

'Be silent; keep yourselves in curb. We are watched in look and word'

An Empire of one hundred and thirty millions of prisoners and of one million gaolers – such is Russia.[27]

Even the free-thinking Kemp had complied. Rather charmingly, she wrote 'To May MacDougall, from her fellow tramp, the author...' in the copy of *The Face of Manchuria* that she gave to her companion.[28]

1912 Crossing the Karakorams

We learn from the 1911 Census that Emily, describing herself as an 'artist and author,' had established a London base, with staff, in an apartment at Harley House, a grand Edwardian building in Marylebone Road, on the south side of Regents Park. Her flat – Number 26 – remained her English home for almost 30 years. She was very sociable, and an attentive listener. Among her friends and acquaintances was Francis Younghusband (1863-1942), a fellow member of the Royal Scottish Geographical Society. He was a spiritual man and also a writer. Younghusband had been an intrepid explorer during the 'Great Game' between Britain and Russia, an 'imperial play of cat and mouse set in the deserts and mountains of Central Asia that ranks as one of the most colourful periods of Silk Road history.'[29] The Game was all about control of India. Younghusband's contribution – in the late 1890s – was connected with mapping rivers and passes in the Pamir Mountains,

'Habib' and a fellow caravanner, Ladakh, 1912 (E.G. Kemp/ ©
Ashmolean Museum, University of Oxford)

a 'strategic vacuum where the Russian, British and Chinese empires converged.'** The Pamirs lie mostly within the south of modern-day Tajikistan. Flanking them to the east is the Karakoram Range. Did Emily's conversations with Younghusband both inspire and give her itchy feet once again? This time the Karakorums and Xinjiang, the far-western province in China, beckoned. Once again, she called on May MacDougall and made her preparations; she would cross from India into China following, in reverse, the footsteps of a traveller called Robert Shaw in 1868.[30]

Emily Kemp and May MacDougall left Leh in the Ladakh Region of India on 17 August 1912, following the ancient caravan route from Ladakh in India to Yarkant (formally Yarkand) in China. Their party consisted of four personal staff plus two members of the caravan organiser's team to look after the eight pack animals hired to carry their tents, stores and luggage. After a gradual ascent by pony via desert, valleys and passes flanked by snow-capped mountains, they had climbed over 2,000m to reach the highest part of the Karakoram Pass (some 5,540m high) on 28 August. The track

---

** Passes held the key to military movement

there, saddled between two mountains, is barely 50m wide. This bleak and barren pass experiences very high winds (which keep it relatively snow-free), frequent blizzards and low temperatures. As Emily noted later 'glaciers made great demands on our ponies, and the high altitudes claimed a heavy toll of life. The vast solitude was haunted by the dismal cry of vultures ... Breathing became difficult, and the cheery spirits of our men failed: faces are skinned and lips became so sore ...' [31]

Having begun the gradual descent towards Yarkant, they reached the old fort at Shahidula (3,750m), sited near the headwaters of the Karakash River. Their arrival sparked considerable interest among the locals. As Emily commented, 'it was red-letter day for these lonely dealers in the wilds, for we were the first European women who had ever been there, and we were glad.' As Younghusband himself recalled after his own visit in 1889:

At Shahidula there was the remains of an old fort, but otherwise there were no permanent habitations. And the valley, though affording that rough pasturage upon which the hardy sheep and goats, camels and ponies of the Khirghiz find sustenance, was to the ordinary eye very barren in appearance, and the surrounding mountains of no special grandeur. It was a desolate, unattractive spot.[32]

Once in Turkestan they needed three interpreters to communicate – traversing from Chinese to English via Turkmen and Hindustani.

Predictably, they had planned their journey and the related formalities well. They were feted along the way with great respect and received warm welcomes and hospitality from all whom they met. The 'charm of the people's kindly dealings with us in Chinese Turkestan which will always remain engraved on our memories.'[33]

While many explorers focus on the physical and environmental aspects of their journeys, Kemp was again more concerned with the people she met along the way; their culture and religion, and particularly the role of women. At the same time, comparison with the Chinese always appeared to be at the back of her mind.

They journeyed on over the desert to Kargalik, where they took on a guard of four Chinese soldiers who accompanied them as far as Kashgar, stopping at Yarkant (1,190m), the principal city in a large oasis area fed by the Yarkant River; a 'thoroughly Mohammedan city' of some 100,000 people.

There, an Imperial Chinese government official invited Emily into his residence to paint his portrait. He horrified her by insisting on posing wearing 'an extremely ill-made and ill-fitting Russian suit – dreadful experience.' Later she commented 'it will be a sad day for the Chinese Empire when all the poetry and charm of the national dress is lost to the world by the adoption of our thoroughly prosaic western male attire.'

Emily arrived in Yarkant at the end of Ramadan. She painted one of the many paintings and sketches that illustrate her book during Eid prayers at the mosque where there were 'many thousands of men (but no women) ... a space had been reserved for us, and seats on a special carpet whence I was able to sketch.'

She also led a seminar to consider means for reducing the high rate of mortality among the pack animals (ponies, yaks and mules) engaged in the trade between China and India. The Hindus and Turkmens (but no Chinese) that attended were intrigued that 'the first person to think of trying a remedy [to reduce animals' death] was a woman.' Later she sent out supplies of medicine from England.

From Yarkant, just three of them (Kemp, MacDougall and a Pathan interpreter called Robert) set off across a stony plain leading to Kashgar 200km away. She describes it as 'ploughing through heavy sand under a broiling sun; one on horseback, the other on a cart and Robert in another.' Kashgar, at 1,230m, was a Silk Road crossover hub, connecting caravan trails from north, central and southern routes from China in the east to Istanbul and countries en route in the west. When welcomed at Kashgar by Sir George and Lady Macartney at the consulate, Emily wrote that it

Walls of Kashgar, 1912 (E.G. Kemp/ © Ashmolean Museum,
University of Oxford)

was 'almost like coming home.' While enjoying her stay there, she
was oblivious of the fact that the wording in the coded telegram
that she had sent her brother George and sister Lydia telling them
that she had arrived was garbled, and that the two were very
concerned about her safety (*qv*). In the event, Sir George cabled the
Government of India on 22 October to report that 'the two ladies
were well and living at the Consulate,' which must have relieved
concerns in England. [34]

On 25 October the party left Kashgar to begin the journey
home. This took them across the Alai Mountains, and after five days
they reached the Russian border [now Kyrgyzstan] at Irkeshtan.
There were difficult moments:

> Toiling across stony wastes and very small passes, with wind
> and stinging dust to try our tempers... One night we got
> belated, and in a dark and forbidding gorge lost track of one
> another, which caused me great anxiety for about an hour,

as I had supposed Miss MacDougall was following me close behind; her pony had proved stubborn and fell a long way to the rear. I sent Robert [the Pathan interpreter] back to hunt for her while I got fire and food ready, for it was very cold.' [This one of the rare mentions of May MacDougall in her texts.] Then, 'on up 10,000ft [3,050m] to mountains barring the road to Russia.[35]

The journey into Kyrgyz lands had involved crossing the treacherous Terek Dawan Pass (3,880m), which Emily recalled as the toughest stretch of their journey. It was 'so steep that the ponies found it difficult, and one went rolling down the snowy side till we felt he must have most of his bones broken when he landed among some rocks; but no, he just shook himself and was ready to continue.' Once over the top they descended down to delightfully open country and journeyed on to the railway terminus at Andijan. By this time the two Britons had crossed some of the highest and most dangerous mountain passes in the world – thrilled to feel they had walked 'in the footsteps of Chinese state envoys and merchants of two thousand years ago.' Their trek from Leh had taken eleven weeks, covering around 1,550km and averaging around 20km daily including rest periods.

In stark contrast to their harrowing experience in Ukraine two years earlier, Russian officials at the frontier post at Irkeshtan welcomed them, taking half a day to process their visas. Emily happily noted the Russians' warm-heartedness regardless of the fact that they had no language in common.

Emily Kemp wrote up her travels in *Wanderings in Chinese Turkestan,* published in 1914. At 28 pages this is a very short book. Typically, Emily dedicated the proceeds to medical missionary work in China.

Rochdale connections

And so, in October 1912, Emily Kemp became the second woman recorded to have crossed from the Ladakh region of India to

Chinese Turkestan via the 5,540m Karakoram Pass. Several English newspapers took up the story, the *Sheffield Evening News*, writing on 28 October 1912:

> Miss Emily Kemp, sister of Sir George Kemp, who left for the Far East last April, has telegraphed home that she has safely negotiated the Karakoram Pass, which lies between India and East Turkestan. The pass is 18,500 feet above sea level, and the journey through it takes about a month.

The reference to George Kemp is interesting, although Emily herself would probably have preferred to be recognised in her own right rather than as her prominent brother's sister. Educated at both Oxford and Cambridge, and a former first-class cricketer, George had been elected to parliament as Liberal Unionist member for Heywood in 1895 and served until 1906. He took time out from 1900 to 1902 to serve with the Imperial Yeomanry in the Boer War.

In 1909 he was knighted for his war services, and at the General Election of January 1910 was elected MP for Manchester North West, this time as a Liberal. Having become disenchanted with politics, he retired in 1912 to focus on his work in the Rochdale woollen industry.[36] He had become a man of influence and wealth, and in 1913 was elevated to the peerage as Baron Rochdale. He returned to the army, leading the 6th Battalion, East Lancashire Regiment at Gallipoli in 1915 where many of his men became casualties. Kemp himself suffered: his eyes in subsequent photographs show that empty stare associated today with PTSD.

One can only guess at the extent to which Emily Kemp used her brother's networks to access individuals, funds and other resources in pursuit of her later campaign to support those suffering in France. But it would be surprising if she had not.

What we do know is that her brother and sister Lydia became extremely anxious about her during her adventures in Chinese Turkestan because of what they saw as an unsafe country.[37] Emily had promised to cable Lydia the word 'good' as soon as she could after completing her traverse of the Karakoram Pass. On 7 September Lydia received a cable with five words that were undecipherable. George Kemp turned to his Foreign Office connections. This resulted in a series of telegrams between London, New Delhi and Kashgar that caused the Foreign Office no little irritation. Their view, as reported by Tessa Morris-Suzuki, was that had the two women attempted to secure official support before setting out 'they would have been advised not to go,' since her Majesty's foreign office was 'not at all sure that Kashgar is a suitable tourist resort for ladies.' Had Emily Kemp ever read the ensuing confidential correspondence, she would probably have been infuriated by the British bureaucratic views of women travellers that it exposed. Would she have laughed or cried?

Tessa Morris-Suzuki's study of these Foreign Office files had an unexpected spinoff. Both she and I, separately, had pondered over the identity of the mysterious 'Miss MacDougall' – Emily's travelling partner on at least three occasions. Apart from referring to her as 'Miss MacDougall' at the beginning of her 1909, 1911 and 1914 books, I have found no references elsewhere beyond the quotes about her as they entered Burma from China in 1908 and then as they almost lost each other in the mountains of Turkestan in 1912. Who was she? Emily does not even mention her first name [May] apart from the hand-written dedication [passim] in the copy of The Face of Manchuria that she gave her friend.

The answer lies in a letter dated 16 February 1912 from the Chinese Legation in London to Sir Edward Grey, the Foreign Secretary, providing him with an English translation of a passport issued to 'Miss Emily Kemp and Miss Mary Meiklejohn MacDougall, who are travelling together, to travel to Chinese Turkestan...' While no one of exactly that name appears in British records, a May Meiklejon MacDougall was born in the Scottish Borders in 1875. May's mother was a 'Meiklejon.' Her father was a surgeon and May grew up in Carlisle. She died in 1932.[38] This name tallies with the references to 'Miss MacDougall' in France and the related entry in the medal roll for the British Committee

French Red Cross (*qv*) that refers to 'May M MacDougall.'[††] This must be her. She would have been 32 when she and Emily set out for China in 1907. How the two of them met remains a mystery.

Regardless of the official view, if the extent of the eventual newspaper coverage of her adventures in the Karakorams is anything to go by, the Kemp publicity machine had become a well-oiled apparatus by the beginning of 1914. The *Rochdale Observer* in particular devoted many column-inches to Emily's activities in 1914, recording her growing experience as a public speaker in several different contexts: leading devotional activities and describing her travels. She had become prominent in London, becoming an early member of the Royal Central Asian Society.[‡‡] On one occasion in 1913 she:

> ...lectured on An Artist's impressions of Western Tibet and the Turkestan. The title was an understatement; she may have had pen and brush, but she carried them on an adventurous journey from Kashmir across Chinese Turkestan and into Tibet. Sir Francis Younghusband, who introduced her talk, said it was a journey 'such as no lady before had ever undertaken.' [39]

Perhaps her thriving confidence fuelled her condemnation of the German war effort as it gathered strength? When the war broke out, she determined to do something to help.

August 1914 – The French army bleeds

The French army had a tragic start to the Great War. Their soldiers died *en masse* in Alsace in August 1914 because of poor and misguided leadership, ignorance of the power of machine guns, and archaic insistence on brightly coloured uniforms that

---

[††] May's surname in the FO correspondence is spelled 'Macdougall.' Elsewhere I have found it written as 'McDougal,' with other variants. For consistency I have used the spelling that May herself used in her later WRNS file.

[‡‡] Now the Royal Society for Asian Affairs

provided easy targets for modern riflemen. By 29 August 1914, French casualties in the fighting along their frontiers had reached 240,000 of whom 75,000 were dead. More French soldiers died at the Belgian village of Rossignal and other actions fought by the five French armies deployed on 22 August than all the casualties on the first day of the Battle of the Somme in 1916.[40]

While the extent to which this news reached England is debatable, the more well-to-do classes displayed a surge of concern for their neighbours in France and in particular, the plight of French wounded. In *For Dauntless France* the poet Laurence Binyon reflected that:

> During that long time [in 1914] when our armies were preparing, and while the French were supporting along so immense a front, the whole brunt and burden of the Western War, how many of us in England were impatient and restless! What a glorious relief it was to those who could engage in this work and feel that in some small way they were helping heroic France! It was a privilege and joy...
>
> We all remember in the earthquake suddenness – for the general public at all events – of the war's explosion. Everyone felt the terrible urgency of the moment. It seemed as if in six months, in six weeks even, all might be lost. Young and fit men could enrol in the great army that England was preparing, but what could others do, the older men and the women? Happy then were those who were in any fashion prepared for the crisis and the occasion.

Emily Kemp felt this call keenly. She was then 54 and held very strong views on the struggle. On 7 November 1914, the *Rochdale Observer* reported her recent addresses to two Rochdale audiences on aspects of the war, when she began by:

> ... dealing [at a Brotherhood meeting on Sunday] with the conflict as a battle of ideals – the British ideals of liberty

for individual and for subject races, and a conception of the moral law as applying to nations as well as individuals. These things stand in contrast to the ideal of triumphant force, military discipline, and naked materialism which dominates modern Germany.

Two days later, she went on to elaborate the same theory nearby at St Chad's Fold in Water Street, Rochdale:

> ... she showed how the German people had been systematically preparing for the war for forty years, their guiding principle being world supremacy for which in their arrogance they imagine they are divinely appointed. In every detail of their educational system, in their autocratic military policy, in their control of industry, and in their elaborate plan of espionage and bribery abroad, Miss Kemp sees their carefully prepared scheme for world power, for which of course, the destruction of Britain now appears to be a preliminary. All this makes it doubly necessary that civilised nations should deliver such a crushing blow as well [will] in Mr Lloyd George's phrase tear the bully from his seat.

Had the Francophile student's views begun to ferment during her schooling in Germany, some ten years after the Franco-Prussian War?

Now, she turned her mind to a more practical measure; support to injured French soldiers. What she may not have realised at the time was that military nursing in France had suffered as a result of the expulsion of the religious orders from France that began in the Revolution and continued on to the 1880s, when lay women were substituted for nuns in hospitals. Consequently, nursing generally in the French military hospitals was unsatisfactory, and the need for professional nursing was stronger that Emily may have realised.

Her solution was to recruit and pay trained nurses with the intention of sending them to work in a French military hospital. Characteristically, she turned to her missionary network and hired a small team through the Nurses Missionary League in London. Then she faced a brick wall. While she was able to register her party of nurses on the British Red Cross's list of reserve nurses, she had neither the hospital nor the key medical staff required to obtain permission for a civilian nursing corps to go to France. Until this could be satisfied her nurses could but wait in England for Emily's signal to mobilise; she needed to find an organised and approved hospital unit aiming for France. She was to receive help from unexpected quarters.

1914-15 *Hôpital Temporaire d'Arc-en-Barrois*

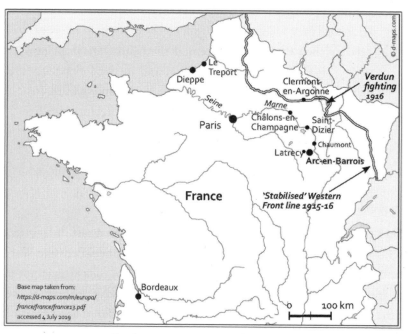

Emily Kemp in France, 1914 - 18

Early in the war a Worcestershire woman named Madeline Bromley-Martin, then County Secretary for the Worcestershire Voluntary Aid Detachment, became disturbed about the plight of wounded French soldiers in Vichy, and decided to act. She eventually secured an option to establish a hospital at Arc-en-Barrois, a small town in the Haute-Marne department of the

Champagne-Ardenne region in north-eastern France. This was at least her second initiative in this area, having also tried to set up a hospital to be called 'The Hospital of the *Entente Cordiale*' at a very large hotel at Le Tréport.[41] Laurence Binyon recalled that Bromley-Martin's initial intention was to 'take out a small party to nurse in a French hospital' but that 'so many good workers joined the group that it soon grew into a complete unit of the St John Ambulance Association.' [42]

This began to take shape in November 1914 when Miss Bromley-Martin secured the services of two doctors, a matron, four trained nurses and six VAD probationers through the Order of St John. Supported by her three sisters Susan (who begun to raise money), Eleanor and Nora she offered the services of her party to the French.

Madeline was very well connected, and had managed to secure the help of Sir Claude MacDonald, a soldier and diplomat who had led the defence of the Legation in Peking during the Boxer Uprising. By now he was vice-chairman of the Anglo-French Hospitals Committee that resulted from a merger of the British Red Cross Society and the Order of St John in October 1914. He was responsible for co-ordinating the volunteer medical resources funnelled through St Johns Gate, the headquarters of the Order of St John at Clerkenwell in north-central London. In particular, he was responsible for the approval of hospital proposals.

Thus, it fell to Sir Claude to inform Madeline that the government would not support her initiative by funding volunteer nurses' salaries as she had hoped. Rather, he had a committee obligation to try to stop the project from getting approval, as swarms of willing but unqualified people were crossing to France, and the French government was now requesting that an authority should be set up to examine both the efficiency and financial position of those intending to come. This resulted in War Office pressure to end civilian projects going to France.

But Sir Claude did put her in touch with Sarah Swift, the Chief Matron of the British Red Cross and with Miss Kemp, a 'well-heeled lady who was by then paying the salaries and the expenses of twelve trained nurses.[43] The consequence of this introduction was that Miss Kemp joined her and impressed [Madeline B-M] as very capable, energetic and 'masterful'.'[44]

Macdonald did however advise the group unofficially to set up a complete hospital from scratch and avoid attaching itself to a going concern.[45] And so, the search for a suitable site for a hospital began.

Emily Kemp's intervention was timely. Her nurses and their assured salaries were a convincing addition to Bromley-Martin's list of personnel and were instrumental in Sir Claude Macdonald and his committee's ability to approve the Bromley-Martin party for work in France. While Sir Claude helped to clear other obstacles in London, the search for a suitable hospital continued.

In parallel, two other individuals wanting to join the Bromley-Martin project offered to find a suitable hospital building in France, settling eventually for the Triannion Hotel at Le Tréport, just north of Dieppe.

> But the exercise hung fire: authorisation to start work at Le Tréport was not yet coming from Bordeaux. Miss Kemp, understandably impatient with twelve nurses [11 in fact] financially dependent on her, went out to France with her Chief Lieutenant, Miss McDougall, in order to be on the spot.[46]

Emily reported from Le Tréport that the Royal Army Medical Corps had already taken the hotel to set up a military hospital for the British Expeditionary Force.§§ As there appeared to be no other suitable buildings in coastal France, and with no other options, she telegraphed Bromley-Martin that she and her nurses had no interest there. This ended all discussion about Le Tréport and moved her to withdraw from the project altogether. At

---

§§ The Triannion Hotel, a grand 300-bed luxury house built in 1912 on a high cliff overlooking Le Tréport harbour. It became the BEF's General Hospital No. 3. (Ruth Cowen, *A nurse at the front* ... (2013) 213)

this point Kathleen, Lady Scott – widow of Captain Scott, the Antarctic explorer – who had supported the project from London, volunteered to travel to Le Tréport, reenlist Kemp and together visit Paris to investigate the availability of suitable sites. There they met the *Vicomte* d'Harcourt, President of the *Croix Rouge Française,* who offered them several sites, including the chateau at Arc-en-Barrois, which had already been placed at the disposal of the *Croix Rouge* by Pierre, Duke of Penthièvre. They found that sites offered in the vicinity of Paris were in ruins or unsuitable. This left the chateau as the last remaining option.

Having visited Arc and confirmed this offer with the duke, Lady Scott and Miss Kemp proceeded together to Bordeaux, where they were received by M. Millerand, the Minister for War, who:

> ... authorised the conversion of the Chateau into a temporary Military Hospital to serve the Third Army and offered beds and a complete installation together with a grant of two francs a day per patient and all their necessaries for the hospital ...[47]

Madeline had sent Miss Maud Banfield, her candidate for matron, to check on progress. She arrived in Paris as Kemp and Scott returned from Bordeaux, was disturbed by their description of the chateau's hygienic arrangements and delivered a very unfavourable report; citing fundamental flaws in location, water supply and sanitation. These matched the opinion of the *Service de Santé*, which had never approved the building for hospital care. But this was too late. Kemp and Scott had secured approval for the chateau, and Bromley-Martin brought family pressure to bear on Banfield and the local *Service de la Santé*. While wheels of the hospital project continued to turn unchecked, Banfield's concerns were to prove well-founded over the life of the hospital.[48]

Having met Miss Banfield in Paris, Emily Kemp then encountered Miss Susan Strong, an opera singer specialising in Wagner who had come to France from London offering to organise a kitchen staff along with several volunteers. She happened also to be proprietor of a laundry shop in Baker Street that specialised in cleaning luxury clothing and stage wear.[49] She agreed to join the party as a cook. Shortly afterwards, Sir Claude and others in London succeeded in obtaining French Government consent for Madeline and her party to travel to France.

Madeline arrived in France to confer with Miss Banfield, and to tackle reluctance from Miss Strong and Miss Kemp to accept Miss Banfield's authority: this pair of strong-willed women simply did not understand the discipline and associated bureaucracy required to run a hospital and its staff effectively.[50] This did not bode well.

After further administrative skirmishes, the French Ministry of Foreign Affairs finally authorised the hospital on 30 December 1914. Next day Madeline began a series of meetings at Chaumont with the director of the *Service de Santé*. These began badly: the French – faced with a hospital group led by female foreign civilians – were very uneasy. Worse, these foreigners sought to operate within a military context that they did not understand. Fortunately, French wariness eventually softened, and the party finally arrived at Arc.

Emily soon made an impression on the party, although not the impression that her leader sought; she pressured Madeline to define a structure and associated responsibilities for the administrative members of the party. This put Banfield, the only professional administrator at Arc, into an invidious position.

> On the first evening at Arc, they were entertained by the Gazins. Miss Kemp asked [Madeline] for a scheme of responsibilities, a request for which Madeline was unprepared. She probably dithered for a moment. Miss Banfield urged her to show authority from the start, a necessity which does to seem to have particularly occurred to her.[51]

Nevertheless, following three weeks of busy preparation, the hospital opened on 27 January 1915, when the first consignment of wounded arrived from the fighting 80km to the north. Its official title was *Hôpital Temporaire d'*Arc-en-Barrois. While the '*Temporaire*' indicated its presumed temporary existence, the hospital was known locally as the '*Hôpital Anglais.*'

Of the early promoters, Madeline Bromley-Martin, as *Directrice*, undertook most of the correspondence and organisation in France. Supporting her in London, the banker Martin Holland acted as treasurer, while Eleanor Martin-Holland, her sister, took on personnel administration.

At first, Emily Kemp's main task was to register the soldiers admitted to the hospital. While her work at the hospital may not have been arduous, her early financial support by paying the salaries of the eleven trained nurses who underpinned the launch of the hospital in January 1915 was crucial. As we have seen, without this resource Bromley-Martin and her fellow promoters would not have been able to clear the numerous administrative, military and international obstacles that stood in the way of getting the project off the ground; it was relatively simple to recruit volunteer orderlies and VADs, but trained nurses were not available without salary support.[52]

Lady Scott followed up her early involvement in securing the site at Arc by organising the hospital's small ambulance service with donated vehicles imported from Britain. Dr Tonks – another early supporter – gave up his work as an artist and teacher in the Slade Art School to offer his services. As he had not kept his surgical skills up to date, he became the hospital anaesthetist and provided general medical care in the wards.

By early February the 106 beds in the hospital were fully occupied, and it became apparent that some spare capacity was needed. Fortunately, there was an old monastery at the higher end of the town, 600m or so east of the chateau that had been used previously as a hospital. The authorities in Arc duly agreed that this building, known as the 'Hospice', should be used as a facility for convalescent men.

Under Emily Kemp's direction, the wards were furnished with 40 beds. Later transformation of a detached building into a ward

The first team of sisters at *Hôpital Temporaire d'Arc-en-Barrois*, 1915;
EGK is centre, front row. Eva Smith is 3rd from left, 2nd row
(© Marjorie DesRosier PhD, USA)

raised the total number of beds to 71. Initially, Dr Tonks oversaw routine medical care of patients at the Hospice and the three nurses who made up the staff, followed – in April – by Dr Edwards, Emily's brother-in-law. May MacDougall was the supervisor.[53]

Laurence Binyon gives a delightful description of the hospital establishment in *For Glorious France*:

> Arc-en-Barrois – the Barrois is the old name of that Arc-en-district of Eastern France of which Bar-le-Duc is the centre – is a large village or little town lying in a pleasant valley among the rolling uplands and vast forests of the Haute Marne. It is about forty miles from the firing line.
>
> … The large rooms of the chateau made excellent wards on two floors: but there is no hot water laid on, no gas or electricity, no system of heating, and the same difficulties had to be overcome as in similar cases already described. All sorts of hospital furniture, such as the little tables which the

patients like to have by their beds to keep their belongings on been made by amateur carpenters among the orderlies. An out-of-door ward, with a penthouse against the southern wall of the chateau, was also made, for the medicine of fresh air has been used as much as possible. The chateau looks on a park, with streams running through it. No hospital is more fortunate in its surroundings; a matter of great moment for the wellbeing of the convalescent...

The entire staff at Arc-en-Barrois is English, with the exception of the French Administrateur and French Vaguemestre but local workers have given useful help. [Not so: there were citizens of Australia, New Zealand, Scotland, Ireland, Wales, Denmark, Canada and the USA].[54]

The staff at Arc – generally ineligible for military service – included some particularly erudite volunteers. The biographer John Hatcher records that Binyon went to Arc in July 1915 as an orderly, only to find himself working in hard, unpleasant circumstances in a building with few basic services. He also learned simple carpentry and contributed to the hospital's growing inventory of homemade furniture. On occasion he wheeled patients in from the wards for operations and assisted in theatre.[55] This was a world for which the 46-year-old Binyon had received absolutely no preparation in his earlier life. Moreover, neither he nor many of the other volunteers were accustomed to taking orders. This inevitably led to tensions.

Binyon himself demonstrated unusually high empathy with the French wounded, being particularly impressed by their fortitude. He found the inspiration for his poem 'Fetching the wounded' during a midnight drive to Latrecey.

That his fellow volunteers should have struggled with their new environment is hardly surprising. Many came from comfortable backgrounds, either as a result of distinguishing themselves in their own right, or as the sons and daughters of eminent families. As well as Binyon and Tonks, we have already met Madeline Bromley-Martin, Susan Strong, and Lady Scott. Others who served during Emily Kemp's time at Arc included the barrister Robert Charles Phillimore; the artists Wilfred de Glehn and his American wife Jane Emmet de Glehn; the artist and former obstetrician and physician William Radford Dakin; the lithographer Arthur Cadogan Blunt; Britain's future Poet Laureate John Masefield; the architect Edmund Fisher; Lady Lillian Robertson, daughter of the 8th Duke of Grafton; the children's book illustrator Frank Adams; the author and Japanese art curator Wilson Crewdson; and Susan Bromley-Martin, the second 'Worcestershire sister.' Most were born in the 1860s and 1870s.[56]

They fulfilled a variety of roles: Phillimore provided two ambulances that he and his chauffeur drove, Dakin was a surgeon, Fisher and Crewdson helped with X-ray work, and Lady Keppel was a VAD nurse. All the non-medical men were classified as orderlies. Few had any medical training: hence the necessity for Emily Kemp's professional nurses.

That this disparate group of civilian volunteers – many well over military service age – should have received British war service medals is only fitting.

At least two of the doctors, including Emily's brother-in-law Eben Henry Edwards, went on to become officers in the Royal Army Medical Corps. Henry Tonks, the artist went on to partner Sir Harold Gillies in his pioneering work on plastic surgery, contributing by drawing the faces of soldiers with severe facial injuries to record progress with their treatment.[57]

For one who wrote prolifically of her travels and other interests, Emily Kemp is almost silent on her wartime activity. For this we have to rely on others such as Eva Marion Smith, one of the first cohort of nursing sisters to work at Arc, who kept a diary. In *A Nursing Sister and the Great War*, we learn not only of her personal experience but also of her relationship with Kemp and related internal politics.

Eva had written to the War Office to volunteer for war service as soon as war broke out in August. Having been approved, but hearing nothing, she learned in October that Madeline Bromley-Martin was recruiting staff to work with the French. She met her and was accepted. In mid-November 1914 Eva went to London to prepare, knowing that while her travel expenses to France would be paid, she would not receive a salary. She was the last of twelve nurses recruited for Emily Kemp's Nurses Missionary League Unit and the only one who was unpaid.

After some delay, she reported to the Headquarters of the Order of St John on 30 December, lodging at an establishment at Newington Causeway where she and five other nursing sisters lived in some squalor. On New Year's Day they met the other six sisters at Charing Cross station and began their journey to France and the challenges they would face there. They were accompanied by May MacDougall, Dr Graham Ashland, and his wife Ada (who had been appointed Assistant Matron).

After a rough crossing to Dieppe, they moved on to Paris by train arriving, hungry, at a hotel at 11.00 p.m. There, to her horror, she had to share a single bed with a complete stranger. Her diary for the following day reads:

> 2 Jan. Up at 6am. Too early for breakfast, so we had bread and coffee. Went to Chaumont on the train. There we were met by Miss Kemp. She was running the hospital with Miss Bromley Marten. Miss Kemp took 11 Sisters, paying their salaries and Miss B.M. organising the place. As these two could never agree, things were very unhappy the whole time we were at the hospital. It was a great pity, because it was a beautiful place and everyone was so keen to give of their best. Could not get a meal at the station, because the train came in before they could serve us. Went on to Latrecey, which was our stopping point. Then we found we had another 7km to do before reaching the hospital. Two very broken-down carts picked us up, and our luggage was put in another cart drawn by two bullocks. We arrived at the hospital quite cold, dirty, tired and hungry, about 4pm

and we were told we could not have any meal till 7pm! Miss Kemp came to our rescue and gave us tea and biscuits.[58]

One of Eva's colleagues elaborated in a letter that she wrote to the Nurses' Missionary League:

> We are really beginning to be busy – doctors, ambulance and chauffeurs have arrived today, with all their etceteras...
>
> We have a prayer meeting each evening after supper, which is a great comfort, and we are truly thankful to know you are thinking of us. We hear daily the bell at noon, as the Church is at our gate: last Sunday we all went to the Intercession service at 4.30; the little ones I fear were more attracted to the nurses than the prayers.
>
> The village people are greatly attracted by us. There are about five small shops, grocery, etc., and a boot shop, which we swarmed the first day, and brought up all their rubber heels and few pairs of galoshes. We have also brought teapots, cups and kettle, and chocolate, so you see we are bringing trade to the place. They have never seen an English person before.
>
> The chateau is situated in the village square, and the park reaches away at the back. It has a river and a lake, also a boat half under water, but we hope as time goes on we may be able to get it out and make it clean, so that we can do a little rowing to keep ourselves in trim.[59]

It is worth noting the misery that the French wounded endured to reach the hospital. Most of the wounded came from the French Third Army – the Army of the Argonne. In 1915, the French line ran roughly from Verdun to Rheims, and casualties were taken by ambulance to a railhead at Clermont-en-Argonne, 30km west of Verdun. There they were loaded onto an ambulance train, which then picked up more casualties en route at the nearby field hospitals at Les Islettes and Sainte-Menehoud. Then began a tortuous twelve-hour rail journey that traversed Chalons-en-Champagne and St Dizier in an enormous S-shaped loop, before finally reaching Latrecey-Orme-sur-Aube, the station where Eva Smith and her nursing colleagues had arrived at the beginning of January. The train would usually reach Latrecey at around eleven o'clock at night. Emily Kemp was later very critical of the carriages in which the French wounded reached hospital, likening them to horse boxes, without windows or ventilation.

Ambulances – crucial to the hospital operation – then brought the wounded the final twelve or so kilometres of their journey to Arc. While it normally fell to the hospital ambulance corps and orderlies to transfer the wounded from the trains, Eva Smith wrote of a visit to Latrecey on 24 March 1915:

> The train came running through and as it passed it slipped off several carriages. These were brought to our siding where the ambulances were drawn up. When the doors opened the atmosphere nearly knocked one down. The carriages were like closed cattle trucks, no windows, only open slits for ventilation. In each truck were 4 iron frames each holding three stretchers, one over the other. To get the stretchers off, the whole frame had to be dragged out to the middle of the carriage; the vibration must have caused horrible pain. We saw the first lot off [on the ambulances] and waited till the ambulances returned from their 14-kilometre journey.... Outside the station all was quiet except for the rumbling of guns away in the distance, the flash on the skyline and nearby the croak of an occasional frog. A beautiful night, the stars twinkling and the moonlight glinting on the bayonets of the silent sentries. In the station were the trucks with their wounded. Some silent, some talking quietly to each other, others restless with pain and constantly asking 'how much longer before we will be in hospital?' We were back at the hospital by 4.30am. On duty again at 6.30am.

Buoyed by the professionalism and dedication of the foreign staff and steadily improving medical facilities, the small hospital soon began to yield results. This process was surely underpinned by the skill and dedication of the trained nurses who took it upon themselves to lead the hospital's nursing service, supervise bed care, and train this disparate group of amateur volunteers.[60] While cynics might observe that its main purpose was to return the wounded to battle once more, they could not dispute its value as a healing facility. It was a strong demonstration of the purpose of the foreigners to offer humanitarian aid to French allies facing a common foe. The authors of *The Hospital of Arc en Barrois* commented happily on the level of friendship that developed:

> ... At last the time comes when the man is fit to return to the military authorities. The day of evacuation was usually a Sunday, and, clad once more in their uniforms, a dozen or more men might be seen making their farewells at the hospice. It was always a difficult matter to cut short the adieus and get them seated in the motors. To the hospital staff, this, the last episode, was almost the saddest of all, for it meant the permanent sundering of ties which were both warm and close. It was a remarkable memory, that of red trousers in a khaki motor from which proceeded the strains of 'Tipperary' in a perceptibly French accent, and of cries of '*Vive Angleterre*' raised in response to those of '*Vive la France*' with which the cars were greeted on the road...[61]

As Eva Smith's diary continues, we glean detail of the hospital infrastructure and staff, medical facilities and care for the wounded, recreation and friendships. There are various references to Emily Kemp:

> [Generally] In the evenings we spent the time by sitting round the log fire, talking, or having French lessons or being read to. We were only allowed one candle. After supper we

went to Miss Kemp's room. There we had prayers and some
of us stayed on talking well into the night.

One of her diary entries highlights the friction between Kemp
and Bromley-Martin. This was extreme; a conflict between two
determined women competing fiercely for administrative control
while their trained staff and volunteers kept their shoulder to
the wheel and made it work.[62] In mid-March 1915 the schism
between the two of them erupted over Bromley-Martin's
continued claim to authority over the trained nurses whose
salaries and board Emily was paying. Kemp duly withdrew
her financial support from the chateau hospital and handed the
nurses' contracts over to the Bromley-Martins. This prompted
Matron Banfield to resign.

Emily in turn assumed charge of the newly opened Hospice
facility where she and May MacDougall supervised the care of
soldiers discharged from the hospital. As Eva Smith's diary affirms,
Emily Kemp was a true supporter and ally of 'her' trained nurses
while she was at Arc, and it is not surprising that this spawned
mistrust in Bromley-Martin:

About this time [probably in February] Miss B.M. [Bromley-
Martin] and Matron sent for me for an interview. They
offered me the post of assistant matron, working under Miss
Banfield. I was still on a different footing than the others.
They were paid by Miss Kemp and I was under Miss BM
and not paid. This did not make any difference to the way
the Sisters treated me. They were always kind and friendly.
When I was told one of my duties would be to report to
them (Miss BM and Matron) what the Sisters were doing in
their off duty time, needless to say I turned it down. It made
me very unhappy and unsettled. So, I asked for advice from
Miss Kemp and she suggested that I should be paid like the
others, and then I would be under her. This I did and was
paid £1 per week. Soon after this Miss Banfield left and a

Miss Watson came instead. Unfortunately, she was given the wrong impression of us all and the friction continued.

Having relinquished her original 12 nursing sisters, Emily may well have lost her early enthusiasm as the Hospice operation became fully established and her work fell into what she perhaps saw as a rather mundane supervision task. 'It is all over at the Hospice,' wrote Sister Elizabeth Bromley on 20 September. 'In a few days we shall be disbanded and return to England. The Chateau takes over the management here, so Miss Kemp will take us all away with her.'[63] Emily Kemp and May MacDougall departed for Paris at the end of September 1915 and returned to England. Madeline Bromley-Martin's sister Susan then took over the administration of the Hospice. It seems that Emily completely severed her ties with the hospital and its management.

Speaking at public meetings in Rochdale in October to raise more funds, Emily Kemp may have given the impression that she managed the hospital and that it was her creation, having 'taken out with her a staff of surgeons and trained nurses;' some exaggeration, but understandable perhaps as she had recruited and personally funded the nurses. (Madeline Bromley-Martin's own paper on the hospital, written in 1919, completely ignored Emily's contribution – along with that of others closely associated with her).[64]

A listener at one of these meetings wrote that 'the remarkable experience in wandering about the world which Miss Emily Kemp has had, doubtless stood her in good stead many a time during the last ten months, which she had spent in France managing a hospital 'just on the border of the war zone'.'[65]

In conclusion, he went on to note Emily's admiration for the 'bravery and high spirits' of the French soldiers and the 'wonderful sympathy' between the English and French that was rising from 'the trials we were undergoing in common.'

A few weeks later, her brother-in-law Eben Edwards (who had left the hospital at Arc to join the Royal Army Medical Corps) had also returned to Rochdale. He too spoke at a fund-raising meeting there, where his focus was on the acute shortage of doctors in China. His former hospital at Taiyuan – destroyed during the Boxer Uprising – had been rebuilt, and it was with some pride that he revealed that one of the wards was to be a 'Rochdale' ward to reflect the generosity of the Rochdale community. Some 95,000 Chinese labourers, organised as the Chinese Labour Corps volunteered to fill acute worker shortages in the British Army between 1916 and 1918, and Edwards himself went on to serve at the Chinese Base Hospital at Noyelles in France.

Hôpital Temporaire d'Arc-en-Barrois ran for four years, closing in January 1919 having treated 3,071 wounded Frenchmen, of whom 76 died. During this time, over 350 temporary and long-term personnel from abroad worked there and, through their voluntary, unpaid service, did much to keep the venture financially viable. They worked alongside French support staff, who provided laundry facilities and local skills in such areas as building repair. Marjorie DesRosier notes the 'contribution of the large dynamic network of individuals who got it off the ground' [of whom Emily Kemp was undoubtedly one] and the strong teamwork among the staff that accounted for its success.

When the hospital was set up in the Chateau d'Arc-en-Barrois in January 1915 it was a rear evacuation hospital designated to the French 3rd Army Corps, at that time buried in the Argonne Forest. A reorganization of the *Service de Santé* in 1915 got rid of corps designations and divided geographic territory into Regions, of which *Hôpital Temporaire* was shifted between Region XX and XXI under a central authority in Chaumont, Haute-Marne. There is a direct correlation between spikes in hospital admissions and major battles: Ardennes, Champagne, Verdun, Meuse-Argonne, etc. Verdun features terribly throughout most of 1916.

Hôpital Temporaire was never a 'frontline' emergency hospital. It was a rear stop along an organised system of hospital trains that evacuated wounded soldiers from the frontline to a regionally designated collection depot.[66]

French gratitude and respect for the hospital remains to this day. A celebration in July 2015 to mark the centenary of the hospital's founding culminated in the unveiling of a plaque in honour of Susan Bromley-Martin at the Hospice, a building that remains to this day. Her sister Madeline had already been honoured with a plaque placed on the chateau in the 1920s.

France 1916-1918

For someone whose media exposure early in the war had been so prominent, Emily's activities in France after the success of Arc-en-Barrois were almost unreported. Yet she was there: her entry in the medal roll for the British Committee of the French Red Cross reveals that she was in France almost continuously from December 1914 to November 1918 except for around three months at the end of 1915. Happily, an entry in the 30th Annual Report of the Somerville Students' Association, dated November 1917, elaborates:

> KEMP, EMILY 26, Harley House, Regent's Park, N.W.1; 20, Avenue Victoria, Paris (temp). 1914, Organiser and Registrar of Hospital for French soldiers at Arc-en-Barrois. 1915, Formed aux. Hospital of 70 beds. 1916, worked for 18 months as Masseuse in French Military Hospital, Paris. Organised and took responsibility for canteen and rest rooms for French soldiers in Verdun zone (to continue till end of war).

Following her return to France early in 1916, she came home to Rochdale from time to time. On one visit, probably shortly after beginning her canteen work for Verdun, she addressed girls at Rochdale Secondary School, where she spoke of her hospital and canteen work in France. Expressing gratitude to the school for the parcels of tea, coffee, writing materials and games sent out to France, she noted that the French soldiers 'seemed to be acquiring a liking for tea as a stimulant less injurious than their usual coffee.'[67] She went on to highlight the plight of the French refugees moving towards Paris from devastated regions evacuated by the Germans, distressed that these crowds of refugees consisted principally of the old and the young. 'Girls and young women were completely absent; they had been driven eastwards by the barbarous Boches.'

A few days later, the *Rochdale Observer* of 19 May 1917 noted Emily Kemp's keen sense of humour. Reporting a ceremony at which her brother presented medals to two members of the 18th (Rochdale) Battalion, Lancashire Fusiliers who had distinguished themselves in the Gallipoli campaign:

> Later, in seconding a vote of thanks, Miss Emily Kemp said her brother had missed the most important part of his duty. Every French officer decorating a soldier kissed the recipient of the decoration. (Laughter). Lord Rochdale replied that he would leave it to his sister to repair his stupid omission (Loud laughter).

We know from May MacDougall's WRNS service record that, having worked for three months in a hospital as a VAD in 1916, she returned to France to run a 'foyer' for French soldiers in the area southwest of Verdun for 18 months, returning at the end of February 1918.[68]

French troops taking coffee at the *Cantine des Dames Anglaises* at Revigny-sur-Omain (Verdun sector), June 1918 (IWM Q106438/ © IWM)

It would not be surprising if Kemp had somehow linked in to MacDougall's work in the Verdun area.[69]

And so, Emily's war ended. Regardless of the little detail that we have of her work from 1916, it is clear that the French valued Emily's services highly. She was energetic, courageous, persuasive and a fluent French-speaker. The French honoured her three times, with the following decorations: *Médaille d'Honneur des Epidemies en Argent* [silver], *Médaille de la Reconnaissance Française en Bronze* [bronze], and the *Médaille d'honneur pour actes de courage et de dévouement en Argent.* (*qv*)

In the last two years of the war, Emily Kemp lost two of her sisters: Susannah Florence, who died in August 1917, followed by Lydia Peto in April 1918. Emily returned to England just in time to see Florence before she died. The two were particularly close following her visit to Taiyuan in China, when she had abandoned her studies at the Slade. As well as further reinforcing her interest in missionary work, this experience had spawned her lifelong interest in China and the Chinese. Later, at the beginning of the war, Emily would persuade Florence's husband Eben to join the team at Arc-en-Barrois. Emily's book *Reminiscences of a Sister*, published in 1919, is testament to her love. By May 1922, when Ellen Constance died, Emily had lost all four of her female siblings.

Chinese Metal

At the beginning of February 1920, Emily Kemp returned to China yet again. She was almost 60. This time she took one of her nieces, a doctor, to show her what the Chinese Empire was like. ¶¶ She also thought this a timely opportunity for an artist to attempt a snapshot of China at that time of fast political, social and economic change. Considering her long association with the country and its culture, she was worried about the struggle between honest, incorruptible, educated Chinese and self-seeking, ambitious, unscrupulous Chinese who were 'dragging China to the verge of the precipice.'[70]

¶¶ This must be Florence Edwards (Kemp, *Chinese Metal*, 11)

The pair sailed to Shanghai via the USA, and then travelled on by rail to Taiyuan via Jinan and Peking. Their trip back to Shanghai took them to Tsinan, where Emily was particularly interested in tales of coolies who had returned from the Great War and the value of their new income on the local economy.[71] From Shanghai they diverted to Hangzhou, the capital of Zhejiang province. A combination of steamer and boat took them on to Hong Kong and then Haiphong in Vietnam. There they boarded a train for Kunming, where they stayed at a CIM mission. Even at the age of 60, Emily had not softened her approach to travel, for here she introduced her niece to more traditional methods: a 480km journey to Anshun in Guizhou Province by four-bearer chair that lasted 17 days. Their entourage included 17 coolies (who carried them, their interpreter and cook), four luggage porters and an escort of ten soldiers. Not surprisingly they attracted much attention along the way. Emily later wrote 'it was a thriving sight for the assembled crowd to watch the barbarians wielding knives and forks instead of their familiar chopsticks.'

From Anshun they set out to research largely unexplored mountains left, mainly, to the aboriginal tribes concentrated there. Emily was particularly interested in the Miao and the I-chia peoples. The Miao are believed to have originated in Guizhou Province, where the rugged mountains and deep valleys provided refuge from the Chinese (who held them in great contempt). In Emily's words:

> The character of the people is in striking contrast to that of the Chinese. They are warlike, frank, lawless, primitive, openhearted, opposed to trading and city life: some are great riders, but we never saw one on horseback.[72]

Leaving with a CIM guide, they climbed up into the hills. Typically, they trekked between elevations of 450 and 1,750m, but once ascended to 2,200m. Worries about robbers operating in ravines required them to be heavily guarded. But they remained untroubled.

After the rigours of the hills they left Yunan Province on 14 May and relaxed for ten days on a houseboat that took them down the Yangtze to Shanghai. From there, their various interests and curiosity took them as far as the three coastal provinces that extend southwards; Zhejiang, Fujian and Guangdong. After a return voyage from Shanghai, Emily Kemp landed in London on 29 August 1920.

Writing *Chinese Metal* in the months that followed, she included specific chapters on aboriginal tribes in Guizhou Province (formerly Kweichow), present day women and the youth of China. In conclusion she wrote that she had:

> Tried to show any channels through which the new spirit of the Chinese race is flowing. I've taken advantage of the knowledge of men of all sorts and nationalities, in order to appeal to men of all sorts and conditions in the West. For we have the right of brotherhood in all work movements, and there is an infinite variety of mutual service possible to those who have undergone and are still undergoing the pangs of new birth. My task has been to draw pictures with pen and brush and my consolation in the inadequacy of its fulfilment is the poet's view that 'a man's reach should exceed his grasp.' If the book proves a ladder's rung by which others mount, it will have served its end.[73]

As well as continuing her focus on CIM, women, girls, education and politics, Emily elaborated on hospitals and doctors' training. She cautiously welcomed the influence of western learning and the numbers of Chinese now sending their children to Britain and the United States to study. She also championed the survival of unaccounted tribes, including aboriginals. *Chinese Metal* was her fourth book on Asian travel.

Here is a summary of the extent to which she documented her travels and the eventual inclusion of photographs. Her published watercolours – more than 90 in all – provide a remarkable contemporary record: a legacy that stands true today.

Images in her travel books

Title	Published	Pages	Ink sketches	Paintings	Photos
The Face of China	1909	271	24	47	0
The Face of Manchuria, Korea & Russian Turkestan	1910	247	3	21	0
Wanderings in Chinese Turkestan	1914	31	-	9	0
Chinese Metal	1921	227	16	14	5

Emily bequeathed some 200 artworks of all sizes to the Ashmolean Museum in Oxford. These all relate to her travels between 1895 and 1925. Mainly watercolours, they include some ink sketches and a few photographs. She went to considerable trouble, and probably expense, to reproduce many of the watercolours in colour in her books. Her bequest to the Ashmolean also contains a very large number of glass lantern slides – all 83mm square. Many are hand-coloured, probably by Emily herself, which would have further delighted the audiences who attended her many lectures.

In April 1921, she gave one of several lectures to the Royal Scottish Geographical Society titled 'Among the aborigines of China.' By this time Emily's book *Chinese Metal* was within weeks of publication. This was the first of her books to feature photographs. Her revelations concerning the Miao and other forgotten tribes of Guizhou Province – the focus of one of *Chinese Metal*'s chapters – began to attract recognition. So much so that the world's oldest geographical society – the French Geographical Society – honoured her with its *Grande Médaille de Vermeil*. As the *Dundee Courier* of 15 June 1922 reported:

> Recently she lectured in Paris to the French Geographical Society, being the only woman who has done so, and Prince Buonaparte, who presided, presented her with Médaille d'Honneur a high distinction. Miss Emily Kemp is author and artist as well as traveller. Her lecture in Paris was on her recent travels in the interior of China, and she spoke in French, being complimented on her excellent delivery.

1920s – Books, exhibitions and lectures

By now firmly entrenched in her Regent's Park apartment, Emily spent the 1920s writing, lecturing and – in 1924 and 1927 – holding exhibitions of her paintings. She was a member of the Council and a Trustee of Selly Oak Colleges, a loose federation of non-conformist colleges in southwest Birmingham with a long history of training and sending women missionaries abroad. She was also a Member of Council for Cheeloo University in China and continued her financial support to various Chinese causes.

In her letter to the Principal of Somerville in January 1940 just after Emily's death, her friend Margaret Roberts recalled how well she set herself up in London and what a sociable person she was:

> She was generous in her friendships as, with her strength and substance through life. Her beaming, genial welcome must have warmed many hearts.
>
> How she would have missed her life in London had she lived! She told me once of having the Chinese Ambassador and some other important Chinese guest to tea at her flat and she enjoyed sitting at the table with one at either hand and just listening and then talking. She sent out promptly great quantities of warm clothing and surgical necessaries and medicine to Madame Chiang Kai Shek whom she also knew personally when the war troubles began. Do you remember a description by Winifred Holtby of a lecture she had heard given by Miss Kemp? ... Her sense of humour counted for much in her contacts with people. She could always relax or brace people up with a laugh. What a gift it is.

There is a fine photograph of a family group taken in 1929 that backs this. In it you see Emily, aged 69; a happy woman with a twinkle in her eye who looks fondly at other members of the family while they all look on rather sombrely.

In 1927, Emily Kemp focused on the women's side of the work of the Baptist Missionary Society in her book *There followed*

Kemp family group, 1929; EGK in 2nd from right, middle row
(© Jonathan Kemp)

him women. This prompted the *Dundee Courier*'s reviewer to observe that:

> In preparing this, Emily G. Kemp has been inspired by near kinship with many who obeyed the gospel injunction, and by her own observation of missionary work in far lands. She has planned her task so as to survey and appraise Baptist activities in China, India, and the Congo region; and the result is a record of religion in experience that leaves printed in one's memory personages and incidents of benignant import.

A review from the *Western Daily Press* a couple of days earlier had commented in greater depth:

> ... Miss Kemp's picture of the missionary women of the Baptist Missionary Society may stand unashamed beside Dr Townley Lord's picture of the men [*Man and his Character* (Christian Manuals No. 2), 1926]. The author was born, she

tells us, a few years before the Women's Association of the BMS, has lived all her life in the atmosphere of missionary loyalty, taking an active share in furthering the cause of Christ in Foreign lands. Thirty-four years ago, she went out to China and spent a whole year in the far interior. She visited all manner of missions and learnt on the spot what the missionaries' work was like. She endeavours in this book to show to the women 'who have not the good luck to travel some of the glorious adventures of faith of women missionaries that they may be filled with pride and joy in it, and with a determination to take some share.' One hopes that both books will fall into the hands of the 'grouser' and 'little faiths' in our churches and convert theory grumblings into hopefulness.

Emily continued to travel, revisiting China in 1923. Late in 1929 she sailed from Liverpool to South America on a six-week-long voyage that would take her up the Amazon. The 60 or so travellers included a party of Franciscan nuns setting out to nurse lepers. The nuns fostered an 'atmosphere of love and service' on the boat. They belonged to a community, widespread over Europe, dedicated purely to missionary work. Emily learned that seven of their number had been put to death along with her sister and others at Taiyuan in China in 1900.

This inspired to Emily to write *Mary, with her son Jesus*, which was published in 1930. She dedicated the book to Captain R.H. Buck, Master of the cruise boat, the *Hildebrand*, on which the party sailed. The book – essentially her biography of Christ and his mother – contains ten chapters. One chapter, tellingly, is titled 'Jesus and the world of nature,' reflecting Emily's lifelong love of the natural world.

The Chapel

In mid-1932, Emily Kemp embarked on her final mission – one that led to a lasting memorial at her former *alma mater*

Somerville College. She resolved to build a chapel there. And so began a tortuous year that led eventually to the college's acceptance of concept, site, and plans for a building within the college that was dedicated early in 1935. Controversial though the project was at the time, it embodies the values, feel and functions of many a university chapel built today: visionary in its own right.

To describe Emily's brief as a 'big ask' would massively understate the challenge that she set the College with her vision; a 'house' where 'students of all kinds and of various beliefs would be welcome.' 'The name I would like it to bear is Christ House; but that would be for your consideration.' Her prescription for the building ran roughly as follows – it would:

- have non-denominational purposes; a 'beautiful, simple and significant house for purposes of meditation, prayer and other spiritual activities;'
- require 'a maker of stained-glass windows and an architect of imagination collaborating to work out the special conception;'
- be small – seating about 200;
- not have an altar 'only a raised chair with table, chairs and a lectern';
- not be consecrated, but it would be dedicated;
- be designed by her own architect – not the college's (a controversial requirement in itself within Oxford University circles.)

To complicate the matter further, she insisted on being anonymous, beginning by appointing one Mr Marcus Tod to present her offer to the Somerville Council (effectively the College's governing body). No doubt she chose Tod carefully. Marcus Niebur Tod, Fellow of Oriel College, had been a member of the Council for 18 years. During his last year he was its Vice-Chairman (1930-31) and was still involved with the college in the autumn of 1931.[74] As a former member of the Council he would have been well aware of what to expect, and indeed how to make his pitch.

Mr Tod submitted Emily's proposals to the Council on 8 June 1932, putting the proverbial cat firmly among the pigeons. Emily was alarmed by what she perceived as the outcome. Following the Council meeting, no doubt with much confusion ringing in her ears, Helen Darbishire the Principal of the College from 1931 to 1945, wrote to Emily to prepare and hopefully soothe her before their first meeting in London saying:

> The Council did not criticise your plans, nor even start any full discussion... everyone felt the great importance and significance of it, and there was general sympathy with the idea of the value to the College of having some building which could be dedicated to religious purposes, as well as a general deep sense of gratitude to you for your thought of the College in this connection... the two main questions which... we must make it our duty to think out carefully are:
>
> What kind of religious building, with what kind of definition of purpose, does the College want, taking into consideration our traditions and our permanent needs as a college? Everyone is familiar with the idea of a college chapel. Everyone again is familiar with the idea of a hall or other secular building which can be used for Prayers and other religious purposes. But your idea is something new to us. The general feeling expressed at that meeting was that any such building should be called the College Chapel.
>
> The other question is the strictly material one of where the building could stand and how it would be brought into relation with present buildings and any future building scheme ... the college would appoint its architect to help them think this out... I am sure you will understand that the more we feel the momentousness of this gift which you offer to the permanent life of the college, the more we must devote thought and far-reaching consideration to it.

Emily replied immediately: 'it has greatly relieved my mind, as your last note had led me to suppose the Council had not grasped my idea of something new and beautiful, instead of the stereotyped old tradition, tied down by clericalism…'

She was unbowed. Darbishire noted after that first meeting that Kemp had chosen her own architect and 'will not consider employing any other.' Moreover, regardless of being informed that it would inevitably be called the College Chapel, she [Kemp] 'is adamant that it be called Christ's House'.

She had also accepted that she would be Emily's sole contact with the college and had promised to uphold her anonymity. In so doing she – without resource to any help – had accepted *de facto* that she alone would have to deal with what became the plethora of letters that Kemp wrote during that first year. (I counted 84 letters between the two). Caught between an inevitable rock and a hard place, she also had to contend with a combination of college Fellows and past and present students that fiercely opposed the chapel project as Emily required it.[75]

The correspondence between the two women is remarkable, not only for its extent, but also for the highs and lows of the news and views that it communicated. [76] The related diplomacy in its language is extraordinary.

On 21 June, Miss Darbishire wrote 'I want to say more fully than before how deeply I feel the value of your gift & how much I believe it will contribute to the spiritual life of the college'… but… 'I have come to the conclusion that [to press to call it] 'Christ's House' would defeat your purpose (i.e. it would not suggest something simple being fundamental as you wish, but something odd, even freakish).' Emily conceded the next day.

In a long letter on 1 November an irritated Kemp included her views on the uses of the chapel – a question batted around for several months.

They [the uses] are briefly – daily prayers, private prayer and meditation; praise and thanksgivings with frequent Te

Deums and psalms; occasional services and addresses and Holy Communion… much music, especially Bach, because he is so cheering and inspiring; mystery plays.

After much detail about the outward looking and community-related work of an international Christian university in China, she concluded that 'the long and the short of it is that I am most anxious that Council should come in contact with the live progressive work of today and in the appropriate setting. It is not easy with the multiplicity of claims in college life.'

On the other hand, arguing that worthy Oxford speakers should speak in the Chapel, she warned 'it is vitally important too, I think, to keep out the wrong kind, populous cranks, like Gandhi – whom the students might probably be keen to have;' perhaps not her most progressive or even-handed comment?

On 11 November Miss Darbishire wrote to report with regret that plans and the site were not approved while hoping and praying 'that the issue may still be good, and that this wonderful gift of yours may come to the college.'[77]

Happily, the next day she was able to report some agreement from the Council; Mr Courtney Theobald, Kemp's chosen architect, was to be invited to submit his plans to the College architect; the building should be dedicated not consecrated; it would always open for silent prayer and meditation and used for daily morning prayers and Sunday evening prayers; and the traditional non-sectarian character of college worship would be maintained. It would be used for occasional addresses from Senior Members or external speakers and for music and religious plays; attendance would always be voluntary. Any texts inscribed on the building should be in Latin or Greek; Emily's request for an inscription 'A House of Prayer for all Peoples' was accepted. Miss Darbishire concluded 'for myself, I am more and more convinced of the value and importance to the college of your offer of the building.'

Emily replied on 16 November:

I am much obliged for the expression of yr. agreement with the views of the uses of the chapel, sent by me, & especially with the text to be placed over the entrance in Latin. With regard to the resolution about a consultation with another architect 'of established reputation' before deciding on the site and plans, I cordially agree with it.

On 8 January 1933, Lord Rochdale's secretary wrote to Miss Darbishire to tell her that Emily was 'seriously ill but obsessed with the chapel (about which Lord Rochdale [her brother] knows nothing!') In time she recovered, and the impressive, resolute and polite ding-dong in the private correspondences between the two soon continued:

2 February. Miss Kemp informs Miss Darbishire that she is 'feeling disappointed that Mr Theobald's plan will have to be put aside. I fully appreciate that he may be able to make another style of design and smaller in size.'

25 February. Miss Kemp is delighted that the site for the chapel is now decided.

27 February. Miss Kemp tells Miss Darbishire that the proposal for a brick Georgian Hall with chairs in unacceptable and 'I feel it is as well for me to let you know that I should never consent to it. If such a proposal were made I should consider it tantamount to refusal by the Council of my offer to build the chapel.'

March 1. Miss Darbishire explains that a gallery 'which might be designed in relation to the organ' would be a solution to the problem of fitting in the extra numbers on occasions when we might have to seat about 160 people. She urges her [EGK] to meet Mr Tapper [the College's architect] and discuss her [EGK's] wish for a stone building. And we have never moved from the ideas of fixed seats as originally suggested by you [no chairs].'

March 3. Emily notes, 'on enquiry I find that Mr Tapper was v. pleased with the plans & he assures me that Mr Theobald will do well for us... I had a talk with Mr Theobald yesterday & we hope to be able to do much to meet the wish of the Council with regard to a gallery...'

May 17. Emily is frustrated that the College had not settled the question of purchasing land for the chapel from University College before offering her the site, and the consequent need for new plans. She objects that 'It will be a year that this matter has been under discussion, and it is not fair to Mr Bell [the window designer], or to Mr Theobald, or to myself to go on temporizing. The matter must be settled in time to get the work started this summer. Otherwise the scheme must be given up.'

7 June. Miss Darbishire finally reports that the Council expressed their unanimous pleasure and satisfaction in the plans for the Chapel. 'We can never thank you enough for your wonderful gift. Its position will be in the very centre of our grounds.'

As the project advanced from planning to implementation, Emily continued her attempts to micro-manage the process; the choice of builders, seating and lighting arrangements, details of the eastern end of the chapel and fit with the adjacent college buildings, the stained-glass window, the chapel woodwork and the alignment of drainage pipes.

One strange aspect of the correspondence between the two is virtual silence regarding costs or the amount of the donation. Even when acknowledging in July 1933 that the footings for the chapel would have to be deeper because of soft ground conditions, Kemp does not raise the matter of rising costs. But when the Fellows objected to running some of the drainage pipes for the Chapel under their garden she pleaded to Miss Darbishire on 31 October:

but I have given way all the time to the Council's wishes –
but I can't afford all the resultant expenditure. They have
made things very difficult for me & taken away much of the
joy of my scheme. I know it is not your doing, for you have
always tried to make things run smoothly... I do beg you
not to urge further expense.

On 25 November she wrote further 'I quite understand the
position, now that you do not realise *my* position, that I have had
to give up some of my cherished wishes on account of the expense.
Builders will always tell you that the expense will be nothing, but
that is because it is not on *their* side. If I were a wealthy person, I
would gladly do all that is wanted, but quite frankly I *can't* and
really hope that more will not be asked. One never knows what
will turn up, and of course there is a margin left for the unforeseen,
but I do expect to be consulted when that happens...'

The work progressed. On 14 March 1934, Miss Darbishire reported
that 'The Chapel is rapidly rising, and is beginning to show what
its final form will be like, and I think it will be a fine building with
an effect of great dignity and simplicity.'

Shortly afterwards, Emily wrote on 6 April 'yesterday was such
a heavenly day that I took the opportunity of paying a surprise visit
to Somerville to see the chapel. I was greatly pleased with it.' She
thanked those who helped her to wheel her chair into the chapel,
and then went on to continue the debate about a wall between the
Maitland Building and the chapel boundary wall, and whether it
should be stone or brick.

Mr Bell's design for the chapel window became the next issue.
Having expressed her unhappiness on 10 June over the revelation
that the Council imagined something abstract, she wrote on 3 July:

I am surprised that you should think of advising such an
artist as Mr Bell with regard to the colour [of the window
glass], and I beg you will do no such thing. The Council

has the right to suggest things, but individual members have not, and the perpetual interference ever since the building was started has been a great annoyance to me.

Nevertheless, she remained courteous, concluding another letter about the window with 'I am sorry to hear that you are in the hands of the dentists and hope you will soon be out of them and able to go away for a good holiday.'

Finally, Miss Kemp tired of the day-to-day details, writing on 19 July in frustration that details of the lighting were not resolved. 'I am extremely worn and tired by the continual correspondences about the chapel ever since the building was started, and feel that it must stop. Will you please kindly take note that I am not to be consulted in future? No doubt you will be glad also to leave off writing about it.'

Miss Darbishire replied the next day, expressing her thanks for this, but not hesitating to add a robust correction to Emily's version of the process of deciding not to have a small vestibule at the east end of the Chapel.

Emily Kemp began her campaign for the chapel noting that 'I have not the means to carry it out in my life time, but wish to make all the preparations for it before my death, which I trust, may not be long delayed.'

This probably reflects her health at the time, particularly her serious illness in January 1933. In the event she lived to see it come to fruition. After much discussion about its form, a moving service to dedicate the Chapel took place on 16 February 1935.

Fittingly, the inscription written in Greek on the outside of the chapel translates as 'A house of prayer for all people'; Emily had achieved her ambition to create a place of prayer for people of all religions and nationalities. To this day, Somerville College has a Chapel Director rather than a Chaplain, in keeping with her vision.[78]

While Emily Kemp paid for the Chapel, her offer in 1934 to provide an organ was short-lived. The whole question of the organ

Interior of Somerville College Chapel from the west, 2018

gathered prominence in mid-1935, and Kemp herself consulted her friend Albert Schweitzer following his visit to the chapel that November. Schweitzer came up with a proposal to utilise an existing organ at Edinburgh or alternatively to commission Harrison's, the organ specialists, to build one. Following the Council's decision in March 1936 to commission a new organ, Miss Darbishire herself took out a loan of £2,000 to advance the money, provided that she 'be repaid a certain interest during my lifetime after which the organ will belong to the College.' Margaret Roberts and others later sought to compensate her for this.

Emily Kemp was too frail to attend the dedication service for the organ on 17 November 1937. As Helen Darbishire reported to her, it was a 'beautiful and triumphant service'... 'Everyone was impressed, and many spoke so warmly of the tranquil beauty of the Chapel itself'... 'Mr Harrison said he did not think that he had ever seen one [organ case] more beautiful... Mr Theobald was much pleased.'

Her mission accomplished, Emily Kemp died on Christmas Day 1939 at Gunnerside Lodge, Richmond in Yorkshire. She was 79. Still a wealthy woman, she left an estate worth £28,572. 2s. 7d. She left her paintings, embroideries and other artefacts related to China and other Asiatic countries to the University of Oxford, and about £10,000 to house them.[79]

What is interesting is that Somerville College has no record of what the chapel cost Emily Kemp. The college committee files reveal what the college spent to acquire a small area of the site, landscaping, drainage and architect's fees for Somerville's representative, but apparently no overall account of the cost of the chapel. (The East Quad, built at around the same time, has the total cost recorded and indexed). The Council minutes for 24 October 1933 concerning the builders are interesting:

> The donor asked for the approval of the Council for her acceptance of the estimate submitted by Messrs. Wooldridge & Simpson whose name had not been in the list of builders previously considered by the Council.
>
> Resolved: that Messrs. Wooldridge and Simpson be approved.

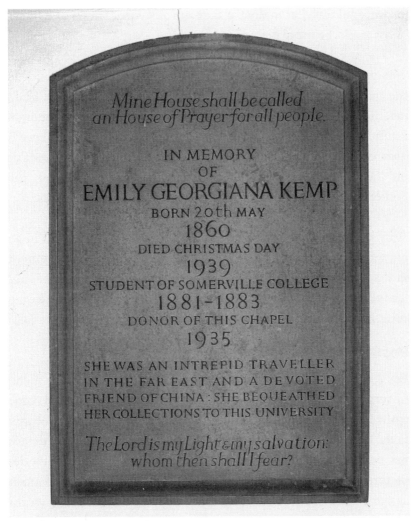

Memorial to Emily Kemp in Somerville College Chapel, 2018

'There is no copy of this estimate or even record of the sum involved. I therefore think that Emily Kemp literally gave the college a chapel, rather than the money with which to build it.'[80]

Not surprisingly, Somerville sought the family's consent to erect a memorial to Emily in the chapel that she built. This was duly done, her brother in law having touchingly reminded the college that the memorial wording should not refer to Emily as a missionary, because she was not. The final wording describes her as

'an intrepid traveller in the Far East and a devoted friend of China.'
What could be more fitting?

The memorial sits proud above a small group of ten smaller
memorial plaques on the south wall of the Chapel, just outside
the apse-like enclosure at the east end that encloses Reginald Bell's
magnificent window. Two of the smaller plaques commemorate
Emily's friends – Edith Coombs and Margaret Roberts.[81] There is
only one other plaque of its size in the chapel: directly opposite
on the north wall is the memorial to Margaret Thatcher, the
Somervillian who became Britain's first female Prime Minister.

Why no biography? This woman excelled in so many ways in an
era where marriage so often spelt the end of female achievement
in the wider sense, and perhaps the only way that a woman could
'go places' was to remain single. By any measure, Emily Kemp
certainly 'went places.'

Post-script

For a woman who whose life could be seen as a wonderful string
of surprises, perhaps it is inevitable that the last word should come
from Emily herself. Her will is unusually lengthy and probably
taxed her solicitor to no small extent. Clause 4, which details
her bequest of 'paintings scrolls jades brasses books embroideries
pictures and other objects' to the University of Oxford for 'deposit
at the Indian Institute Ashmolean Museum' contains 457 words
with no punctuation apart from the occasional capital letter.[82]

Other clauses bequeath 'paintings, engraving and etchings by
Alphonse Legros... for the use of the Ashmolean Museum,'
three oil paintings by Sauti to her brother (to be passed on to
the University of Oxford upon his death) and one thousand
Cumulative Preference shares in Kelsall & Kemp Limited to her
niece, Florence Edwards.

She did not forget Somerville College: she asked for her terra-
cotta 'The Annunciation' derived from the work by Andrea Della

Robbia to be placed in the college chapel, along with predictably clear instructions on how it should be moved from the wall of her flat in London to the chapel, how this would be paid for, and who should supervise its erection [Courtney Theobald].[83] On 25 January 1940, Helen Darbishire wrote what was probably the last piece of her lengthy correspondence regarding Emily Kemp: charmingly, she informed the solicitors handling Emily's estate that she and the Fellows had unanimously agreed that the college would accept the donation, and would they agree that it would 'expedite matters' if Mr Theobald would visit and that 'we might have his opinion before the Council as to what he considers to be a suitable place for it in the chapel?'

Handwritten notes on these pages value the Clause 4 bequest to the University for probate purposes at £177. 13s, the Legros works at £43. 3s, the bequest to her brother at £450 and the Della Robbia terra-cotta at £100.

Arguing that 'by reason of the War in China and the damage arising therefrom it is apprehended that the said paintings, sketches and objects etc. are now of unique interest,' her brother, Lord Rochdale, held successfully that the value of these bequests to the University of Oxford should be free of death duties (to a total value of £770. 16s. 0d). And the last piece of the jigsaw fell into place.

So how do we interpret this wonderful lady? Maybe it all boils down to the Somerville Chapel Director's description of her as an old eccentric.[84] What drove her? Does her refusal to reveal her financial support for the chapel stem from her deep religious beliefs, or is it more a question of rejecting the public persona that some might see as related to her brother's high profile? I have found nothing of any relationships with men. Her description of her early governess as a 'man-hater' is the only comment I have seen on the sexes. She was clearly very sociable, with all the confidence that it takes to cultivate the great and the good. I suspect that as one who did not seem remotely constrained by a 'comfort zone,' and as many other pioneering women of the time, she could not have taken on all the challenges that she did if fettered with a man. Eccentric or not, she was only going to achieve all this if she was truly independent. And from time to time – as evidenced by her standoff with Madeline Bromley-Martin – this required some stubborn and not always peaceful behaviour.

Emily Kemp's medals

Emily Kemp wore a group of five dress miniature medals in respect of her war service – two from her own country and three from France

Her entitlement to the two British medals is confirmed on page B.11 of the medal roll for the British Committee French Red Cross. In 1922, she received the *Grande Médaille de Vermeil* from the French Geographical Society for her book *Chinese Metal*.

Emily's brother George Kemp, the 1st Baron Rochdale, had bought a house near Keswick in the Lake District in 1900. It became the family home and was called 'Lingholm.' In 2013 his great grandson St John Durival Kemp (the 2nd Viscount Rochdale) and his second wife sold 'Lingholm' and auctioned the contents. St John Durival Kemp died in 2105.

As well as a magnificent collection of furniture and other artefacts, the sale included Emily Kemp's full-size war medals, her miniatures, and the full-size French gold medal. They came onto the market at Lyon & Turnbull's sale of 22 October 2013. A dealer at Aberdeen bought the medals (Lot 133), and then sold the miniatures to me.

While I have not had the opportunity to research French records in respect of the French decorations, the two full-sized medals included in Lot 133 are both issued by the Ministry of War and inscribed 'Miss E. G. Kemp 1919' on the reverse. The full sized *Médaille d'honneur pour actes de courage et de dévouement (en Argent)* is missing, presumably lost. How interesting that the only record of her full medal entitlement seems to come from her miniatures.

As a direct recipient of French medals (as opposed to Lucie Toller, whose award of the *Médaille d'Honneur des Epidemies* came via the British Authorities, and *The London Gazette*), Emily would have had to pay for her medals.

The *Médaille d'Honneur des Epidemies* was instituted in 1885 following the cholera epidemic of 1884. In the Great War, it was issued separately by the ministries of War, Interior, Marine and Colonies, and has four classes: *Or* (gold), *Vermeil* (silver-gilt), *Argent* (silver) and *Bronze* (bronze).[85]

The medal of 'honour of the epidemics' rewarded individuals who had shown exceptional devotion combating epidemic diseases, either by caring for infected patients or by undertaking actions to contain the spread of an infectious disease, while exposing themselves to dangers of contamination. (See too Lucie Toller's story.)

The *Médaille de la Reconnaissance Française* (French Medal of Recognition) was instituted in 1917 to signal the nation's thanks to those civilians who had voluntarily come to the aid of the injured, disabled and refugees, or who had performed an act of exceptional dedication in the presence of the enemy during the First World War. Issued in three classes (bronze, silver, and gold) it was conferred on French citizens and foreigners, including those who helped support the French war effort through lobbying, recruitment, fundraising and the provision of aid. Nearly 15,000 people and communities were recipients of this award. [86]

The *Médaille d'honneur pour actes de courage et de dévouement* was originally created in 1820 and was eventually given its present name in 1901.[87] It recognises those who, at peril of their life, conduct themselves in the rescue of one or more persons in 'danger of their life.' It can also be awarded collectively to whole units.[88] As with the *Médaille d'Honneur des Epidemies,* during the Great War there were Gold, Silver-gilt, Silver and Bronze grades, but Silver was differentiated into Class 1 and Class 2 to make five grades altogether; it seems that the class of award was progressively raised as the receiver carried out more rescues.

Notes

1 Manchester Evening News, 'The 1860s', *http://www.manchestereveningnews. co.uk/news/local-news/the-1860s-1145209*, accessed 19 Dec 2016

2 Rochdale Pioneers Museum, 'Our Story', *http://www.rochdalepioneersmuseum. coop/wp-content/uploads/2013/02/Our-Story.pdf*, accessed 19 Dec 2016

3 Emily Georgiana Kemp, *Reminiscences of a Sister, S. Florence Edwards, of Taiyuanfu* (1917) 10

4 Somerville College Register 1879-1971 (1971) 2

5 Originally titled 'Somerville Hall,' in 1894 Somerville became the first women's hall to adopt the title 'College'

6 Somerville College, 'Fuller History', *https://www.some.ox.ac.uk/about-somerville/history/fuller-history/*, accessed 9 Mar 2018

7 Somerville College, 'History', *https://www.some.ox.ac.uk/about-somerville/history/*, accessed 9 Mar 2018

8 Pauline Adams, *'Somerville for Women' an Oxford College 1879-1993* (1994) 34

9 Adams, *'Somerville for Women'*, 172

10 The BMS was formed by twelve Baptist ministers in 1792. It began its overseas work in India in 1793 and went on to serve elsewhere in Asia (including China), and in the Caribbean, Africa, Europe and South America

11 Somerville College Archive: Letter to Miss Darbishire, 10 Jan 1940

12 University College London Calendar for 1892-93 – Department of Fine Arts

13 Invariably spelt Taiyuanfu in Kemp's writings

14 New York Times, 'A Short History of Shanghai', *http://www.nytimes. com/fodors/top/features/travel/destinations/asia/china/shanghai/fdrs_feat_145_5. html?n=Top/Features/Travel/Destinations/Asia/China/Shanghai*, accessed 21 Dec 2016

15 Emily Georgiana Kemp, *The face of China; travels in east, north, central and western China; with some account of the new schools, universities, missions, and the old religious sacred places of Confucianism, Buddhism, and Taoism, the whole written & illustrated* (1909) 78

16 Kemp, *The Face of China*, 75

17 History of the Boxer's resistance to the Great Powers' Division of China (*The Guardian* 5 Aug 2000)

18 Women's Missionary Association of the Baptist Missionary Society (Baptist Zenana Mission), Jubilee: 1867-1917 'Fifty years' work among women in the Far East' (1917) 23 (*https://archive.org/stream/MN41453ucmf_0/ MN41453ucmf_0_djvu.txt*, accessed 7 Feb 2018)

19 Baptist Missionary Society, '139th Annual Report', *imageserver.library.yale. edu/digcoll:354056/500.pdf*, accessed 7 Feb 2018

20 Marcus Dods, *Later letters of Marcus Dods, D.D.* (1911) 269 (Dods (1834 –1909) was a Scottish scholar who was elected to the Chair of New Testament Exegesis at New College in Edinburgh University in 1889 and became Principal in 1907. Previously he was minister of the Church

of Scotland at Renfield Free Church, Glasgow, from 1864 to 1889. He was a prolific correspondent, and his son's second volume of his father's letters includes four to Emily Kemp. One dated 11 April 1904 mentions Emily's 'preparations for India.')

21 Kemp, *The Face of China*, 195

22 Kemp, *The Face of China*, viii

23 Manchuria – the 'land of the Manchus' – is the name given to a large tract of North East Asia. While it can have wider meaning, depending on context, Kemp refers to what might be termed today as Northeast China – Heilongjiang, Jilin and Liaoning provinces.

24 Emily Georgiana Kemp, *The Face of Manchuria, Korea & Russian Turkestan* (1912) vii

25 Kemp, *The Face of Manchuria*, 119

26 Insight Guides, *The Silk Road* (2008) 242

27 Kemp, *The Face of Manchuria*, 239-40

28 pers. comm. Marjorie DesRosier PhD, USA, 3 Jan 2015

29 Insight, *The Silk Road*, 70

30 Robert Barkley Shaw was a British merchant resident in India who explored Chinese Turkestan in the 1880s

31 Emily Georgiana Kemp, *Wanderings in Chinese Turkestan* (1914) 2

32 Francis Younghusband, *Wonders of the Himalayas* (1924) 108

33 Kemp, *Wanderings*, 27

34 Letter from Foreign Office to Sir George Kemp of 7 November 1912 in TNA, FO 371/1618 (courtesy of Tessa Morris-Suzuki)

35 Kemp, *Wanderings*, 31

36 The Kelsall and the Kemp families were partners in the wool textile business Kelsall & Kemp, in Rochdale.

37 Letter from Lydia Kemp to Foreign Office London of 16 October 2012 in TNA, FO 371/1342 (pers. comm. Tessa Morris-Suzuki 9, 19 & 29 Dec 2016, 22 May 2017)

38 pers. comm. 22 Dec 2016 Elaine Hunt (who has researched the Meiklejon family in depth)

39 H. Leach, S.M. Farrington, *Strolling about on the top of the world. The first hundred years of the Royal Society for Asian Affairs* (2003) 100

40 Max Hastings, *Catastrophe: Europe goes to War 1914* (2013) 181

41 The 'Hospital of the *Entente Cordiale*' was intended to offer hospital care to wounded French, Belgian and British soldiers as a sort of alliance hospital. This scheme was in name only--the start of a fundraising initiative to appeal to potential British donors--and never received official approval. (pers. comm. Marjorie DesRosier PhD, USA 6 Jun 2017)

42 Laurence Binyon, *For Dauntless France: An account of Britain's Aid to the French Wounded and Victims of the War* (1918) 145

43 She began by recruiting eleven nurses and took on the twelfth once they were in France

44 Nicholas Bromley-Martin, 'The Hospital at Arc-en-Barrois' in IWM: Documents 13070, Papers concerning the British Hospital at Arc-en-Barrois, France' 2

45 This strays from official policy in effect. He advised them to obtain a guarantee of funding and a fully equipped staff of trained nurses and qualified surgeons, locate a hospital facility in France, rework the proposal and submit it for committee approval. (pers. comm. Marjorie DesRosier 30 May 2017)

46 Nicholas Bromley-Martin, 'The Hospital at Arc-en-Barrois' in IWM: 13070 3

47 *The Hospital of Arc en Barrois, Haute Marne, France; being a brief record of British Work for French Wounded* (1915) 1

48 Banfield, an internationally renowned British nurse, hospital administrator and educator--who had retired to Worcestershire from her distinguished American career and knew Madeline in the local community--was entirely opposed to the Chateau d'Arc-en-Barrois. Her detailed reports outlined the building's massive flaws and its location--lacking light, heat, hot running water and modern plumbing as well as without railway service for supply and travel. ... This was also the beginning of emergence of conflicts between Madeline and Kemp as Kemp took it upon herself to assume more authority over the project than Madeline had granted. (pers. comm. Marjorie DesRosier 30 Jun 2017)

49 pers. comm. Marjorie DesRosier 17 Aug 2018

50 pers. comm. Marjorie DesRosier, 30 Jun 2017

51 Nicholas Bromley-Martin, 'The Hospital at Arc-en-Barrois' in IWM: 13070 5

52 pers. comm. Marjorie DesRosier, 30 Jun 2017

53 *The Hospital of Arc en Barrois, Haute Marne* 13

54 *For Dauntless France* ... 145

55 John Hatcher, *Laurence Binyon Poet, Scholar of East and West* (1995)

56 Developed from data in 'Hôpital Temporaire d'Arc-en-Barrois', *Wikipedia* (last modified 23 Dec 2017), https://en.wikipedia.org/wiki/H%C3%B4pital_Temporaire_d%27Arc-en-Barrois#Personnel, accessed 26 Feb 2015

57 J.F. Bennett, 'Henry Tonks and his contemporaries', *British Journal of Plastic Surgery* (1986) 39, 1-34. Also see ch. 15 of Pat Barker's *Toby's Room* (2013)

58 IWM, Documents 16098 – Private papers of Miss E.M. Smith (sheets One and Two of 'Miss E. M. Smith: War Work 1914-1916')

59 Nurses' Missionary League, Leaflet No. 46, February 1915

60 The hospital was routinely inspected and certified by the chief military surgeons of the *Service de Santé* and received high marks for its efficiency and adherence to modern hospital standards of surgical care. (Which is all the more reason why Kemp's nursing corps was key to the hospital's foundation and ongoing success.) (pers. comm. Marjorie DesRosier 12 May 2017)

61 *The Hospital of Arc en Barrois, Haute Marne* 21

62 pers. comm. Marjorie DesRosier 6 Jun 2017

63 IWM, Documents 14947 – Private Papers of Miss E. Bromley

64 Madeline Bromley-Martin – 'Hotel Temporaire at the Chateau at Arc-en-Barrois' in IWM 13070

65 *Rochdale Observer* 23 Oct 1915

66 pers. comm. Marjorie DesRosier 3 Jan 2015

67 *Rochdale Observer* 23 May 1917

68 ADM 318/188 Service Record of MacDougall, May Meiklejohn

69 May MacDougall was appointed Principal in the WRNS in April 1919 with the initial intention that she should run the Royal Navy hostel at Inverness. Having made an excellent initial impression (an early assessor wrote 'great resource. Extremely understanding. Practical to a degree. Full of common sense') she soon ran foul of service etiquette by taking 'too much independent action' and irritating her male superiors. 'She talks too much whether spoken to or not.' After temporary secondment to an RAF seaplane base at South Shields she left the WRNS in January 1919. (correspondence in ADM 318/188)

70 Emily Kemp, *Chinese Mettle* (1921) 12

71 95,000 or so Chinese workers served on the Western Front between 1916 and 1920 in an organisation that came to be known as the Chinese Labour Corps. Apart from vital work in the dockyards and other manual labour activity some were engaged in specialist tasks such as tank maintenance. CLC workers also served in other sectors, such as the 6,000 based in Basra, Iraq. Many of the CLC personnel were eligible for bronze issues of the British War Medal 1914-1920. (Brian Fawcett, 'The Chinese Labour Corps in France, 1917-1921', *Journal of the Hong Kong Branch of the Royal Asiatic Society, Vol. 40*, (2000) 50

72 Kemp, *Chinese Mettle*, 117

73 Kemp, *Chinese Mettle*, 222

74 pers. comm. Kate O'Donnell, Somerville College Archives 21 Oct 2016

75 In *Somerville for Women* Pauline Adams lists three petitions from the Junior Common Room in November 1932; one from 30 supporters of the chapel proposals, a second from 58 opponents and a third from 96 opponents to the proposed chapel site.

76 By the time the correspondence stopped in November 1937 Kemp and Darbishire had exchanged almost 240 letters, including 165 up until February 1935 when the Chapel was dedicated.

77 The college had required a more sympathetic site and demanded collaboration with an architect 'of greater experience.'

78 Somerville College *http://www.some.ox.ac.uk/196/all/1/The_Chapel.aspx*, accessed 4 Nov 2015

79 *Birmingham Daily Post*, 15 Mar 1940

80 pers. comm. Kate O'Donnell, Somerville College Archives 26 Oct 2016

81 Kemp had specifically asked the College to remember Combes; in her words 'the first Somerville Martyr.'

82 TNA, IR 62/1905 Bequests to the University of Oxford and Somerville College respectively: E G Kemp

83 The Somerville Annunciation is a 19th century Italian terracotta relief derived from the Annunciation lunette in the *Ospedale degli Innocenti* or 'Foundlings' Hospital', Florence by Andrea Della Robbia (1435-1525), (*http://blogs.some.ox.ac.uk/chapel/2012/02/08/the-somerville-annunciation/*, accessed 27 May 2018)

84 Somerville College 'Cracking the Chapel Code by Daniel Moulin – Chapel Director' , *http://www.some.ox.ac.uk/wp-content/uploads/2015/08/Somerville-Magazine-2013.pdf*, accessed 14 Oct 2015

85 Adapted from *http://www.france-phaleristique.com/medaille_honneur_epidemies.htm*, accessed 17 Jul 2018

86 Adapted from *http://www.france-phaleristique.com/medaille_reconnaissance_francaise.htm*, accessed 17 Jul 2018

87 Adapted from *Fiche de Procedure pour l'attribution de la Médaille d'honneur pour actes de courage et de dévouement*, accessed 17 Jul 2018

88 Ibid

Jack Nunn

The gunner: Jack Nunn

*For goodness sake don't mention
anything to Mother...*

Jack Nunn's group of miniature medals (Military Cross (GRV) with
Second Award Bar, 1914 Star with '5ᵀᴴAug.: 22ᴺᴰ Nov. 1914' bar, British
War Medal 1914-20, Victory Medal, General Service Medal 1918-62
with 'NORTH WEST PERSIA' and 'IRAQ' clasps)

At first light on 16 August 1917, a young artillery forward
observation officer and his party struggled across shell-cratered
farmland in Belgium, the ground boggy from heavy rainfall. He
was a tall man; his height would have made him an easy target.

The small group followed closely behind British infantry who were assaulting the German lines at a town called Langemark. Men fell from the enemy machine gun and mortar fire that raked them all along the way. Reaching their objective, they sought whatever cover they could find in a shallow ditch, which was churned up by shellfire.

Connecting up the telephone wires that they had unwound during their scramble from their trenches, they set about their task of observing the German response to the British attack and calling up supporting artillery fire. Looking for preparations for enemy counter-attacks and SOS signals from their own front-line infantry, their link between the forward troops and the heavy artillery batteries behind them was crucial.

The enemy artillery soon found them, and their situation deteriorated further. By mid-morning the enemy had begun to counterattack. Despite heavy hostile shellfire, dense smoke, noise and general confusion the officer and his team managed to keep the vital communication lines open. Their position became increasingly vulnerable, even the more so when repairing telephone line cut by the bombardment.

By the end of the day, almost all of the young officer's party were dead or wounded. Exhausted, filthy and wet, dazed and lucky still to be alive, he had somehow kept going and maintained a steady flow of vital information to the supporting guns behind him from his sodden and muddy hiding place. He had

WJN c. 1919 (courtesy Paul Rocky and © Virginia Barnes)

struggled to see the forward infantry's SOS signals and preparations for the German counter-attacks through the intense fog of battle. But by late afternoon the British had driven back the counter-attacks and had taken Langemark.[1]

He was unhurt. And he would survive the war.

Eight years ago, I bought the miniature medals worn by an artilleryman along with a photograph that showed a young subaltern proudly wearing the ribbon of the Military Cross, with a rosette to indicate the second award that followed the exploit I have just described. But in a way, the photo is misleading. It gives no hint of his earlier life, which was far removed from the established officer class. How did this happen? Was it his brothers' example that motivated a youngster from rural Suffolk to join the army? For this is what William John Nunn did at the age of 15, when he enlisted with the Royal Garrison Artillery as a Boy on 16 April 1909. Did he simply want a change from rural England, or did he just yearn for adventure?

Whatever his motives, he not only survived the horrors of the Western Front but also rose to win rank and distinction.

Known to all as Jack, William Nunn was born on 16 August 1893 at Onehouse, a village in rural Suffolk, just west of Stowmarket. Soon the family moved to Buxhall, the parish next door, where he grew up. He was the fifth of eight children. All four of his brothers served in the Great War. Three, including Jack, were to find themselves in France as members of the BEF in the autumn of 1914 and, remarkably, all survived the war. Their sister Nell, who gave birth to her daughter Enid in October 1914, gave her a third name, 'Frances', remembering her brothers and where they were at the time.

Reuben and Eliza Nunn, Jack's parents, were both from farming families and employed in-service with landed-gentry households. While described in several census returns as a 'coachman domestic,' Paul Rocky, Jack's great nephew, recalls Reuben Nunn as a 'stud groom to a horsey family.'[2] Jack and his brothers grew up on the fringes of rural high society. Their parents brought them up well and taught them how to behave. Horses shaped at least two of his sons, Ernest and Frederick, otherwise known as Ernie and Fred. Fred Nunn's deep affection for them resonates in letters that he wrote home during the war. Ernie 'who "had enough skill with hounds to draw them off when in full cry," something that allegedly no others had' became a professional huntsman.[3]

Jack Nunn grew up in a small, picturesque village, with farms devoted largely to barley, wheat and clover. In his *History of the Parish of Buxhall*, W.A. Coppinger tells of an old village listed in the Domesday Book, where 'the majority of the houses and cottages forming the village are of picturesque design and well situated. They are mostly built of the clay of the neighbourhood and thatch with straw.'

The population in 1891 was 421.[4] Fortunately for Jack and his brothers, Buxhall had had a primary school since 1877, and they all studied there – Jack from April 1897 to November 1906.[5] He then moved on to continue his schooling at nearby Stowmarket.

Around two and a half years later, he chose to follow two of his elder brothers Frank and Fred into the army as a gunner. At that time, following a reorganisation in 1899, there were three separate arms to the artillery from which to choose; Royal Horse Artillery (RHA), Royal Field Artillery (RFA) and Royal Garrison Artillery (RGA).

The RHA was the *Corps d'élite* of the artillery. It was armed with relatively light, mobile, horse-drawn field guns known as 13-pounders.[6] These provided support to cavalry units, but as cavalry actions in the Great War were relatively rare, the RHA was used to a great extent to supplement the Royal Field Artillery. Fred Nunn served in D Battery, RHA. (A 'battery' is the basic unit in the artillery organisation structure. Depending on the British Army units at the time, a battery in the Great War would have between two and six guns, depending on whether it was part of the RHA, RFA or RGA).

Fred has particular significance in this story, as he wrote some remarkably perceptive letters during the Great War. His letters are insightful and informative, with sharp comment on the geo-politics of the war itself, the engagements in which he fought, and the terror of being shelled. He laments human devastation, senseless leadership and its obsession with spit and polish. He thinks about the effects on the war of the February Revolution of 1917 in Russia.

He witnesses the impact of tanks at the Battle of Cambrai. Above all, he reflects on his love of the horses that hauled the guns. It would be very surprising if such a wealth of detail and opinion had survived the slightest attempt at censorship – perhaps this is why only three letters written in 1917 survive? As a long-suffering 'ranker' at the bottom of the military pile, he was also bound to have his more contemptuous moments, writing on 19 September 1917:

> Our late Major, who went on leave in June, did not return. Thank Heaven he did not. A more unreasonable man could not be found in the whole army! The whole time he was in command of the Battalion, the order was – burnish and polish! And inspection of harness was made every Saturday, when he used to pull the whole lot of it to pieces, look behind the buckles, etc., and should he find a tiny speck of rust, the man concerned got an extra turn out, and on the Somme last year he stopped a man proficiency pay because he turned out with dirty boots... there was at least 4 inches of mud at the time!

Fred's teachers at Buxhall Primary School would have been proud of his writing.

The RFA, armed also with horse-drawn guns, was the largest branch of the British artillery. Its role was to support infantry. It was organised into brigades and typically equipped with batteries of 18-pdr guns (generally firing shrapnel) and 4.5-inch howitzers, in the ratio of three to one, near the front line.[7] Howitzers are built to 'lob' heavy shells at a steep trajectory at relatively low velocity, as opposed to medium field guns that fire at relatively high velocity over flat trajectories. The RFA was reasonably mobile, each battery with six guns.

Frank Nunn had joined the RFA in 1899 and seen service in South Africa against the Boers in 1901. He left the army in 1911, aged 30, and was later to re-join the army in September 1915, as a driver in the Army Service Corps.

The Royal Garrison Artillery manned the largest guns, especially those mounted in coastal and colonial forts – essentially for garrison defence. While the army possessed very little heavy artillery in 1914, the RGA grew into a sizeable component of the British forces, divided into Heavy, Siege and Mountain batteries. It was armed with heavy, large calibre guns and howitzers that were normally positioned some way behind the front line and had immense destructive power.[8]

With exception of the largest RGA weapons, one thing that each of the three artillery arms did have in common was a reliance on teams of horses to tow the guns; the bigger the gun, the larger the number of horses required to tow it. Later on, tractors were used to tow the heavier RGA guns.

Trumpeter

Did the heavier ordnance of the bigger guns of the RGA batteries appeal more to Jack Nunn than the RHA's lighter horse-drawn guns? Whatever the reason, he enlisted for twelve years as 31554 Boy, RGA in 1909. At that time, he was 1.7m (5' 7") tall, with grey eyes and dark brown hair. In November 1910 he was appointed Trumpeter, joining 44 Company RGA, stationed at Pembroke Dock. [9]

Where did Jack Nunn fit into all this? What purpose did boy soldiers and trumpeters serve? What drew them to this life?

Whether they sought it or not, education was an essential part of a boy soldier's development. Boys could enlist from the age of 14 years and 8 months, provided they had permission from their parents. This gave them access to a military and civil education and a coveted Educational Certificate. Jack Nunn had joined aged 15 years and 8 months.

Boy soldiers had no pay or pension entitlement and were a good source of free labour. But their education gave them a great advantage over those who joined as adults, many of whom were illiterate. Boy soldiers were often promoted soon after they reached 'adult' status at 18 partly because they could read and write. Even today, the Army uses colours to aid recognition for those who can't read labels.

In November 1911 Jack Nunn was one of 3,826 boys serving in the British Army, of whom 2,984 were musicians – 975 more than the then current regulations allowed. The explanation for this excess (compounded by suspicions that some boys reported as Tradesmen were in fact training as musicians) was that many cavalry and infantry units considered the Army regulation limits on men insufficient for them to maintain their bands. The artillery was one of the army units that *did* comply with the regulations, having its full allocation of 400 musicians. Jack Nunn was one of 144 trumpeters employed by the RGA.[10]

The general level of over-recruitment of boys, and variations in service conditions between different army units, concerned the Army Council. It not only regarded the 12-year service period granted to the boys when they enlisted as adult soldiers as a financial liability over the twelve years but was also concerned that this period would enable the former boys to become pensionable. This applied to musicians and tradesmen alike.

At the end of 1911, the Army Council appointed Col R. J. Strachey to 'consider the system of boy enlistments in the army' and formulate recommendations for the 'terms of service on which musicians and tradesmen boys should be enlisted and the numbers of each class [musicians or tradesmen] to be allowed.' Strachey's committee assembled data that concluded that there was indeed over-recruitment of boy soldiers and led to recommendations that for boys enlisted for 12 years at 18, the first 6,7, or 8 years should be spent with the 'Colours', and the remaining 6, 5 or 4 years with the Reserve.[*]

While not solving the question of total numbers (which could not be addressed until the boys' conditions had been fixed), this did address the financial concerns. This proposal, which aligned boys' conditions more closely to enlisted soldiers as a whole, was adopted on an experimental basis in 1913.

Trumpeters had an important function in the army; to transmit orders. This practice continued until the late 1930s, when radios at last became more reliable. Consequently, it paid the army to teach boy soldiers to play, particularly intelligent ones who could interpret and communicate instructions clearly. As an organisation that relied on horses to tow its guns and related baggage, the artillery had a further interest – horses respond to tunes.[11]

On 24 February 1911 Trumpeter Jack Nunn embarked from Pembroke Dock to join the Royal Garrison Artillery establishment at Gibraltar. He landed five days later and joined 54 Company RGA, which had been deployed there since 1905. Manned by five officers and 195 NCOs and men, including three trumpeters, 54 Company's role was to defend the 'Northern Sector' of Gibraltar.

The members of the company trained hard, developing skills in laying and operating the guns, range and position finding, telephony, signalling, semaphore, blacksmithing and wheel maintenance and repair.[12]

Jack progressed well, attaining a Good Conduct badge on 16 April 1911. One month later he mustered formally as Gunner. His height was now 1.8m (5' 11"); well above average height in those days. Three years later, having passed a course in ambulance instruction and attained a second Good Conduct badge, he advanced to Lance Bombardier on 17 September 1914.

---

[*] Colours: reference to the British Army regimental flags used to denote regular army service (as opposed to the army reserve)

Call to arms

What might well have been a reasonably relaxed station changed dramatically at 9.55 p.m. on 29 July 1914, when the alarm guns on Gibraltar fired and 54 Company RGA proceeded to its War Stations.[13]

We can sense the mood on Gibraltar from a letter that Jack Nunn wrote to his sister Nell on 22 August:

> My Dearest Sister
>
> Many thanks for your letter and good wishes, it was quite a pleasant surprise as I thought that all my brothers and sisters had forgotten me as I have only had two regular letters for months ...
>
> Well, old girl, you must excuse short letter as I am on duty tonight at 10 o'clock until 4 a.m. in the morning so I will tell you as briefly as possible what we are up to here.
>
> In fact there is not much to tell. Of course you know that we are mobilised. The alarm was sounded on the 29th July. I was at a mixed 'Whist Drive' at the time so had a fine joy ride back to barracks in a gharry [horse-drawn cab]. The population here was very excited but we soon quietened them down when they started crowding round a bit too much!
>
> We arrived on our battery at about 12 o'clock. Of course we were working at night. We never had a sleep or smoke for 36 hours as it was very heavy work getting the ammunition up from the magazine. This is a 3-gun battery of light 2.24-inch guns for repelling ... boat attacks, so naturally it's all night work.[†] We are not very busy now – that is as regards hard work – as all the heavy stuff is completed, but it's the continual suspense that tells and besides we are not living too well, being on fortress war rations. This place is a picture at night, Nell. I should like to see it from the Straits as we have 22 powerful lights continually sweeping the sea and heavens for miles around and woe-betide any ship that comes in the

---

† QF 6-pdr Hotchkiss was a light 2.24 inch (57 mm) naval gun and coast defence gun

beam as there are 72 modern guns, both heavy and light, ready to fire by just laying on the target and pressing the button, but I don't suppose there will be any such luck. We are all very anxious to have a shot at something, if only to fire a round. Everybody is saying 'why don't they come round for volunteers?' but I suppose there is no chance of that for the Artillery as we are under-manned as it is, and this is a far too important place to leave open to attack, as we can fire into Africa and Spain…

I wonder if Fred [their brother] will have to join the expeditionary force. I hope not for the sake of Mother. Poor dear, she must be worrying about us. I have written to assure her that I shall be safe enough, but one never knows as the O.C. of Infantry here have asked for 33 of our Company to man the maxim guns, as the 2nd Battn. Wiltshire Regiment have packed up ready for the front. They are expecting to leave for the front on the 27th. I will cable you through my O.C. if I have the luck to go – but for goodness sake don't mention anything to Mother until I am actually gone, as the Infantry will not leave here if our brave troops are successful in the field, or until a battle squadron can be spared from home. I should love to go, dear Sister – anything better than this terrible suspense, but…

Well goodbye, Sister, I hope you are all in the best of health. I am in the pink. Give George [her son George Kent], the young rascal, a soldier's kiss for me and write again very soon.

Your ever-loving Brother, Will xxxxx

In time-honoured fashion, he added amusing comments on their war rations that apart from anything else, lacked milk or butter. What was he to do with a ration of tobacco 'as we get no pipe or matches?' He concluded with 'if ever anyone offers me jam after this, I will fling it at them as it's bread and jam for breakfast and tea every day!'

In spite of his anticipated jealousy 'if old Fred goes to the front' he did not have to wait long. The company's diary for 10 September 1914 records that Gunner Nunn was one of 21 NCOs and men who were posted to the home establishment for Active Service. They departed five days later: Jack was on his way to France and the Western Front.

He was promoted to Bombardier while at sea. Once onshore in England he and the other members of his draft from Gibraltar joined 114 Heavy Battery, RGA, and a new unit that had formed at Woolwich on 17 September 1914 in response to the outbreak of war. His Medal Index Card reveals that he crossed to France on 3 October.

By this time, two of his three older brothers were already in France. Fred (now with 3rd Brigade, RHA) had landed on 15 August 1914 – a fully paid-up member of the 'Old Contemptibles.' Ernest, a driver with 32nd Brigade RFA, followed a week later. His mother Eliza must have begun to worry. (After the war she was to receive a telegram from the King congratulating her that her five sons had all served in France).

Gunner on the Western Front

114 Heavy Battery RGA (114 HB) landed at Le Havre on 4 October 1914 – well after the British retreat from Mons. The Germans had been held at the First Battle of the Marne, fought between 7 and 12 September. Paris had been saved. The allies had recovered and turned north, where – following fighting between 13 and 28 September – the Germans dug in on the heights along the Chemin des Dames, north of the River Aisne. This concluded a month of highly mobile advance and retreat and heralded the onset of static trench warfare that would soon follow. The First Battle of Ypres, fought from 19 October to 22 November, halted the German advance to the coast and key Belgian ports. Before long, a 750 km trench line would link the Belgian coast to the Swiss border, with no space at either end for one opposing side to outflank the other.

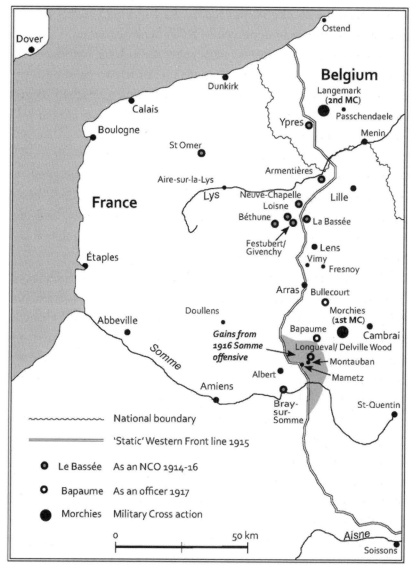

Jack Nunn in Northern France, 1915 - 17

The strength of 114 HB, including its ammunition column, numbered six officers, led by Major F.C. Poole, and 198 NCOs and men. There were 144 horses to haul the guns and associated wagons. Its firepower came from four breech-loading Mk. II 120mm (4.7-inch) guns. These fired 20kg high explosive shells, lighter than the 26.8kg shells used by the 127mm (5-inch) '60-pdr' guns more commonly deployed in RGA heavy batteries.

Nevertheless, these guns, with their 4.8m long barrels, could hurl HE shells up to around 11km at a rate of five to six rounds per minute. The guns were heavy – 3.8t each. Once attached to gun carriage limbers, it took a train of four pairs of horses driven by a rider for each pair to move each one. [‡]

Regarding ammunition – the gunners could fire shells loaded with shrapnel (for anti-personnel use), Lyddite (designed to detonate into fragments) and high explosive (a newer TNT-based explosive also designed to fragment with great force), and gas. Each gun was served by an ammunition wagon, itself attached to a horse-drawn limber when on the move.

Having established itself at Le Havre between 4 and 19 October, 114 HB moved on via St Omer to establish itself at Loisne, just NE of Bethune, which it reached on 24 October. To the north, heavy fighting to hold back the main German assault around Ypres continued. But large German concentrations in the area in front of Armentières and behind La Bassée led to unanticipated, bitter battles in the last half of October. [14]

The battery went into action three days later, engaging hostile guns and supporting attempts to stem German attacks in the La Bassée area. Along with 108 HB and 2 SB, their divisional commander congratulated them for their excellent shooting on 29 October, which had driven out three German batteries, and probably two more.[15]

The gunners' activities quickly settled into a hazardous game of hide-and-seek played between Anglo-French and German artillery as each supported infantry striving to control the area around Neuve Chapelle and La Bassée. The RGA's role was to silence enemy guns that shelled entrenched infantry under attack, and then keep them quiet during infantry counter-attacks. Both sides strove to locate and neutralise their opposing batteries first, and deployed aircraft and observation balloons to do this.

---

‡ Limber: a two-wheeled cart to support the trail of a gun while on the move.

Artillery observation post, Loos sector, 1916
(Morris Meredith Williams/© Phyllida Shaw)

Having located a hostile battery and deployed a battery to retaliate, the gunners relied on front line observers to advise corrections for range and direction as the opening shots were fired. More often than not, communication between the observers and the batteries relied on telephone messages, or runners if, as happened often, the vulnerable telephone wires were broken. Visibility from trees, church towers and high ground was prized. Aircraft later became equally valuable as spotters. And as Fred Nunn later wrote, there was apprehension about spies behind the lines who might betray the locations of gun batteries to the Germans.

As the records for 2 and 3 November show, 114 HB (now part of Meerut Division of the British Indian Army) had to be light on its feet:

2nd November: Battery engaged a hostile battery located N.W. of Bois du Biez and later on near Ligny le Petit, fire being observed by an airman. At midday our troops were attacking in the direction of Neuve Chapelle to recover trenches which had been lost on the previous night, and the Battery supported the attack by engaging a battery near the

Richebourg distillery. The enemy shelled the Battery but their fire was ineffective... At 2.30 p.m. a heavy shellfire was directed on our battery from the direction of Violanes, the fire being very accurate. During the night the Battery changed to an alternate position.

3rd November: engaged a hostile battery N.W. [of] Bois du Biez, fire being observed by an airman, range and line were speedily found and the hostile battery was heavily shelled and compelled to cease firing. During the afternoon the enemy shelled our late position at Loisne, being no doubt deceived by the dummy guns which had been left there for their airmen to locate.[16]

There were casualties, including Battery Sergeant Major J. Gilbert who died from the 'very accurate' fire reported on 2 November. On 5 November, things became hotter still:

Engaged battery at Violanes and batteries near Ligny le Petit, the Germans replied and searched for us without results. At 12.30 p.m. the Battery was ordered to engage targets located by the airmen. At this time a heavy howitzer (about 8.2-inch) located near La Hue found the range of our battery and shelled it vigorously. The shooting was excellent, four rounds being right into the battery. Thanks to our trenches, no casualties occurred, but two shots over killed three, wounded 12 men and killed four horses belonging to Field Art. [Artillery] Amm. [Ammunition] Column and Siege Coy. The airmen landed and reported the position of an assailant, the battery was turned on to him, and he very shortly ceased firing. Position changed during the night to position recently vacated by 110 HB.[17]

After the best part of two months of mud, cold and hostile gunfire, the battery went for rest in billets at Pacault on 24 November.

It was back in action a week later, remaining in the area around Bethune until late February 1915 in a state of almost continuous action. While aerial observation provided targets when the weather permitted flying, the enemy started to use captive observation balloons.

The Indian troops who formed a large part of the Meerut Division suffered heavily during the winter battle around La Bassée. After bitter fighting around Givenchy and Festubert, the battery's diary for 22 December, the day that it transferred to 2nd Division, noted 'the Indian troops being worn out by the cold and wet of the trenches, and heavy casualties suffered during the past few days, were withdrawn.' It gives no hint of 114 HB's Christmas, simply noting that 'the enemy's activity has died away for the present. The ground has been sodden and movement difficult all this month.' Not much fun for gunners trying to manhandle guns weighing almost four tonnes.

Apart from a vigorous bombardment prior to a successful infantry attack just south west of La Bassée on 10 January and 'occasionally shelling hostile batteries,' 1915 began with general 'quiet all along the front.' Jack Nunn probably did not see it quite this way, as he was admitted to hospital in Rouen on the 19th, awaiting surgery for a hernia.

After almost two months' rest and recovery, he returned to duty – this time to 118 HB, also equipped with 4.7-inch guns, which had been engaged in the mid-March fighting at Neuve Chapelle.[18] This battery became his operational home for the best part of two years and remained in the area around Armentières and Neuve Chapelle until April 1916, when it moved south to prepare for the Battle of the Somme. Jack's promotion to corporal in June 1915 marked another step in his way up the ranks.

While their colleagues in the siege batteries tended to concentrate their howitzer bombardment on enemy trenches and barbed wire, the gunners in 118 and the other 4.7-inch heavy batteries concentrated on engaging enemy batteries in retaliation to enemy shelling and firing on enemy working parties. The batteries moved position from time to time; there were brief periods of rest and escape from the mucky chaos around them; and the list of casualties grew.

There were variations. On a hot day in July a tip-off from an RFC observer reported an active battery of 'archies' which 110 and 118 HBs took on, getting many rounds into the battery and silencing it.§

While daily operations were often coordinated battery by battery from Brigade level, there were times for integrated action by all the guns, for example in preparation for large scale offensives such as the Battle of Loos (the first British use of poison gas) which began on 25 September 1915. Typically, this would involve setting targets, firing times and ammunition supply for each battery in the build-up to the assault, along with a schedule of targets once the attack had commenced.

As 1915 drew to a close, there was little or no scope for celebration, and there was certainly no repeat of the unofficial Christmas truce of 1914. The diary entry for 25 December in the diary of 4th Brigade RGA, to which 118 HB belonged, reads:

> Heavily shelled about 11.40 a.m., Brigade engaged hostile batteries and retaliated at Ennetieres & shelling ceased. Three hostile batteries located by flashes and cross bearings were silenced; got 7 OKs on 77mm battery with aeroplane observation. An enemy OP was severely dealt with.

New year's greetings were no different: not long after midnight heralded the arrival of 1916, Jack's battery was supporting two British trench raids, one of which brought in German prisoners.

In May, after another five months of this weary and deadly regime, Jack went home for one week on his first spell of leave. By the time he returned to France he had risen to sergeant, and his battery had moved to 18 Heavy Artillery Group (HAG) and final

§   Archie – British military slang for anti-aircraft fire or anti-aircraft guns

preparations for the Battle of the Somme. At that point 18 HAG consisted of two 60-pdr batteries and two 4.7-inch batteries, of which 118 HB was one.

As we have read in Richard Trevethan's story, the battle began on 1 July. Jack's battery was positioned near Bray sur Somme and engaged in the British attacks of Mametz and Mametz Wood to the east of the town of Albert. 118HB's task was counter-battery fire, to be carried out with 'the greatest vigour' in the daytime, and short bursts of fire on roads and woods where German reinforcements might gather at night. Information from observation aircraft became increasingly important in their work.

Mametz wood fell on July 12, by which time Jack's battery was gearing up for the attack on the German Second Line that began two days later.

As July stretched into August and on into September, 18 HAG continued its support of the British Fourth Army fighting, moving inch-by-inch through such places as High Wood, Delville Wood, Longueval... And there were new threats: while the batteries relied increasingly on the RFC for information, German air activity increased, and the gunners faced machine gun fire from low-flying planes for the first time. Also, the numbers of enemy observation balloons grew steadily. Apart from deteriorating weather (August was particularly wet and muddy) there were increasing fears that the guns were becoming worn out: one 4.7-inch gun had fired 6,000 rounds. Yet ten 60-pdr and four 4.7-inch guns fired 3,300 rounds in support of an attack on Ginchy on 3 September.[19]

On 15 September the British and French troops opened their assault on the German Third Line, and finally High Wood and other key objectives. The fighting involved the first deployment of a new weapon, which the 18 HAG diary recorded thus:

15 Sept: Attack delivered on Switch Trench etc.; a constant fire was kept up by the Group on known batteries until 11.00am and batteries were hard at work all day firing on targets given by aeroplane. The 'tank', a new engine of war,

was used by us for the first time. It consists of a 30-foot armour-plated caterpillar, armed with 6-pdr Hotchkiss and machine guns, and capable of negotiating practically any sort of country... As far as could be gathered the tanks did good work...

Casualty numbers continued to rise, including the death of a young officer from 121 HB and his bombardier while attempting to lay a telephone line to a forward observation post.

By 18 November when fighting on the Somme finally died down in the mire that choked Fifth Army's attacks on the German First Army in the Ancre Valley, 118 HB had been positioned near Longueval since early October. It remained there for the rest of the year. Snow fell. There were some fine sunny days and frosty nights but then the miserable winter and associated stalemate of 1916 set in.

Jack's battery had been positioned near Longueval, a small town SSW of Bapaume, since early October and remained there for the rest of the year. Fighting on the Somme finally stopped on 18 November – bogged down in the deep mud that choked Fifth Army's attacks on the German First Army in the Ancre Valley. Snow fell. While there were some fine sunny days and frosty nights, the miserable winter of 1916 and its associated stalemate set in.

Not only did Jack Nunn survive the thunder and chaos of the Somme, he also distinguished himself to such an extent that he was promoted as Second Lieutenant 'for services in the field.' [20] By this time, he had served seven years and 264 days in the ranks.

1917 – Decorated officer

On 6 January 1917, 2nd Lt Jack Nunn, now an officer, joined 116 Heavy Battery RGA, part of 62nd Heavy Artillery Group, RGA.[¶] His new unit, also positioned near Longueval, was equipped with

---

[¶] Heavy and Siege batteries were organised into Heavy Artillery Brigades (HABs). These were renamed Heavy Artillery Groups (HAGs) in April 1916, before reverting to HABs in December 1917. 116 HB served in seven separate HAGs during 1917.

A 60-pdr gun advancing through the village of Bertincourt, France, 1918 (Wikimedia Commons - *https://www.flickr.com/photos/nationallibrarynz_commons/21500927769/* accessed 18 Mar 2019)

six BL 60-pdr guns; a heavier 5-inch calibre weapon weighing 4.5t that could hurl a high explosive shell up to 9.4km at a rate of two rounds per minute. Each gun had a crew of ten men. Over ten million 60-pdr rounds were expended on the Western Front.[21]

A combination of obliterated and unworkable trenches, devastated ground and low morale on the Somme front had led the German General Staff to set up a series of new lines of defence beginning at the ridge at the north end of the Ancre Valley, and culminating in the formidable fortifications of the *Siegfriedstellung* or 'Hindenburg Line.'[22]

Built over the winter of 1916, these stretched from Lens to Rheims – some distance behind the existing front line. The German plan was to withdraw to these new, secure and strongly defendable positions in February and March 1917 under Operation 'Alberich.' In doing so they intended to destroy everything in their path. Ernst Jünger, a highly decorated German infantryman, suffered much at the hands of British gunners around that time. He wrote extensively in *Storm of Steel* of the withdrawal from the Somme, and the appalling living and fighting conditions that he left behind, sketching the wreckage on the way:

> As far back as the Siegfried [Hindenburg] Line, every village was reduced to rubble, every tree was chopped down, every road undermined, every well poisoned, every basement blown up or booby-trapped, every rail unscrewed, every telephone wire rolled up, everything burnable burned; in a word, we were turning the country that our advancing opponents will occupy into a wasteland.[23]

However, successes in February 1917 following renewed British Fifth Army attacks in the Ancre Valley pre-empted Operation 'Alberich' to some extent, taking some of the new German positions and so prompting a 6.4km German withdrawal on 24 February. Nevertheless, the 'Alberich' withdrawal continued.

During this phase, 116 HB was 'generally employed in neutralising hostile batteries,' having previously provided more tactical support during the 44th Infantry Brigade's earlier attacks on the Butte de Warlencourt at the end of January. The battery had suffered heavy shelling on 30 January.[24]

On 6 February 116 HB transferred to 23 Heavy Artillery Group (HAG) and took over guns at Martinpuich, on the NW outskirts of Longueval, relieving a battery that had moved to rest.

It is around this time that Fred Nunn's letters began to reveal his distinctive slant on the war. Writing to his brother-in-law on 28 March 1917, he reported that 'Willie's battery was only 10 minutes from us in Delville Wood.' A month or so later he went on to say:

> I am very delighted about Willie's success and am sure that all of you at home are very proud of him. I always thought he would get on in the army and the amount of experience he has had with heavy artillery now should make him a very

useful officer. I hope and trust that he pulls through all right.
I shall try and find him if I get anywhere near him again.

Although shelling and counter-shelling was a constant threat and
horror to gunners on both sides, Fred Nunn somehow managed
to inject some humour when writing of one night at Easter 1917:

> I was on picket from 11.30 till 1.30 and they were shelling
> us all the while, more or less heavily. I was all the time
> expecting a couple of rounds to fall bang in the Battery but
> they always, in some remarkable manner, seemed to just
> dodge us, although they were using a searching fire and the
> rounds were dropping all over the place.
>
> At 1.30 I was relieved of picket and got into a shell hole
> with two other chaps and thought I could at least have an
> hour or two sleep, but we were just getting warm when a
> Jack Johnson landed fair beside us and nearly buried us with
> mud and stones.[25] That settled my sleeping arrangements;
> I was never more wide-awake in my life! I thought it best
> to walk about, which I did, and got a bullet through my
> haversack for doing so! I tried to smoke but was shivering so
> much that I could not get a light. At the time, I should have
> been jolly glad if I had been hit.
>
> However, dawn came at last and when it was fairly
> daylight, Fritz, I suppose, thought we had a jolly hard
> neck to be still there and forthwith turned his frightful
> arrangements on us again and I don't know till this day how
> any of us got out of it alive.

Following the sudden withdrawal of enemy batteries along
practically the whole Corps front, 23 HAG had to move its
batteries east in order to keep in range and maintain some sort
of effective counter-battery capability. As for the German
retirement, there were false alarms. On 15 March 'all exits from
Bapaume [were shelled] by all the heavy batteries in [false]

anticipation of enemy withdrawal.'[26] It was not until 19 March that Australian troops finally occupied the town (one of the original Somme objectives).

But roads made impassable for heavy guns and other constraints made it hard to find new battery positions. Eventually, 116 HB received orders on 31 March to prepare a position west of Morchies – a small, thriving village NNE of Bapaume. It lay right in the path of the Australian Vth Division's advance from Bapaume to the Hindenburg Line between 17 March and 6 April 1917.

The battery was to be dug in by 1 April in readiness for the Battle of Arras, intended to start on 8 April. Each 60-pdr battery was allocated 6,000 rounds for the pre-attack bombardment.

A combination of bad weather and extremely bad roads that virtually prevented getting ammunition up by lorry and the fact 'that our line was not far enough forward to allow heavy guns to move so far forward' delayed this.[27] 116 HB did not get back in action until 4 April.

On 8 April it was tasked with preventing the completion of new enemy trenches 'by keeping them under continual fire' as part of the preparations for the 4th Australian Division to capture Bullecourt. There was particular emphasis on cutting the wire to the east of the town. The infantry went over the top at 0430 the next morning, facing determined resistance from Germans dug into the rubble of Bullecourt. Let down by tanks that broke down, the surviving attackers returned to their trenches even though the wire had indeed been 'well cut.'

The Germans shelled Morchies very heavily between 5 and 15 April during their build-up to heavy counterattacks. So great was the threat that arrangements were made to pull the heavier guns out of action. In the event a counter attack at battalion-level drove the Germans back and the retreating enemy were very heavily shelled. During this barrage (which was reported to have left '2,000 enemy dead lying in front of their wire') 116 HB fired 604 rounds.

The German infantryman Ernst Jünger somehow survived the full force of British bombardment and the terror that it caused.

Recalling his experiences on the morning of 28 April at Fresnoy, north of Morchies, he wrote:

> The terrain between the edge of the village and the dressing station was receiving a total artillery barrage. Light and heavy shells with impact-, fire- and time-delay fuses, duds, empty cases and shrapnels all participated in a kind of madness that was too much for our eyes and ears. In amongst it all, going either side of the witches' the cauldron of the village, support troops were advancing.
>
> Fresnoy was one towering fountain of earth after another. Every second seemed to want to outdo the last. As if by some magical power, one house after another subsided into the earth; walls broke, gables fell, and bare sets of beams and joists was sent flying through the air, cutting down the roofs of other houses. Clouds of splinters danced over whitish wraiths of steam. Eyes and ears were utterly compelled by this maelstrom of devastation.[28]

Jack Nunn was 'in the thick of it.' On 4 May 1917, his battery was still working from a position near Morchies – just south of the area fought over during the Second Battle of Bullecourt that ran from 3 to 15 May. This was the last of the series of engagements fought in the Battle of Arras, as the allies continued to assault the Hindenburg Line. The barrage that heralded the attack was massive (one field gun for every ten metres of front and one heavy gun for almost every 18m).[29] Counter-battery fire was also well organised, but buoyed by slow progress by the attacking infantry, the German artillery was able to recover from the initial counter-battery fire and move to new positions. It then began to inflict considerable damage, savaging exposed Australian troops.

While engaging in barrage and counter-battery neutralisation fire itself, 116 HB had been shelled heavily since 1 May. One particular 5.9-inch gun that had been harassing them for two days began to wreak havoc. By 5.30 p.m. on 4 May two guns were badly damaged and out of action, and over 100 rounds of ammunition had been destroyed. Jack was one who responded to the danger. As 23 HAG's war diary for in 1917 reported:

> The battery position was heavily shelled, two guns being hit, and a quantity of ammunition being put up. Lieutenant Temple, the officer [Lt W. J. Nunn] and WO [BSM H.J. Daniels] and two men (volunteers) went out while the position was still under heavy fire and at great risk proceeded to put out the burning boxes of ammunition, thereby saving a large quantity of cartridges which would otherwise certainly have been burnt and also other stores such as sights, etc. Major Swayne was away at the time, but the action was seen by the OC of a 4.5 how [itzer] battery close by and this officer sent in a special report pointing out the gallantry of the action and the fine example set to all ranks of his own battery as well as those of 116 Heavy Battery.

This exploit earned Jack Nunn his first Military Cross.[30] Lt Frank Temple and BSM Henry Daniels also received the MC and the two ORs received MMs.

Two days later Jack began a nine-day stretch of home leave. His brother Fred wrote:

> I hear from Will that he has been on leave and had a jolly time. How did you think he looked as an officer? He has also got the MC so he is going well ahead, isn't he? I am on the lookout for him and I believe he is somewhere not far from me. I might drop across him soon.

He may well have done so, as the two brothers moved north as part of the preparations for the Third Battle of Ypres, fought in a series of actions between July and November 1917, and culminating in the two battles of Passchendaele.

The Third Ypres offensive involved 17 British divisions operating along a 24km (15 mile) long front. In the 'most massive artillery attack ever known until that time' 3,106 guns fired almost three million shells onto forward German positions during an eight-day period.[31] Long downpours of rain interrupted the barrage. Late in July, Ernst Jünger, reeling from heavy fighting around Langemark, a village 8km north of Ypres, remarked thankfully that these rainstorms had been:

> ... a real godsend for us, because it doomed the English push to bog down in its first, crucial days [of the run-up to Third Ypres]. The enemy had to get his artillery through the swampy cratered landscape, while we could trundle our ammunition along intact roads.[32]

On 16 August 1917 an infantry attack was directed at Langemark – the second of the battles of Third Ypres. Jack Nunn took part in this offensive and went on to win a second MC, becoming one of just 71 RGA officers to do so in the Great War. This time, he was one of the forward observation officers, charged with keeping the batteries informed of preparations for enemy counter-attacks and support or suppression (SOS) signals from the front-line infantry. This was very vulnerable work. Many front-line observers lost their lives.[33] The citation for Jack's exploit on 16 August reads:

> ... for conspicuous gallantry and devotion to duty when forward observation officer. Keeping close behind the infantry attack he succeeded in reaching the objective shortly after it was taken, and although practically the whole of his party was killed or wounded, he maintained communications almost uninterruptedly, and continued to send back information of the utmost value under heavy hostile shell fire. But for his gallantry and devotion to duty communication would have been impossible.

Shortly afterwards he travelled home for leave on 22 August. This time bad health intervened, and he was admitted to a military hospital at Ipswich suffering from severe bronchitis. I have often wondered if he had been mildly gassed. His treatment lasted almost three months: it saved him from the ghastly fighting for Passchendaele, which continued until 10 November.

Following convalescent leave, he finally returned to France on 18 January 1918. Meanwhile, the King had invested him with his Military Cross and second award Bar on 19 October.

Writing on 19 September 1917, Fred Nunn reflected 'I hear that Willie is in hospital in England and I hope he is mending. I am sure he can do with a rest and change.'

Kaiserschlacht

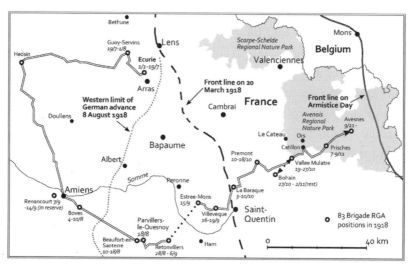

From Aras to Avesnes: 83 Brigade RGA in 1918

By the time Jack Nunn re-joined 116 HB it was part of 83 Heavy Artillery Brigade, positioned just north of Arras where it remained for around six months. At that time the brigade comprised two heavy batteries, each with 60-pdr guns, and four siege batteries, one of which was equipped with 9.2-inch (234mm) howitzers.

The brigade's activity for the rest of the war moved through three broad stages: defensive operations around Arras, about seven weeks on the breakout from Amiens to St Quentin and finally, seven weeks pursuing the Germans northeast towards the Belgian border.

Jack's first two months back in France were relatively quiet, the main emphasis being on neutralising hostile batteries and trench mortars with high explosive or gas shells and occasional harassing fire at night or early morning.[34] ('Harassing' fire involved shelling approach roads, bridges, command posts and other targets to disrupt the movement of reserve troops and supplies to the front line, often at night, and generally apply psychological pressure.)

Incoming German fire was frequent. For example, on one day in February around 300 shells hit Jack's battery over a four-hour period. Ammunition was destroyed, two of the gun pits were damaged and one gun was damaged. But no personnel were injured, and the battery was back in action the following morning.[35] Gas attacks remained a real threat. Many of Jack's colleagues with 135 SB suffered from gas damage in March, when the brigade diarist noted 'this gas appears to linger on the ground… men were affected many days afterwards with bad throats and a burning in the lungs.'[36]

On 21 March, the German Army – now reinforced with forces released from the now-quiet Eastern Front – launched 'Operation Michael' against the British Third and Fifth armies. This was the first phase of a major attack known as the 'Spring Offensive,' which the Germans named the *Kaiserschlacht*. In the mayhem that followed the Germans made deep advances in the Somme area, undoing the hard-won Allied gains of 1916 and 1917 in about four days. British and Commonwealth casualties were great, and many troops became prisoners of war. Fred Nunn was caught in the fighting around St Quentin but managed to evade capture.

Positioned north of the attack area, 83 HAB immediately responded to counter the enemy's barrage on the British front as well as shelling targets that were already programmed. This prompted enemy retaliation with about 250 gas shells. Overnight, guns in the rear positions were pulled out of their pits and repositioned on auxiliary platforms that had already been prepared in case there was a need to fire south. The brigade spent the following week firing on enemy targets to the south; harassing fire on troops seen to be massing along their own front and answering SOS calls.[37]

On 28 March, the enemy launched a second phase of their operation (Operation Mars) against the front at Arras, where 83 HAB was positioned. A substantial bombardment began at 3 a.m., which quickly extended over the front of the 50th Division, of which 83 HAB was part. The brigade responded quickly with howitzer fire on trench mortar emplacements, but soon the battery positions were subject to heavy gas and high explosive shells. Retaliatory fire along SOS lines followed, but hostile fire grew so heavy that the second of the two 60-pdr batteries was put out of action. At this point all of the 'mobile' guns were heavily exposed, as they had been pulled out of their pits to enable them to change their direction of fire if required. Fortunately, some of the hostile guns ranged on battery positions that had already been vacated.

The intense bombardment of the battery positions continued until midday, after which more sporadic shelling continued for a further eight hours. Many of the guns were put out of action for short periods either when damaged or when partially buried by shell explosions. The day's action involved counter-battery shelling, infantry support, and harassing enemy troops massing for attack. Later the gunners fired on enemy batteries in the open and bodies of troops and transport, sometimes at very close range which savaged enemy troops in the open). By end of the day the German attack had failed. Jack's battery had fired almost 2,000 of the 8,400 rounds fired by the whole brigade (which lost three officers and 11 other ranks killed, and five officers and 69 other ranks wounded).

While the enemy did not attack again on the following day, the batteries continued firing throughout. In the event, the final phases of the *Kaiserschlacht* would continue in the south until mid-July, but Operation Mars *had* been contained. For 83 HAB this signalled a return to the 'normal' rhythm of harassing fire, shoots assisted by aeroplane or balloon observers, 'neutralisation' of enemy batteries and working parties, responding to notifications of enemy batteries that were firing, and gas bombardments at night. All the while, enemy batteries continued to retaliate.

On 15 May, the enemy shelled Jack's battery with some 400 rounds. The position was 'much knocked about' and shell splinters damaged three guns. Fortunately, the gun crews had been withdrawn to a flank, and there was only one slight casualty. In the three months from April to June, the brigade fired almost 104,000 rounds, of which over 31,000 were from 60-pdrs.

Despite all this there were rare moments of recreation and relief. At the end of May, batteries of two heavy brigades competed with each other at a horse show held at the 116 HB wagon lines. Jack's battery was pipped at the post for the cup awarded for winning the most events. A week later the brigade won the mile and relay events in the XVII Corps heavy artillery sports, and Jack's battery reached the final of the tug-of-war.

On 19 July, the brigade moved northwest out of the line to Guoy-Servins and began ten days of training in readiness for a move south by rail to Amiens. There they were to prepare for the next battle.

Home run

Operation Michael was running out of steam. On 8 August Jack's brigade took part in the heavy bombardment that preceded the Fourth Army's offensive to remove the German threat to Amiens. It fired over 5,100 rounds in little more than six hours. A rapid enemy withdrawal followed: by 10.50 they were well out of range and by the end of the day had fallen back some 14km.

The breakout from Amiens was achieved through the first real coordination of infantry, artillery, tanks and air forces. This, effectively marking the birth of modern warfare, was decisive.

There ensued what amounted to a game of cat and mouse that lasted three months, during which the Fourth Army moved steadily eastwards in what become known as the 'Hundred days.' Jack Nunn's battery ended up 120km away; he was almost back in Belgium when the Armistice of 11 November came into effect and the fighting ceased. Breakthrough followed breakthrough, and 83 HAB fell into a routine of fighting a 'moving battle' to a new battery position, engaging the enemy, moving on again and so forth. The relatively mobile 60-pdr batteries were in action during these periods of movement, frequently fighting close up alongside the French 75s. (The French '75' or 'soixante-quinze' was a highly successful quick-firing field gun that could deliver 15 rounds of HE or shrapnel per minute at ranges up to 8.5km.) 116 HB's action just 3,000m from the front line on 28 August supporting the French near Ham, a small town southwest of St Quentin, won particular respect from the French gunners.[38]

At the end of September 83 HAB participated in the bombardment of the Hindenburg Line in the area north of Bellenglise, 10km north of St Quentin. This operation carried out by British, Australian and American troops was very successful, and followed two days of concentrated preparatory barrage. The effects of such relentless harassing fire on the Germans was readily apparent; prisoners reporting that as well as causing considerable damage and casualties, the bombardment denied them food and reinforcements for the whole two days period. The Hindenburg Line had been breached; a landmark moment for the allies. By this time, Jack Nunn was second in command of 116 Battery.

As October 1918 unfolded, the Fourth Army, flanked by the Third and then First armies to the north pushed the Germans further east across the Selle and Sambre rivers. Eventually they crossed into Belgium and recaptured Mons, the town where the BEF's war had begun in August 1914.

Jack Nunn's battery moved steadily north-east from positions north of St Quentin towards Le Cateau as part of the Fourth Army's drive towards the River Selle, along which the Germans had set up new defences following their loss of the Hindenburg Line. On 9 and 10 October the Fourth Army advanced some 13km as the Germans withdrew towards the Selle, coinciding with the Canadian forces' capture of Cambrai on 10 October. Meanwhile, the Third Army to the north advanced quickly in the face of stiff resistance and reached the river on 12 October only to be contained on the west of the river by robust German positions on the east bank.

Then began preparations to drive the Germans eastwards from these positions towards the Sambre-Oise Canal. These included massive artillery bombardments. Early on 17 October Fourth Army infantry and tanks moved forward along a 16km front south of Le Cateau in the face of unexpectedly strong German resistance. Le Cateau fell that evening. By 19 October the attackers, assisted by the French First Army to its south had advanced over 8km, forcing the Germans back towards the canal. To the north, the British Third and First armies began the process of dislodging the Germans from its well-defended positions on the east bank of the Selle. By 25 October the Battle of the Selle was over. Trench warfare was effectively over, and the fight had shifted to open ground. The enemy was in retreat, albeit in a planned and orderly way.[39]

During these operations there was a particular moment on 23 October when the First and Third Armies aimed to close up and break through German positions which followed the Sambre-Oise Canal to Ors, a few kilometres north of a strategic canal crossing at Catillon. The Fourth Army guarded the southern flank of this force. Jack Nunn's battery was one of a large group of artillery units, totalling 456 guns that supported this action. Collectively they demonstrated the 'crushing effect of well-co-ordinated, massed artillery' which 'simply swept away the opposition.'

Two days later Jack and his colleagues in the two 60-pdr batteries left their guns and went to rest near the safety of Bohain.

In *History of the Royal Artillery: Western Front 1914-18* Martin Farndale reflected on the sophistication that the British artillery had developed by this late stage of the war. Tactics refined during the September and October advance included deploying RFA 18-pdrs right forward with the attacking battalions; improving infantry-artillery information exchange; maximising opportunities to effect enfilade fire; using field guns as anti-tank guns, (particularly at times of counter-attack) and running single guns forward with infantry protection to engage enemy machine guns.[40]

During the October fighting there was the added problem of dealing with forested areas such as the Forêt de Mormal, north of Ors. One approach was to fire a creeping 18-pdr barrage of shrapnel immediately ahead of the attacking infantry – elevating the guns to achieve shell bursts at treetop height and deploying 4.5-inch and 6-inch howitzers to fire 400 and 600m beyond the 18-pdrs. To deal with small woods it was not unusual to 'creep' a barrage up to a wood, concentrate on it as the infantry closed in, and then bring the barrage to bear on escape routes for any fleeing enemy.

By this late stage of the war British artillery firepower was pre-eminent. It could be deployed in devastating quantities and was very flexible in terms of ordnance – high explosive, shrapnel or smoke. Good communication between infantry and artillery commanders at all levels was enhanced by close contact in forward positions, and produced an entirely new level of cooperation and related responsiveness.

The results were pretty brutal, and underpinned allied tactics for the rest of the war, which fortunately was nearly over. As Farndale concluded:

> It is possible that, in terms of sheer numbers of guns and weight of fire, the Royal Regiment [of Artillery] has never known a more technically proficient period in its history.[41]

On 2 November 83 HAB's 60-pdr batteries moved from their rest billets and returned to the gun positions they had left a week earlier. They were back in action by late afternoon. Two days later the brigade supported the hard-fought but successful assault on the Sambre-Oise Canal, firing 6,900 rounds in a 24-hour period as part of the Battle of the Sambre – a major attack on a 90km front fought by the First, Third and Fourth armies. Two days later 83 HAB's 60-pdr batteries crossed the canal.

116 HB fired its last shot of the war on 8 November in a 'programme of slow harassing fire on distant roads and cross roads...' It took up positions near Avesnes 'in readiness' on 9 November but saw no further action: the enemy was retreating back into Belgium.

During the advance from Amiens, the two heavy batteries and four siege batteries that comprised 83 HAB had been in the line for 70 days and fired over 150,000 rounds – an average of 2,144 rounds per day. [42] The brigade diary entry for 11 November 1918 reads simply 'hostilities ceased at 11 a.m. today. Armistice signed.'

A later entry records proudly that the brigade was 'in touch with the enemy and shooting every day that it was in the line except for 2 days of enforced waiting' for the bridge over the canal at Catillon to be completed. It suffered 220 casualties during this period, including 49 officers and men killed.

Jack had been promoted to Lieutenant on 6 July 1918 and appointed Acting Captain on 27 September. He remained with his unit until May 1919, when the battery left Antwerp for Southampton. By this time, he had volunteered for service in India and the East. Once home he became adjutant at the headquarters for the Second Brigade, RGA.

Both he and his brothers had survived the war. Of his fellow gunners 3,507 officers and 45,442 men did not. [43]

Between the wars

Back at Larkhill Camp in Wiltshire, Jack Nunn met Florence Rushbrooke and they began what was perhaps a whirlwind romance: they married at Amesbury Parish Church on 5 November 1919. Since Jack sailed for Iraq from Tilbury Docks that night they must have been utterly determined to marry before he left. While there is every reason to hope that Florence accompanied him to Iraq, I find no evidence to show that she did.

Florence is something of a mystery. From their marriage certificate it looks as though she was either nine years older than Jack or a year younger. All that we know is that she was born near Colchester, the daughter of an engineer called George Rushbrooke.

Jack had reverted to his substantive rank of lieutenant and was soon involved in operations in Iraq. He landed at Basra in mid-December 1919 and served with 5 Medium Battery RGA in Mesopotamia until March 1921. Equipped with a 6-inch howitzer, a 60-pdr and two Stokes mortars, they were among British forces in Mesopotamia who quelled the Arab revolt of 1920-21. His battery was besieged at Baqubah in July and August 1920.[44]

For ten weeks from 25 September 1920, Jack Nunn was seconded to 97 Battery RFA for service in the North Persia Force 'Noperforce.' In its latter stages this involved some 6,000 troops supporting Persian cossacks and other White Russian troops trying to prevent further Bolshevik advances into Persia. By mid-November opposition to the Bolshevik forces ceased following the defeat of the White Russians, which in turn marked the end of counter-revolutionary activity in Persia. [45] All British forces withdrew from Persia. Jack Nunn returned to Baghdad on 2 December.

His service earned him the General Service Medal 1918-62, becoming one of only 18 RA officers to earn both the 'N.W. PERSIA' and 'IRAQ' clasps on the medal.[46]

Once home from Iraq, Jack Nunn remained with the army, serving mainly with coastal defence establishments: Exeter, Ireland – on attachment to the South Wales Borderers; Portsmouth; Queenstown, County Cork; and Portsmouth again. On 19 March 1924 he sailed to Sierra Leone, where he served for a year with 24 Company, RA on port defence work.

After further coastal defence work at Plymouth and Portsmouth, Jack Nunn became adjutant of the Kent Heavy Brigade in December 1925. This was a Territorial Army unit based

WJN at home in Singapore, c. 1930
(courtesy Paul Rocky and © Virginia Barnes)

at Rochester. He remained there for four years – his longest posting in one place. Promoted to captain on 23 November 1929, he and his wife left shortly after for Singapore. There he served first with HQ Malaya and then with 22 Heavy Battery. After nine months he and Florence moved on to Malta where, but for a couple of weeks' leave in 1933, they stayed until February 1936.

On his return to UK early in 1936, Jack Nunn held appointments with coastal fixed defences at Portsmouth for the remainder of 1936 before moving north to Leith Fort on Fixed Defences for Scottish Ports. He was adjutant there from January 1937 until April 1941, having been promoted to Major early in 1938.

World War 2 and thereafter

Jack was 46 when the Second World War broke out. Was this too old for him to be considered for active service overseas, or was he not fully fit?

At the start of WW2, Jack remained with coastal defence in Scotland. After a brief stint in Orkney, he moved to Kent on 20 May 1941 as acting lieutenant colonel to command 26 Coast Artillery Group, headquartered at Walmer. Redesignated as 563 Coast Regiment on 6 June 1941, Jack remained in command until

1 April 1944. On 15 April 1944 he moved to Broadstairs to take over 549 Coast Regiment – his last command.

The regimental war diaries during these periods indicate a fairly quiet war, interspersed with the occasional engagement of enemy aircraft, although two gunners were killed at St Margarets Bay during counter-shelling on 8 July 1942.

Those gunners manning Bren and Lewis light machine guns seem to have been the busiest. For example, on 10 May 1941, the Lewis gunners at 235 Coast Battery at Deal engaged five Messerschmitt fighters flying low, some 200m offshore. They claimed to hit one and succeeded in nudging the enemy aircraft out to sea.

The entry in the war diary for 31 October 1942 reports that 'enemy aircraft approximately 50 in number believed to be FW 109s [190s?] flew in at sea level between Sandwich and St Margarets Bay. All Bren gunners and AA [anti-aircraft] LMGs in action, also concentrated rifle fire. Many planes observed hit. One aircraft observed down in the sea and one in direction of Manston. Three minor casualties were sustained by personnel of regiment. No damage to WO [War Office] property.'

Jack's last entry in the war diary records the disbanding of his regiment and all but one of his batteries, noting with some humour on 22 June 1945 that '296 Coastal Battery lapses into suspended animation.'

While his Second World War service earned him the Defence Medal and the War Medal 1939-1945, both these are missing from his miniature medals. Assuming that he would have had reason to wear his miniatures post-war, I imagine that either I have an earlier set, or he simply was not bothered to add the last two.

After the war, Jack Nunn continued with the RA until 10 June 1946, when he was admitted to hospital at Canterbury. He remained in hospital care for almost two months but did not recover fully. The Army classified him as 'Unfit – category D' on 31 October 1946. Granted the rank of Honorary Lieutenant Colonel, he retired from the army on 9 January 1947. He had served almost 38 years, working in seven countries outside what is now the UK and fighting in three of them. Not bad for someone who began as a trumpeter!

Jack Nunn never regained his health. Like many soldiers, he had settled near his last military station – at Broadstairs in Kent. He died in hospital at Ramsgate on 13 January 1951, aged 57. His death certificate records that he suffered from heart failure due to fibrinous pericarditis resulting from pulmonary tuberculosis.

Florence Nunn remained at Broadstairs and was living at 23 Queens Road when she died in 1964.

What of Jack's brothers? Frank Reuben Nunn, the eldest born in 1881 (who changed his surname to 'Lane' and who had served in the Boer War) re-enlisted in the ASC in 1915 and was discharged in 1918. He too died in 1951.

Fred Nunn remained in the army after the Great War. Following the unification of the RFA and the RGA into the Royal Artillery in 1924, he became 1036207 Gunner, RA. He was awarded the Army Long Service & Good Conduct Medal in 1927. He died in 1959, aged 72. When in France he was always on the lookout for Jack, his 'little' brother.

The third brother, 36960 Driver Ernest Nunn, RFA (born in 1891) served in France with 32nd Brigade, RFA from 23 August 1914. He became a huntsman of some legend, and recordings of his hunting songs from the 1920s still exist. He died in 1994.

Their youngest brother Albert, born 1897, also served in the latter stages of the war. Without having identified him conclusively, I suspect that he was L-41184 Driver Albert Nunn, RFA.[47] He served overseas during the later stages of the war.

Somehow, they all survived.

Fred Nunn's legacy

Since Jack Nunn spent a lengthy time in hospital and convalescence, I suspect that Fred Nunn spent more time in action than his brother. Fred's was one of the very first BEF units to land in France. His unit 'D' Battery Royal Horse Artillery was part of III Brigade RHA, which was – for most of the war – part of the 2nd Cavalry Division.

D Battery was in action near Baur during the Battle of Le Cateau, a rear-guard action fought on 26 August 1914. This was the occasion of the famous retrieval of howitzers of 37 Battery RFA, when three men won the Victoria Cross.

The battery endured the retreat from Mons. 'The BEF had covered 140 miles in 13 days... The infantry managed about four hours rest in twenty-four, the gunners only got two or three.' 'D' Battery was in action along the way, for example on 1 September when, together with 'E' Battery, they 'drove off six German squadrons [of cavalry] with their fire.' [48]

Following the recovery at the Marne, the battery moved north to the fighting around Ypres where, on October 15, it 'closely supported a highly successful attack by the 16th Lancers driving the Germans back from the Mont des Cats. The cavalrymen were dismounted, and D Battery kept up its fire to the very last moment, contributing solidly to the success of the attack.'

We know from Fred's letters that he was at the battles of Neuve Chapelle and Loos in 1915, the Somme in 1916, and Arras and Cambrai in 1917. In 1918, 'D' Battery was in the thick of the Battle of St Quentin during the Germans' 'Spring Offensive.' It ended its war at Mons on 11 November 1918. I would like to know what stories we are missing from those years before and after 1917?

One gap in his letters, or more of an omission perhaps, is that he does not write about the relationship between him, his 13-pdr and the devastation it caused.

Bearing in mind that they were regularly fighting in support of infantry and fighting in plain sight of their targets, there must have been times when the German infantry were uncomfortably close – as noted in D Battery's diary for 22 March 1918:

… when our attention was attracted by seeing a number of our men get up out of the long grass about 1000 or 1500 yards ahead and start coming back in a thin and straggling line. Simultaneously, we had a good deal of machine-gun fire and next minute out of the grass rose a German attack. They outnumbered the defenders by 5 to one at least and seemed to be formed in two or three waves – each wave composed of men apparently about two at yard intervals.[49]

Here are more extracts from Fred Nunn's letters to his brother-in-law, Will.[50]

After Arras – 24 (probably June) 1917
Well, what do you think at home of our lads' performances at Arras, etc. I bet old Fritz wont [sic] forget it in a hurry as there is no doubt they had a terrible bending and one that will take a bit of getting over. We were up at Arras during Easter week and the experience was not that is likely to remain in one's mind a long time. I will try and explain it a bit – without colouring:

We left our billet on the Thursday before Good Friday and the weather then was cold but dry, but two days out there was a change and the following fortnight was some of the vilest weather I have ever been out in. The wind was bitterly cold with constant storms of snow and sleet with, of course, inches of thick sticky mud. We stayed the night of Easter Sunday a few miles from Arras and turned out the following morning in a blinding snowstorm and reached Arras about dinnertime, nearly frozen stiff. The whole of my Division was on the move. We, of course, kept with our own Brigade. Arras is a big town very much like Leeds but it is awfully smashed up, now German shells are dropping in it all day. We marched through a good part of it and then turned up a track that had been made for us. Bridges had also been placed across the trenches for us. We went ahead over what had that morning been the German lines. It was my first experience of crossing a newly won battlefield and it was not a pleasant one. We arrived at our position of readiness and all of us thought we were in for a real good hunt but there was nothing doing for us that day but to look on. I was surprised at the large number of tanks that had come to grief. They were sticking about all over the place. I believe the Germans have a dodge of making some very wide deep trenches which are very difficult for them to get over, but I saw one of them crawling over barbed wire and shell holes quite easily. They are really funny things on the move, they wobble along like a tipsy man. We were well under cover that day and not many shells came near enough to hurt us, except two which fell in our Cavalry quite close to our gun and killed and wounded a number of men and horses. A lot of coal boxes** were, however, dropping on the roads in our rear and our bombardment was at its height then and the noise was terrific.

One could only converse by shouting and the very earth shook and the weather was steadily getting worse. The cold was intense. I did not see a Boche aeroplane that day but the air was full of ours. A never-ending stream of wounded were coming down from the trenches and those that had been killed in the morning were still lying there, both British and German. If one turned one's head to avoid seeing one of them, one's eyes got fastened to others.

We stayed there till dark, about 8 p.m., and them got the order to return to billet, which was a muddy field about 6 miles from Arras. Just as we got mounted, a terrible blizzard started which lasted about 2 hours and which turned the whole plain into a perfect sea of mud. We were the last Unit to move and we had not gone a hundred yards when all the guns and wagons were stuck fast. We had about 2 miles to go to get on the hard road and we did not get there till 5 o'clock in the morning and we got to the billet, the aforesaid mud field, at 6.30 and about 9 o'clock had our first meal since the previous morning. The weather was terrific, no one thought of sleep, the snow was at least 3 inches deep then.

** Coal box – British nickname for a low-velocity German howitzer shell emitting black smoke, used by the German army; opinions differ as to whether this is another word for a 'Jack Johnson.' Fred Nunn refers to both in the same sentence in his letter of 19 September.

That was Easter Monday, but worse was to come. Very soon, that same day, about 2 o'clock we got the order to saddle up and off we went across the track again. I noticed a lot of dead horses lying by the roadside and a lot more stuck in the mud on the track. Many had dropped exhausted – by the way they had been on reduced rations all the winter. We arrived at the same position of readiness, as the previous day and word came down that the whole of the brown line was ours, that our Infantry were pushing on and it was – hunt! You can imagine how pleased we all were. In our gladness of hearts we forgot even the cold, which was all the while getting worse.

Well, we got mounted again and away we went, through a little village, a slight turn to the right, and we were on the top of a valley side which sloped gently down, crossed a road, a level field or two, and then gently up the far side where we halted just below the haw of the crest [time about 4.30 p.m.]. The German trenches were about 800 yards over the crest. As we came down the valley side, a good many whiz-bangs†† came over but we got through all right, but I remember passing a Cavalryman who had been hit in the waist by one which had cut him completely in two. His horse's head was missing as well. He had been just ahead of us. A good many Infantrymen were lying there as well, that had been hit in the morning. We had been halted about 5 minutes when one of our gunners was hit by a rifle bullet, a great many of which were coming over. Just after, 2 horses and another man were hit. A good many shells were also going just over us and falling in the other Regiments of our Brigade who were in the rear of us. As the shells were coming closer, we got the order to split up, which we did and stood shivering with our horses in little groups. It was just then that the enemy became aware of our presence – I think they could observe us from our right flank – and he started sending over a perfect hail of shell and machine gun fire for about a half hour. They fairly had us on toast and we had to stand there

†† Whizzbangs – 14.4lb shells from 77mm (3.1-inch) field gun – range up to 7,000 yds. (*http://www.gommecourt.co.uk/weapons.htm#German,* accessed 08.03.2018)

and stick it. We lost several horses and a few men just then and the marvel is that we got off so lightly. The other Regiments did not fare so well. No doubt the crest saved us a bit, but they had no cover at all. A shell would fall fair in the middle of a little group of them and the result was always the same when the smoke had cleared, there would be on the ground the remains of what had, a second before, been horses and men. It was generally about 5 or 6 of each. It filled one with an intense pity to see it but one could do nothing.

It was nearly dark now and we got the order to close up and form mass as we were staying there the night. We had to remain saddled up. You can imagine what a joyful night it was. It was freezing very hard and we could not light a fire to make a drop of tea, but it was wonderful how calmly everyone took it. Those that were not on picket crawled into shell holes under the wagons, etc., and got what little sleep they could ...

[The next afternoon] About 2 o'clock we got the order to go back to the crest and leave the guns there in action, which we did, but as a heavy blizzard was on at the time, we were not molested by Fritz but it was bad enough to have to keep turning one's horse aside to avoid treading on the remains of our chaps and their horses. We fired on a village that was holding our chaps up and were told afterwards that we severely strafed a lot of German machine gunners there. The guns were in action till about 5 o'clock, during which time a gunner was killed and 3 others wounded. During the afternoon, 4 German planes came over us, quite low, firing at one of ours whom they brought down, and afterwards turned their machine guns on a battalion on the road and killed a lot of horses. ...

About 5.30, when the teams came to take us out of action, a tremendous snowstorm was raging, which lasted till 9 o'clock. It, however, prevented Fritz from seeing us and we got out of action all right but I remember a bullet passing most uncomfortably close to my face. On the way back to our mud field, it quite hurt one to see the wounded and lame horses trying to keep up. Many had not had a drink or food for two days and yet they would try to follow on till they finally got stuck in the mud, when they would sob and look up at one in the most pitiful way. The greater part of them never got up again. The whole place was in fact dotted with dead horses – and men.

Well, we got back to the mud field about 2 o'clock Thursday morning and the next day marched on to a better billet, with our horses like hat racks, the weather of course having punished them severely. Since then our time has been entirely taken up with them and as there is plenty of grass about now, they are coming on well. My horse, in fact, which is a really good one, is looking a treat.

The above is how I spent Easter 1917 and I am sure you will agree that I am not likely to forget it. That was the fourth time our high hopes had been dashed to the ground and it seems to confirm my original opinion that Cavalry actions on a large scale are now a thing of the past. Aircraft and machine guns have taken their place.

Apropos of the cavalry 22 December 1917

No doubt you have read a good deal in the paper of the show that started on November 30th and which resulted in us breaking up a good bit of the Hindenburg line, and we are all very well satisfied at the success we obtained, but at the same time it imposed upon those engaged a very severe test – both as regards hardship and real 'Active Service'. We were again greatly disappointed – as Cavalry – at the little fighting that came our way, the actual Cavalry action which my Brigade took part in being practically nil and, as I have often told you before, I do not think that we shall ever get Fritz into a retreat rapid enough to permit of the use of Cavalry on an extensive scale. He has too many prepared positions in his rear. We have no doubt gained a lot of first rate experiences and the sights that we have seen are such as do not often fall to one's lot, but it seems so bitter that when you have a prize almost in your grasp that it is snatched away again. Still, we hope for better luck next time.

Losing friends 19 September 1917

When we had time to look round a bit, I was very sorry to find that one of the killed was a special chum of mine. He and I had shared a bivouac and, in fact, everything together all the time I have been in the Battalion. He was a splendid little chap and his death has hit me hard. He came out here with the Battalion and had driven in the gun team all the time and the cruellest part about it is that he should have gone on leave the very next day. For some time he had talked of nothing else. I saw him on the stretcher and he was smashed to pieces and, as I looked at him, I thought how bitter is the price we have to pay for the great causes for which we are fighting and how hard is the task we have – for the sake of our future – to complete. My little friend has gone on that last long leave from which there is no returning, cheerfully doing his duty. He laid down his life for Britain's sake and his tiny grave is another little stepping stone to Britain's future greatness... 32 horses were killed, and my old horse was one of them. He was a spanking old horse and I had him a long time... To lose one's horse and best chum in one day is rather a shock to a fellow.

We left that particular spot and it has since been blown to pieces. These high velocity guns are the very devil, you don't have an earthly chance. A Jack Johnson or Coalbox comes along quite lazily and gives one plenty of time to take cover, but with this particular gun there is just a scream and it is on you.

The wider picture 19 September 1917

While the harvest moon lasted, the Germans bombed a good deal during the night but I hope it will cease a bit now. The bombing of hospitals and the C.C. [casualty clearing] stations was a deliberate act on their part and I hope we shall make them pay for it in due time. They know quite well that the war is lost for them and they are out to do as much damage as possible – hence their raids on England etc. If only Russia had stood firm, the end might now have been in sight but to take a look at things now, we find that the result of the summer fighting has been to inflict heavy losses on them in both men and material, but we have not been able to get them into that general retreat that we thought we should; and I should say that the present condition of Russia is worse for us than if she was neutral because the Germans are sweeping up such a lot of booty that is extremely useful to them. What they lose here on the swings, they are able to win back there on the roundabouts.

Of course there is no doubt that the German people are heartily sick of the war and longing for peace, but the powers that be have them in such an iron grip that they cannot possibly protest. What they will do when they are finally awakened, remains to be seen. In any case, the Kaiser will go down in history as the biggest blackguard that ever trod the earth and I doubt if his scamp of a son will every wear the crown.

My opinion now is that the war will never be decided by military power, that is to say by great battles and armies opposed to armies in the field. The summer's fighting has proved that, and therefore we have to look elsewhere for a deciding factor and we shall find it – in the air – and the only way to do that is sufficient aeroplanes and with America's aid I think we should, next summer, be able to employ sufficient planes of all kinds…

The submarine warfare is, of course, a very serious matter for us and although we shall feel the effect of it very strongly before the war is over, in my opinion the Germans will not have time to make it the deciding factor. As far as we are concerned, they – luckily for us – started wholesale sinking a bit too late and their idea of winning the war by their U-boats will be a false one.

Cambrai and tanks 22 December 1917

[This is in the context of the 1,003 guns and howitzers at the Third Army's disposal at the beginning of the battle. Major Norton, Fred's CO wrote 'the batteries were literally flank to flank in two lines as far as the eye could see, the rear tier firing over the front tier at 200-300 years distance. The synchronisation was excellent and it was a most impressive sight to see the hillsides burst into a perfect sheet of flame.']51

We left the wood the evening before the attack – no lights, no smoking – and arrived about midnight at a place about 8 miles from Gouzeaucourt. I slept the remainder of the night in a tin hut and although the papers say there was no bombardment in the sector we were in, there certainly was one – exactly at 6.30. I was getting up when a most mighty roar broke out, the floor of the old tin hut danced that much that I had to go out to lace my boots up. We watered and fed, had breakfast, watered again at 10 o'clock and then our troubles started. No-one must leave the lines. Be ready to saddle up at a moment's notice. We got things fixed, the wind turned very cold, we shivered – and waited – the bombardment meanwhile had ceased.

Before long, groups of prisoners came down and then rumour got busy again – it had been a walk-over, the Hun was in full retreat, the Cavalry were through, etc. We looked up the road again and yes, by Heaven the Cavalry were going up, regiments of them at the trot! Our hopes were high and about mid-day we got the order 'saddle up'. We were soon on the road, a main road it was, this we followed till just through Gouzeaucourt, when we struck the tracks prepared for us and we were soon over what had that morning been the German first line. Our Artillery had gone ahead and was firing heavily and we marched on and arrived at the rendezvous. It was getting dusk. Rain was falling heavily. We dismounted and awaited orders.

While coming across the tracks, one could see it had been a battle of tanks. There were tanks and their tracks everywhere and they were all creeping forward. A tank is a really wonderful arrangement, one would get under way, stick his snout into a big trench or hole, disappear, his snout would come up the other side and, with quite a graceful bow, he would drop on his middle and calmly crawl over piles upon piles of barbed wire. I only saw two that had come to grief that day and there were very few dead of either side lying about. I don't believe I saw more than a dozen the whole afternoon. I spoke to some of our wounded coming down and they were full of the good news, thousands of Cavalry were ahead of us, Cambrai had fallen and Fritz had been fairly taken by surprise.

There is no doubt he was taken by surprise, as although we were in easy range, not a round had come near us…

More casualties…

Quite close to where I stood was a Hun dugout being used as a dressing station and all day the wounded were coming down and how strange are the fortunes of war – here would be one fellow hit in the leg, a Blighty one, a fag in his mouth, the war for him was, for a time at least, over. He was content with all the world but how different the poor fellow badly hit, groaning in agony on the stretcher. One poor chap I saw was racked with pain. He constantly threw the blanket off him, leaving himself exposed to the bitter wind. We would put it back and speak a word of comfort to him. It was no use, he fought hard for his life but died in front of our very eyes. But one never heard a grumble of any sort. They took what came their way with real solid pluck.

Notes

1 Gen Sir Martin Farndale, *History of the Royal Artillery: Western Front 1914-18* (1986) 204

2 pers. comm. Paul Rocky 02.02.2012

3 'Experience teaches wisdom' by Neil Lanham *http://oraltraditions.co.uk/wording/files/orality_metaphor.pdf, accessed* 09.02.2017

4 Kelly's Directory of Suffolk 1900, pp.102-3, *http://specialcollections.le.ac.uk/cdm/ref/collection/p16445coll4/id/278595*, accessed 14.05.2017

5 National School Admission Registers & Log-books 1870-1914 from Suffolk Record Office, Ipswich, *http://search.findmypast.co.uk/record?id=gbor%2fschool%2f3644%2f588933*, accessed 10.02.2017

6 Guns are commonly named by the weight of the shells they fire e.g. '60-pounder' or the internal diameter of their barrels (e.g. 4.7-inch)

7 Dale Clark, *British Artillery 1914-19* (2004) 9

8 The Long, Long Trail: British Army in the Great War, 'The Royal Artillery in the First World War', *http://www.longlongtrail.co.uk/army/regiments-and-corps/the-royal-artillery-in-the-first-world-war/*, accessed 10.02.2017

9 Army Personnel Centre, Support Division: Army Service Record – William John Nunn

10 TNA: WO 32/6896, Report on Evelyn Wood's Boys Enlistment Committee (Colonel Strachey's committee work with related papers)

11 E. Lawrence Abel. *Singing the new nation: how music shaped the Confederacy, 1861-1865* (2000) 130

12 Abstracted from 54 Company RGA records at Royal Artillery Museum, 16.09.2014

13 Ibid

14 Max Hastings, *Catastrophe: Europe goes to war* (2013) 472

15 TNA: WO 95/2995/5, 114 HB 2

16 WO 95/2995/5, 114 HB 2

17 Ibid, 3

18 Farndale, *History ...*, 82

19 TNA: WO 95/540, 18 HAG

20 *London Gazette* 30 January 1917 1125

21 Clark, *British Artillery*, 36

22 Remembrance trails Northern France 14-18, 'The Hindenburg Line', *http://www.remembrancetrails-northernfrance.com/history/the-battlefield/the-hindenburg-line.html*, accessed 27.02.17

23 Ernst Jünger, *Storm of Steel* (2004) 128

24 TNA: WO 95/476, 73rd HAG

25 Jack Johnson: British nickname used to describe the impact of a heavy, black German 15-cm artillery shell

26 TNA: WO 95/469, 23rd HAG

27 TNA: WO 95/469, 23rd HAG

28 Jünger, *Storm of steel*, 138

29 Farndale, *History ...*, 181

30 *London Gazette* 18.06.1917 5996

31 Farndale, *History ...*, 195

32 Jünger, *Storm of steel*, 172

33 *London Gazette* 26.9.1917 9971; citation in London Gazette 09.01.1918 576

34 The Germans fielded large trench mortars ranging from 75.8mm (3-inch), 170mm (6.7-inch) and 9.8-inch). The 250mm *minenwerfer* could lob a 100kg bomb about 420m; the others could range about twice as far. (*http://www.tandfonline.com/doi/full/10.1080/03071847.2012.714202*, accessed 25 Sep 2017)

35 TNA: WO 95/478/1, 83rd HAB, diary entry for 21 Feb 1918

36 Ibid, entry for 6 Mar 1918

37 Guns were often registered on known enemy targets in 'SOS lines', so that they could be engaged quickly in the event of request from the front-line troops. (*http://www.longlongtrail.co.uk/battles/battles-of-the-western-front-in-france-and-flanders/the-first-battles-of-the-somme-1918*, accessed 25 Sep 2017)

38 TNA: WO 95/478/1, 83rd HAB, diary entry for 30 Aug 1918

39 *https://en.wikipedia.org/wiki/Battle_of_the_Selle*, accessed 06.04.18

40 Farndale, *History ...*, 311

41 Ibid, 311

42 83 HAB comprised 1/1st Highland & 116 HBs 6x60-pdr guns each; 230 & 284 SBs 6x6in howitzers each; 185 SB 6x8in howitzers; 69 SB 6x9.2in howitzers; (General Staff, GHQ Order of battle of the British armies in France (including lines of communication units) November 11th, 1918, Imperial War Museum facsimile reprint series: London 1989, 80-83) (Reproduced and bound by Cedric Chivers Ltd, Bath)

43 Farndale, *History,* 322

44 Great War Forum post by 'Kildaremark' on 11.09.2009, *http://1914-1918.invisionzone.com/forums/index.php?/topic/132843-5th-bty-rga-in-iraq/*, accessed 03.03.17

45 'Noperforce', FIBIwiki, *http://wiki.fibis.org/index.php/Norperforce*, accessed 03.03.17

46 pers. comm. Dick Flory 15.02.17 and 15.04.17 and TNA: WO 212/613, General Service Medal with clasps 'Iraq' (1919-1920), 'Kurdistan' (1919), 'NW Persia' (1920), 'S Persia' (1918-1919), Off/139

47 Medal Roll of Individuals entitled to the Victory Medal and/ or British War Medal – RFA, 223

48 Farndale, *History ...*, 59

49 Ibid, 266

50 Nunn, Frederick C. unpublished letters 28.03.1917, mid 1917, and 19.09.1917

51 Farndale, *History ...*, 218

References

a) Publications

Abbott P.E. & Tamplin J.M.A. *British Gallantry Awards*, Guinness Superlatives: London 1971

Abel, E. Lawrence. *Singing the new nation: how music shaped the Confederacy, 1861-1865*, Stackpole Books: Mechanicsburg 2000

Adams, Pauline. *'Somerville for Women' an Oxford College 1879-1993*, Oxford University Press: Oxford 1994

Anonymous. *The Hospital of Arc en Barrois, Haute Marne, France; being a brief record of British Work for French Wounded, London*: privately printed for the subscribers 1915

Anonymous [Sister Kate Luard]. *Diary of a Nursing Sister on the Western Front, 1914-1915*, William Blackwood & Sons: Edinburgh & London 1915

Army Lists, Apr 1921-Nov 1937, Feb 1939, Jul 1941, Dec 1946, Apr 1947

Arthur, Max. *Forgotten Voices of the Great War*, Ebury Press: London 2002

Ashworth, Chris. *Military airfields of the Central South and South-East*, Patrick Stephens Ltd: Wellingborough 1985

Attlee, Clement. *As it happened*, Odham's Press: London 1956

Barker, Pat. *Life Class*, Penguin Books: London 2008

Barker, P. *Toby's Room*, Penguin Books: London 2013

Bew, John. *Citizen Clem*, Quercus Publishing: London 2016

Bickmore, Miss. 'Life in an Ambulance Train in France in the Great War 1914-17', Hand-written m.s. in Documents 3814, Imperial War Museum: London 1918

Binyon, Laurence. *For Dauntless France: An account of Britain's Aid to the French Wounded and Victims of the War*, Hodder and Stoughton, 1918, from *https://archive.org/stream/fordauntlessfran00biny#page/n21/mode/2u*, accessed 10 Aug. 2012

Brough, Ray. *White Russian awards to British & Commonwealth Servicemen during the Allied Intervention in Russia 1918-20*, Tom Donovan: London 1991

Busch, Briton C. (Ed.). *Canada and The Great War: Western Front Association Papers*, Ch. 12. Canadian Airmen and Allied Intervention in North Russia, 1918-19 by Owen Cooke. McGill-Queen's University Press: Montreal: Canada 2003

Clarke, Dale. *British Artillery 1914-19*, Osprey Publishing: Oxford 2004

Coppinger, Walter Arthur. *History of the parish of Buxhall in the county of Suffolk*, 1902

Cowen, Ruth (Ed) *A Nurse at the Front: the First World War Diaries of Sister Edith Apple*ton, Simon & Schuster/ IWM: London 2013

Crewdson, Wilson. *French Heroes at the Military Hospital, Arc -en-Barrois*, France privately published: London 1916

Davies, C. B., Edmonds, J. E., Maxwell-Hyslop, R. G. B., *Military Operations France and Belgium, 1918 March–April: Continuation of the German Offensives*, Battery Press: Nashville – reprint of 1937 ed. *1995*

Dean, George (for the relatives of Eva Marion Smith). '*A nursing sister and the Great War*', contained in the 'Private Papers of Miss E. M. Smith' at the Imperial War Museum (Documents.16098), 2008

Downing, Taylor. Breakdown*: The crisis of shell shock on the Somme*, 1916, Little Brown: 2016 eBook

Edinburgh Gazette: 19 July 1919

Dobson, Christopher & Miller, John. *The day we almost bombed Moscow*, Hodder & Stoughton: London 1986

Lewis, Cecil. *Sagittarius Rising*, Peter David Ltd: London 1936

Dods, Marcus. *Later Letters of Marcus Dods, D.D.* (selected and edited by his son), Hodder & Stoughton: London 1911

Edwards, E.H. *Fire and Sword in Shansi: The Story of the Martyrdom of Foreigners and Chinese Christians*. London: Oliphant Anderson & Ferrier 1907

Farndale, Gen Sir Martin. *History of the Royal Artillery: Western Front 1914-18*, The Royal Artillery Institution: Woolwich 1986

Fawcett, Brian C. 'The Chinese Labour Corps in France, 1917-1921', *Journal of the Hong Kong Branch of the Royal Asiatic Society, Vol. 40*, 2000 33-111

Faulkner, R. Letter commenting on a draft account of the battle of Sari Bair, dated 11 December 1930, appended to the War Diary of 6 South Lancs.

Franks, N., Guest, R., & Gregory Alegi, G. *Above the war fronts: The British two-seater bomber pilot and observer aces, and the Belgian, Italian, Austro-Hungarian and Russian fighter aces 1914-1918*, Grub Street: London 1997

Fell, Alison E. & Hallett Christine E. (eds) *First World War nursing: New perspectives*, Routledge: New York 2013

Galloway P., *The Order of the British Empire*, Central Chancery of the Orders of Knighthood: London 1996

GB Historical GIS / University of Portsmouth, Berkhamsted RegD/PLU through time | Life & amp; Death Statistics | Decennial Cause of Death by Age. A Vision of Britain through Time. Retrieved through *http://www.visionofbritain. org.uk/unit/10066700/cube/CoD_DS_1880s*, accessed 24 May 2018

Gillings J.M. & Richards J. *In All Those Lines – the diary of Sister Elsie Tranter 1916-1919* published by the editors, 2008

Gliddon, Gerald. *Somme 1916: A battlefield companion*, Sutton Publishing: Stroud, Glous. 2006

Gooding Norman G., *Honours and Awards to Women: The Military Medal*, Savannah Press: London 2013

Hallett, Christine E. *Veiled Warriors: Allied Nurses in the First World War*, Oxford University Press: Oxford 2014

Hart, Peter. *1918 A very British victory*, Weidenfeld & Nicholson: London, 2008

Hastings, Max. *Catastrophe: Europe Goes to War 1914*, William Collins: London 2013

Hatcher, J. *Laurence Binyon Poet, Scholar of East and West*, John Clarendon Press: Oxford 1995

Hayward, J., Birch, D., & Bishop, R. *British battles and medals (7th Ed.)*, Spink: London 2006

Hobson, Chris. *Airmen Died in the Great War 1914–1918: The Roll of Honour of the British and Commonwealth Air Services of the First World War*, Suffolk, JB Hayward: 1995

Insight Guides. *The Silk Road*, Apa Publications: Singapore 2008

Jones, E. & Wessely, S. *Shell shock to PTSD: Military psychiatry from 1900 to the Gulf War*, Maudsley Monograph 47, Psychology Press: Hove 2005

Jünger, Ernst. *Storm of Steel*, Penguin Books, 2004

Kemp, Emily Georgiana. *The face of China; travels in east, north, central and western China; with some account of the new schools, universities, missions, and the old religious sacred places of Confucianism, Buddhism, and Taoism, the whole written & illustrated*, Duffield & Company: New York 1909

Kemp, E. G. *The Face of Manchuria, Korea & Russian Turkestan*, Chatto & Windus: London 1911

Kemp, E. G. *Wanderings in Chinese Turkestan*, 1914

Kemp, E. G. *Reminiscences of a sister, S. Florence Edwards, of Taiyuanfu*, The Carey Press: London 1919

Kemp, E. G. *Chinese Mettle*, Hodder & Stoughton: London 1921

Kemp, E.G. *There Followed Him, Women; pages from the life of the Women's Missionary Association of the Baptist Mission* 1927 (or 1928)

Kemp, E.G. *Mary, with her son, Jesus*, Golden Vista Press: London 1931

Kemp, E.G. *Girls Schools in China*, Article in Somerville College Record, 19??

Kettle, Michael. *Churchill and the Archangel Fiasco: November 1918 – July 1919*, Routledge: London 1992

Leach, H., Farrington, S.M. *Strolling about on the top of the world. The first hundred years of the Royal Society for Asian Affairs (Formally Royal Central Asian Society)*, Routledge Curzon, London 2003

Lloyd, Nick. *Passchendaele: A new history*, Viking/ Penguin Random House: London 2017

London Gazette: numerous issues

Maton, Michael. *Honour the officers: Honours & awards to British, Dominion and Colonial officers during the First World War*, Token Publishing: Honiton 2009

Maynard, Sir C. *The Murmansk Venture*, Hodder & Stoughton: London c.1928

McCrae, Niall and Kuzminska, Katerina. 'The origins of a two-tier profession: nursing school at a Poor Law Infirmary', *British Journal of Nursing* 26.5 2017

Members of the QAIMNS, *Reminiscent Sketches 1914 to 1919*, Bale, Sons & Danielson: London 1922

McCarthy Dame E.M. *War Diary: Matron-In-Chief, British Expeditionary Force, France and Flanders*, Crown Copyright: The National Archives, WO95/3988-91 via *http://www.scarletfinders.co.uk/110.html*, accessed 21 Feb 2014

McEwen, Yvonne. *It's a long way to Tipperary: British and Irish Nurses in the Great War*, Cualann Press: Dunfermline 2006

McEwen, Yvonne. *In the Company of Nurses: The history of the British army nursing service in the Great War*, Edinburgh University Press: 2014

Meynell E. W. *Some Account of the British Military Hospitals of World War I at Étaples, in the Orbit of Sir Almroth Wright*, Journal of the Royal Army Medical Corps, v142; 43-47, (1996), via *jramc.bmj.com*, accessed on 20 Jan 2014 – Published by group.bmj.com

Miller, James F. *FE 2b/d vs. Albatros scouts: Western Front 1916-17*, Osprey Publishing: Oxford 2014

MacPherson Sir W.G. *History of the Great War: Medical Services, General History Vol. III*, HMSO: London 1924 available through *https://archive.org/stream/medicalservicesg03macp/medicalservicesg03macp_djvu.txt*, accessed 23 Feb. 2014

Morley, Robert M. 2006, *Earning their wings: British pilot training 1912-1918*, MA thesis, University of Saskatchewan, Canada and AIR 1/39/15/7, *(https://ecommons.usask.ca/xmlui/bitstream/handle/10388/etd-12142006-161732/RobertMorleyFinalVersion.pdf?sequence=1&isAllowed=y*, accessed 24.11.2016)

Morris-Suzuki, T. *To the Diamond Mountains*, Rowman & Littlefield Publishers, 2010

Mullaly, Brian Reginald. *The South Lancashire Regiment: The Prince of Wales's Volunteers*, White Swan Press: Bristol 1952

North J. *Gallipoli – The fading vision*, Fabre & Faber: London 1967

Piggott, Juliet. *Queen Alexandra's Royal Army Nursing Corps*, Pen & Sword (Famous regiments series): Barnsley 1990

Powell, Anne. *Women in the War Zone*, The History Press: Stroud 2013

Quigley J. *Picardy: a quiet, simple land of dreamy beauty, where artists find much to paint*, 255-[264] Gustav Stickley (ed.) / *The craftsman* Vol. XII, Number 3 (June 1907), *https://www.scribd.com/document/162106722/The-Craftsman-1907-06-June-pdf*, accessed 18 May 2018

Reid, Fiona. *Medicine in First World War Europe: Soldiers, Medics, Pacifists*, Bloomsbury: London 2017

Royal Air Force Museum, Hendon: Royal Air Force Casualty Card Forms 55, 2015

Sebag-Montefiore, Hugh. *Somme – Into the breach*, Viking/ Penguin Random House: London 2016

Shaw, Phyllida. *An Artist's War: the Art and Letters of Morris and Alice Meredith Williams*, The History Press: Stroud 2017

Shaw, Robert. *Visits to High Tartary, Armand and Kashgar (formerly Chinese Tartary)*,

John Murray: London 1871

Smith, E.M. *A Nursing Sister and the Great War (Eva Marion Smith 1.2.1879-3.9.1971)*. Ed George Dean, and privately published by him (2008) (Courtesy of the Imperial War Museum Archives)

Somerville College, Oxford: *Somerville Students Association Thirtieth Annual Report and Oxford Letter, 1917* [in 1917 they used it to record all the war work undertaken by Somervillians].

Register of Students, Somerville Hall, (handwritten book) ref. SC/AO/RG/SH

Somerville College Register 1879-1971, 1971

The SSA *15th Annual Supplement to the Report of the College 1939-40* includes Emily Kemp in the list of deaths of members

Stapledon, Olaf. 'Experiences in the Friends' Ambulance Unit', taken from *We Did Not Fight 1914-18: Experiences of War Resisters*, edited by Julian Bell (London: Cobden-Sanderson, 1935), pp. 359-374. *http://ebooks.adelaide.edu. au/s/stapledon/olaf/friends/,* accessed 24 May 2018

Stevens, J. & Stevens, C. *Unknown warriors: the letters of Kate Luard, RRC and Bar, nursing sister in France 1914-1918*, History Press: Stroud 2014

Taprell Dorling, H. *Ribbons & Medals*, George Philip & Son: London 1960

Thetford, Owen. *British Naval Aircraft since 1912*, Putnam: London 1962

Thorpe A.W., *Handbook to the Most Excellent Order of the British Empire*, 1921; reprinted London Stamp Exchange 1988

'Waterbeach: Manors and other estates', *A History of the County of Cambridge and the Isle of Ely: Volume 9: Chesterton, Northstowe, and Papworth Hundreds* (1989) 243-248, retrieved through *http://www.british-history.ac.uk/report. aspx?compid=15424,* accessed 03 Feb 2014

Whalley-Kelly, Capt Henry. *'Ich dien'; the Prince of Wales's Volunteers (South Lancashire) 1914-1934*, Gale & Polden: Aldershot 1935

Whitton, F. E. (Frederick Ernest). *A short history of the Prince of Wales's volunteers (South Lancashire)*, Gale & Polden: Aldershot 1928

Williamson, Howard. *The Great War Medal Collectors Companion*, Anne Williamson: Harwich 2011

Williamson, Howard. *The Distinguished Conduct Medal Awarded to the Allied Armies by the British Government during the Great War 1914 to 1918*, Anne Williamson: Harwich 2018

Women's missionary association of the Baptist Missionary Society (Baptist Zenana Mission), *Jubilee: 1867-1917 Fifty years' work among women in the Far East,* Carey Press, London 1917 23 (*https://archive.org/stream/MN41453ucmf_0/ MN41453ucmf_0_djvu.txt* accessed 07.02.2018)

Wright, Damien. *Churchill's Secret War with Lenin: British & Commonwealth Military Intervention in the Russian Civil War, 1918-20*, Helion: Solihull 2017

Younghusband, Francis. *Wonders of the Himalayas*. John Murray: London 1924

b) Archives

Army Personnel Centre, Support Division: Army Service Record – William John Nunn

Berkhamsted School Archive:
Berkhamstedian 1919

Imperial War Museum, London (IWM):
Miss Bickmore, 'Life on an ambulance train in France, 1914-1917' (Documents 3814)
Papers concerning the British Hospital at Arc-en-Barrois, France, First World War; contains Madeline Bromley-Martin's 1.5 page summary 'Hotel Temporaire at the Chateau at Arc-en-Barrois' dated 29 August 1919 and Nicholas Bromley-Martin's typed Ms 'The Hospital at Arc-en-Barrois' (Documents 13070)
Miss E. Bromley (Documents 14947)
Sir Theodore Fox, 'A boy with the BEF – Recollection of 1918' signed by him April 1979 (Documents 15735)
Miss M. D. Peel, Self-published pamphlet 1921 (Documents 16722)
Miss E.M. Smith, contains bound copies of diary entries titled 'Miss E. M. Smith: War Work 1914-1916' (Documents 16098)
Squadron Leader R M Trevethan MC (Documents 22390)

London Metropolitan Archive:
'Register of students at the London School of Medicine for Women' (handwritten book) in London School of Medicine for Women and Related Collections 1888-89 (H72/SM/C/01/03/001/0225)

Royal Artillery Historical Trust Collections
War Diaries for 44 and 54 Companies, R.G.A., 26th Coast Artillery Group, R.A., 23rd Coast Artillery Group, R.A., 563 Coast Regiment, R.A., 549 Coast Regiment R.A., April 1941 – June 1945

Slade School of Fine Art
University College London Calendar for 1892-93 (Accessible through *http://digitool-b. lib.ucl.ac.uk:8881/R/?func=collections&collection_id=3186*)

Somerville College, Oxford:
Correspondence 1932-37: Miss Darbishire & Miss Kemp re Chapel (C/TY/BG/CH/8)
Letter from Margaret Roberts to Miss Darbishire of 10 January 1940 in Kemp (R.SH.028)
'Register of Students, Somerville Hall', handwritten book (SC/AO/RG/SH)
Miss Darbishire's tribute 'In Memoriam Emily Georgiana Kemp' in *Somerville*

College Chapel Addresses and Other Papers by Helen Darbishire (posthumously published 1962), 10-13 (SC/PO/PP/HD/1)

The National Archives of the UK (TNA):
ADM 318/188, WRNS Service Record of MacDougall, May Meiklejohn

AIR 1/39/15/7, *Air Ministry: Air Historical Branch. Papers. Series 1:* RFC and RAF casualties August 1914 – October 1918
AIR 1/167/15/156/1, History of 20 Squadron RFC
AIR 1/472/15/312/167, North Russia 'Syren' Force: Operation and intelligence reports – General returns Photography – Report on difficulties, 22 Jun 1919
AIR 1/733/185/4, An account of an air-fight by a formation of FE2ds of No. 20 Squadron in Flanders
AIR 1/864/204/5/508, Return of casualties to all ranks of the RFC (fortnight ending 30 Sep 1917)
AIR 1/1768/204/143/2, North Russia 'Syren' Force. Observers Reports June-Sept 1919 – General return
AIR 10/1839, 1928 Report on the operations carried out in the Southern Desert in connection with the Iraq-Najd borders, November 1927-May 1928

DEFE 69/192, History of the Small Vessels Pool and Admiralty Ferry Association 1939-45 (1973)

FO 371/1341, *Political Departments: General Correspondence from 1906-1966:* China. Code 10 File 3811 – 5601
FO 371/1342, China. Code 10 File 5682 – 8053

IR 62/1905, Bequests to the University of Oxford and Somerville College respectively: E G Kemp

J 77/3349/2270, Divorce Court File: 2270. Appellant: Richard Michael Trevelyan Trevethan. Respondent: Muriel Doris Graham Trevethan. Co-respondent: William Francis Bryan McLellan. Type: Husband's petition for divorce [HD].

RG 12/ 1126, 1891 Census Returns, Hertfordshire. Registration Sub-District 1 Berkhamstead
RG 14/18406, 1911 Census Schedules, Registration Sub-District: Meriden, Civil Parish, Township or Place: Berkswell (part)

WO 32/4965, Decorations and medals: Military Cross (Code 50(G): Decision regarding award of Military Cross to nurses
WO 32/5189, Reports concerning bombing of British Hospitals at Étaples, France
WO 32/6896, Report on Evelyn Wood's Boys Enlistment Committee (Colonel Strachey's committee work with related papers)

WO 95/213, *First World War and Army of Occupation War Diaries*: 8 Brigade Royal Garrison Artillery

WO 95/298, 4 Brigade RGA

WO 95/299/5, 109 Heavy Battery RGA. 114 Heavy Battery RGA. 115 Heavy Battery RGA

WO 95/394/3, 62 Brigade RGA

WO 95/397, 24 Brigade RGA

WO 95/302, 92 Brigade RGA

WO 95/469/2, 23 Brigade RGA

WO 95/476/1, 73 Brigade RGA

WO/95/478/1, 83 Brigade RGA

WO 95/540/4, 18 Brigade RGA

WO 95/1468/1, 4 Division Ammunition Column and 4 Division Ammunition Park

WO 95/3988, Matron in Chief, 1 Aug 1914 – 31 Dec 1915

WO 95/3989, Matron in Chief, 1 Jan 1916 – 30 Jun 1917

WO 95/4027, Vol. No. 37 Étaples Base: Commandant 1917-19

WO 95/4081, 12 General Hospital, Rouen

WO 95/410/7/2, 39 Stationary Hospital

WO 95/4302 Dardanelles, 13 Division, 38 Infantry Brigade, 6 Bn South Lancs. Regiment, Volume I

WO 95/4129/5, Lines of Communication Troops, 1 Ambulance Train

WO 95/4130/..., 2 Ambulance Train; 3 Ambulance Train

WO 95/4131/ ..., 4 Ambulance Train; 5 Ambulance Train

WO 95/4132/..., 6 Ambulance Train; 7 Ambulance Train; 8 Ambulance Train

WO 95/4133/..., 9 Ambulance Train; 11 Ambulance Train

WO 95/4134/1, 12 Ambulance Train

WO 95/4263-4359, 6th South Lancs. Regiment, Volume I

WO 100/120, *Campaign Medal and Award Rolls:* Queen's South Africa, Imperial Yeomanry

WO 100/171, Queen's South Africa, 1st-7th Battalions Royal Fusiliers

WO 212/693, General Service Medal with clasps 'Iraq' (1919-1920), 'Kurdistan' (1919), 'NW Persia' (1920), 'S Persia' (1918-1919)

WO 222/2134, Reports on various Army nursing services in France 1914-1918 (The work of the nursing services with British ambulance trains and station units in France, in 1914)

WO 329/2323, British Committee, French Red Cross: medal rolls. Pages 1-306. British War Medal and Victory Medal

WO 329/3211, Royal Army Service Corps (Woolwich) list RASC 1251-1500. Silver War Badge

WO 364/55, Soldiers Documents from Pension Claims, First World War. 1914-1920 collation. Name Andrews, Charles – Andrews, Harry [includes GSA]

WO 372/1/90678, *War Office: Service Medal and Award Rolls Index, First World War:* Gerald S Andrewes – Army Service Corps MS/527, Acting Corporal

WO 372/15/16639, Medal Card of Nunn, William John –Royal Garrison Artillery, Bombardier

WO 372/23/176173, Medal card of Toller, L M M – Queen Alexandra's Imperial Military Nursing Service, Sister/ Acting Matron

WO 372/20/76715 Medal card of Trevethan, Richard Michael – South Lancashire Regiment ...

WO 399/8376, Directorate of Army Medical Services and Territorial Force: Nursing Service Records, First World War, Queen Alexandra's Imperial Military Nursing Service, Toller, Lucy

Royal Air Force, RAF Disclosures, RAF service record – Richard Michael Trevethan

Index